BRING THE NOISE

BRING THE NOISE

THE JÜRGEN KLOPP STORY

RAPHAEL HONIGSTEIN

NATION
BOOKS
New York

Nation Books
116 East 16th Street, 8th Floor
New York, NY 10003
www.publicaffairsbooks.com/nation-books
@NationBooks

Printed in the United States of America

Published in the United Kingdom as *Klopp Bring the Noise* by Yellow Jersey Press in 2017

First Trade Paperback Edition: February 2018

Published by Nation Books, an imprint of Perseus Books, LLC, a subsidiary of Hachette Book Group, Inc.

Nation Books is a co-publishing venture of the Nation Institute and the Perseus Books.

The publisher is not responsible for websites (or their content) that are not owned by the publisher.

Typeset in Baskerville MT Std by Jouve UK, Milton Keynes

Library of Congress Control Number: 2017963207

ISBN: 978-1-56858-957-2 (paperback)
ISBN: 978-1-56858-958-9 (e-book)

LSC-C

10 9 8 7 6 5 4 3 2 1

For Mama and Papa

CONTENTS

Photo section appears after page 186

It ain't where you from, it's where you at.
Eric B. and Rakim

1. THE SURPRISE

Glatten 1967

The Black Forest isn't black. It's not even a forest. Not any more. Eighteen hundred years ago, the wild Germanic tribes of the Alemanni first tore through the massed gloom that had so scared the Romans, to make space for cattle and villages. Celtic missionaries from Scotland and Ireland, armed with axes and faith, kept pushing inward until nature was bested, iniquity contained. Today, the remnants of the darkness mostly serve as raw material for children's nightmares and cuckoo clocks, as well as a magnificent tourism brand.

From all over the country and beyond, they flock to the low mountain range in Germany's south-westerly corner, to clear their lungs and hearts of all urban squalor. After the war, the Black Forest became a favourite of a film industry searching for an unsoiled backdrop, an idyllic setting for health clinics real and imagined, one of those places where fantasy and reality could blend into one another to enchanting effect.

Cynics beware, because it is, of course, all true – in the picture-perfect town of Glatten. The neat white houses with their gingerbread rooftops and wooden balconies, unpretentiously pushed up against the hills, keeping watch over endless slopes of green. 'Others build on top of the hill, to show off their splendour. But Swabians build their houses into the hill, to hide how big they truly are,' explains former Green party politician Rezzo Schlauch about the modest mindset of the local inhabitants, his kinsmen. 'They will keep the Mercedes in the garage and put the VW in the driveway.'

The river Glatt (Old High German for bright or smooth) flows down from the north into the tiny town that borrowed its name, past the steel-clad J. Schmalz GmbH vacuum technology factory. The river is a discreet chaperon to the high street (car dealership, bank, bakery, butcher, florist, a doner kebab stand) and hesitant supplier to the natural swimming pool, flowing out again next to the sports ground past Böffingen, a village that's been absorbed by Glatten proper.

A difficult climate – there's a lot of rain – makes this a paradise won, not given. They grow grass, corn, piglets and people of fearsome resolve and frugality here; an extreme type of Germans, harder than hard-working, unwilling to give themselves an inch. '*Schaffe, schaffe, Häusle baue*': you work, work, then build a house; that's how the famous saying in this region goes.

'To toil day and night is a big part of being Swabian,' says Schlauch. 'That has its roots in history, as has the Swabians' reputation for being innovative. In other regions, the first-born would inherit their parents' farms. But in Swabia, the land was partitioned equitably among the children. The farmland got smaller and smaller until it was no longer viable, so the descendants were forced to take up other jobs. Many of them became inventors and *Tüftler*, people looking to find new solutions to old problems.'

Local custom demands that everything must be done studiously, seriously. Including fun. One of the fourteen active social clubs in Glatten is dedicated to 'Carnival'. Another one brings together friends of the German Shepherd Dog.

Barns line a little street dotted with lumps of clay left behind by tractors, and then it's here, right next to a field: Isolde Reich's 'Haarstüble', a petite hair salon, discreet meeting place, outlet for charity socks hand-knitted by one of Reich's friends. The proceeds go towards buying shoes for the homeless.

Isolde was born in Glatten in 1962, the younger of two sisters. Her father Norbert, a talented goalkeeper, was a sport fanatic. Thwarted by a serious-minded father – 'he insisted Norbert should have a proper vocation, not try his hand at becoming a football pro,' Reich says – his career was over before it had really begun. His sporting ambitions, however, were undiminished. He played amateur football, handball and tennis, and tried to pass on his passion to his family. When his wife Elisabeth and eldest daughter Stefanie showed no inclination to take up any game, Norbert's hopes centred on Isolde. Before her birth ('In my album of baby photos, he wrote "Isolde, you should have been a boy, actually,"' she smiles), and after. 'I was the first girl in all of Glatten to go to football training.'

Norbert was her coach, his methods exacting and demanding. He took five-year-old Isolde to practise heading on the Riedwiesen football pitch next to the river, where an old heavy ball on a rope hung from a green iron bar. If her body positioning wasn't right or her arms were too high,

Norbert sent her to run a lap around the pitch for
punishment. 'He was tough but just. A man of principle,
full of passion,' Reich says.

In the summer of 1967, her mother left the family home
for a month. Elisabeth was heavily pregnant, and the risk of
complications made it necessary to check into a clinic in
Stuttgart, 80 minutes away to the north-west. The local
hospital at Freudenstadt, just 8.5km up the road, wasn't
equipped to perform caesareans. It was hard for Stefanie
and Isolde to be without their mother for such a long time.
'We were promised: "Mum will bring something amazing
for you when she comes back."'

When Norbert and Elisabeth arrived at the house,
however, they had a tiny baby in their arms, screaming its
head off. After an hour or so, the sisters wondered whether
it couldn't be taken back and exchanged for something
different. A small, shrieking brother – what a lousy surprise!
But Isolde soon realised that she had been given much more
than a second, annoyingly loud sibling that day. 'All of my
dad's sporting focus shifted immediately on to the boy. I was
relieved from practising headers with the pendulum,
allowed to take up ballet and athletics instead. Jürgen's birth
was my good fortune really. He set me free.'

2. ROSE MONDAY: ZERO HOUR

Mainz 2001

Christian Heidel loves the story so much, he's beginning to wonder if it's actually true. 'As a Mainzer, I could say: let's make this up. But it really happened,' he insists, readying himself for a mental hyper-jump: from the corporate blandness of his Schalke 04 office to a city lustily singing and dancing in a confetti rain, and a tiny, hopeless second-division team banished to a distinctly unsexy, provincial exile forty minutes away by car.

The day before, on 25 February 2001, FSV Mainz 05 had played their bogey side SpvGG Greuther Fürth and lost 3-1 at the Playmobil-Stadion. 'Klopp was a little bit injured and the worst man on the pitch, he had to come off twenty minutes before the end,' Heidel says. The defeat plunged Mainz deep into the relegation zone. 'We were *am Arsch*,' the former FSV general manager smiles. Quite literally in the bottom of the table, with no discernible light at the, ahem, end of the tunnel. 'We had 3,000 people at games on average, nobody cared about us any more. Everybody was sure we were going down.'

His colleagues on the Mainz board were all in the city centre, revelling in the Rose Monday carnival festivities for which the capital of Rhineland-Palatinate is famous in Germany. Half a million people dress up in silly costumes, get a little tipsy and a little flirty. State broadcasters ARD and ZDF devote an entire evening to the four-hour meeting of the city's carnival clubs at the Electoral Palace, a potpourri of beer-soaked gags and political satire.

Eckhart Krautzun, the well-travelled Mainz coach (nickname: 'Weltenbummler', globetrotter), deemed the temptations of the carnival too great for the team ahead of a very big game at Duisburg on Ash Wednesday. 'After losing in Fürth, the shit had hit the fan in Mainz. We knew that they would either axe the coach or set light to our backsides. We were secluded in a hotel in Bad Kreuznach for three days, so that no one got out and about,' says FSV midfielder Jürgen Kramny, Jürgen Klopp's roommate at the time.

Christian Heidel had stayed at home in Mainz. He wasn't in the mood for partying; the team's situation was too dire to act the fool. It was obvious that the coach had to go. Krautzun was a very pleasant man, no doubt, an experienced operator who had once coached Diego Maradona in a game for Al-Ahli FC in Saudi Arabia, the national teams of Kenya and Canada, as well as a raft of clubs around the world, but six points in nine games since he had taken over in November was the kind of run that was heading straight for relegation. Heidel also felt that Krautzun had somewhat tricked him into getting appointed in the first place.

His predecessor, the former Belgian international René Vandereycken, had been a gruff, monosyllabic coach whose refusal to communicate with players, board members and officials was matched only by his reluctance to put forward a coherent playing system. He was fired twelve games and a meagre twelve points into the 2000–01 season, with Mainz in the relegation zone once more. Heidel wanted someone in charge next who could re-implement the successful back four/zonal marking system that the former Mainz coach Wolfgang Frank had introduced six years earlier, a tactic seen as so modern and advanced at the time by Bundesliga standards that almost no one knew how to make it work.

Heidel: 'I told everybody that I wanted a coach with a sense of understanding of a back four. Somebody who could practise it, who could teach the players. All of a sudden, I get a call from Krautzun. I have to be honest, I hadn't thought of him at all. He'd been at Kaiserslautern before, it hadn't really worked out for him there, and I had the feeling there was no point. But he kept on talking and talking until he convinced me to meet him. So I went to see him in Wiesbaden. He proceeded to explain everything about the back four in great detail to me and I thought, "Fuck me, he really does know his stuff after all!" I had seen so much of Frank's training that I knew exactly what the specific exercises had looked like. So I appointed him coach. About two weeks later, Klopp came up to me and said that Krautzun had called him a month before. "He wanted to know how the back four works, we spoke for three hours." And that's what it looked like on the pitch. We won one game in the beginning and then it all went tits up.'

Getting rid of Krautzun was the sensible, easy decision. Finding the right successor proved much harder. Heidel tore through a mountain of *Kicker* yearbooks, hoping to excavate a suitable candidate. 'There was no World Wide

Web then. You didn't know who coached at Brugge, for example. In any case, these types of teams were five times our size. Different times. There were almost no foreign coaches in the Bundesliga either. You were fishing in the same pond the whole time.' After a while, Heidel closed all the books and admitted defeat: 'I thought the only chance left for us was to somehow get to the point where we played like we had under Wolfgang Frank. But I couldn't find anyone. I had no idea who could do this job.'

Maybe Heidel found inspiration in the jesters parading through the Mainz streets on the day when normal rules didn't apply. He was out of sensible answers. The only logical move left was to plump for the downright absurd. If there was no right coach to be found, maybe the answer . . . was to go without one?

'I thought "Let's do something spectacular. We should coach ourselves."' There were 'enough really good guys and intelligent players in the squad', he says, to make that crazy idea work, they could teach those who had arrived after Frank's time at the Bruchwegstadion. But football being football, someone still had to be in charge. Heidel chewed over putting himself up. 'I could have told them how the system works after attending so many of Wolfgang's sessions, but I had never played a single game in the Bundesliga, not even in the Oberliga [fourth division]. That would have looked stupid. That's why I gave Klopp a call in his hotel room in Bad Kreuznach. He had no clue what was coming.'

Heidel informed the veteran right-back that they couldn't carry on with Krautzun, that they had to make a change. 'I said to him: "I think you are uncoachable. The stuff we play here – or want to play – to be successful, nobody in Germany understands. You, the team, understand it. But it doesn't work out with any of the coaches." Klopp still didn't know what I was getting at. Then I said: "What do you think about us coaching ourselves? Someone has to front it, and that should be you." There was silence on the other side of the line, for maybe three, four seconds. Then he said: "Great idea. Let's do it."'

Heidel called captain Dimo Wache, the goalkeeper. 'Kloppo was the real captain, but Dimo had the armband. Dietmar Constantini [the coach prior to Krautzun] had taken it off Klopp, because he always complained about tactics. He was into tactics unlike any other player, he spent a lot of time thinking about it. Constantini had also taken him out of the team for a spell. Kloppo on the bench, that doesn't work at all. It's funny when he complains about players complaining today, you should have seen him then . . .

Harald Strutz, the debonair Mainz president, was busy fulfilling carnivalistic duties as a leading member of the *Ranzengarde*, a nineteenth-century guard of faux soldiers mocking Prussian militarism. 'Heidel called me and said: "We have to sack the manager, urgently,"' Strutz says, sitting in his neat office at Mainz's administrative headquarters in a corporate block outside the city. In the lobby, there's a glass cabinet with FSV merchandise, including a special version of Monopoly with Klopp and Heidel on the cover. 'Krautzun was very proper. He wanted to stay in the job but we told him it's over. So I took off my *Ranzengarde* uniform and drove to Bad Kreuznach. Everyone's partying on Rose Monday in Mainz but that doesn't mean everyone's drunk. Well, I wasn't, otherwise I wouldn't have driven there. We asked Kloppo: "Do you think you're up to it?" He didn't hesitate for a second: "Yes, absolutely. Yes, of course."'

Strutz pauses for a moment, taken aback by the incongruity of the most important decision he's ever presided over at Mainz. He's a local politician for the Liberal Democrats and works as a lawyer, there's a copy of the Bürgerliches Gesetzbuch, the German civil code, on his conference table. Strutz is, in summary, a pretty serious man. Not the kind of club boss you'd expect to get swept up by the *Schnapsidee* (flight of fancy) of his general manager. 'It's a very special story,' he continues. 'That was the beginning. Why should we change that? If you knew what it looked like here then . . . It was an extraordinary achievement to keep the whole team together. An extraordinary start to such a coaching career. This extraordinariness still fizzes in the mind.'

The ten local journalists who arrived for the FSV press conference at Bad Kreuznach the next day weren't as elated. Heidel: 'They already knew that Krautzun was gone. We confirmed it. Then this one journalist, Reinhard Rehberg, who still works today, said, "What is Klopp doing here?" They all thought we would appoint the assistant coach as caretaker manager but I don't think we even had an assistant manager at the time. So I said, "Kloppo will be the coach here." The whole table roared with laughter. They all cracked up. They took the piss out of us the next day in the papers. People believe that everybody cheers Klopp all the time but he wasn't the Klopp of today, he was the Klopp of then. He was a player, he didn't have a professional coaching badge, he had studied sport science.'

Klopp knew that the reporters didn't believe he was in any way qualified to save Mainz from the drop. He made a joke about his own inexperience, pretending he didn't know the script. 'You have to tell me what I have to say here,' he commanded the press corps with a broad smile.

'The next thing, I'll never forget this,' Heidel says. 'The journalists left and Klopp said: "We're off to train now." We boarded a couple of buses and drove to Friedrich-Moebus-Stadion. And I got there and I saw something that made me think: "Ah, there's life here." There were these poles on the pitch everywhere. The team were practising moving side to side in formation again. That's when I knew: we had returned to the times of Wolfgang Frank.'

The squad was as surprised as the journalists that Klopp was the new boss. 'All of a sudden, there's Kloppo in the meeting room addressing us as coach,' former FSV midfielder Sandro Schwarz remembers. 'He was still one of us, really, you didn't have to address him formally or keep your distance. He had a natural authority but we were still close, and he followed through on things. The team didn't mind because we were in such difficulties in the relegation fight. Nobody believed in us any more. The boys who had been there for a while longed to play the 4-4-2 system again, the system that had made us strong. With his positive demeanour, he got us to adopt the old behavioural patterns once more.'

The first-ever team meeting left a lasting impression on Heidel. 'I still remember how that room looked. This guy had never addressed a team before. Never. I was a bit leaner then, fitter. If somebody had given me a pair of boots right then, I would have dashed out to play against Duisburg after hearing him talk. I had witnessed ten, eleven coaches before. But nothing like that. You wanted to go out and play straight away. I left the room and encountered many doubters. They said, "He's only a player . . ." I told Strutz and my colleagues on the board that we would win, 100 per cent. If the team were as sure as I was, we had to win, we *would* win. I can't tell you the exact words but it was a mixture of tactics and motivation, more of a lecture. We could have played immediately. He talked and talked until the team believed they were good.'

'Taking the job felt like a kamikaze mission,' Klopp admitted to spox.com a decade later. 'There was only one question I asked myself: what can we do to stop losing? I didn't think about winning the game at all. The first session was all about running across the pitch tactically. I put up these poles and wondered what the right distances between the lines had been under Wolfgang Frank. Most players still had the right moves lodged in their long-term memory from the days they had practised it under him until they had been blue in the face. We wanted to play a game that was independent of the opposition.' As far as the motivational part of his pep talk was concerned, it too echoed one of Frank's themes: that 'investing the final 5 per cent' (Klopp) would make the difference.

Klopp made 'simple decisions', Kramny says. 'I moved from right midfield into the centre. One or two more changes. Heidel told us that we all had to pull together after giving previous coaches such a hard time. We all felt responsible. There wasn't much time to do a lot, so the idea was to inject a bit of fun, to practise our shape and dead balls. And then we said: Okay, let's go. Run, run, run. It was pissing down on matchday.'

Heidel: 'There were 4,500 people in the ground. Playing on Ash Wednesday is something special in Mainz. Duisburg were the much better side, a hot contender for promotion. I have to honestly say we played them off the park. We won 1-0 but they never got near our goal. They couldn't deal with our system at all. The people in the stadium went berserk.'

Those in the main stand had a particularly good time. They saw a Mainz coach 'behaving like the twelfth man, effectively playing the game on the touchline', Heidel adds. 'The stand only held 1,000 people at the time but they were in stitches laughing about that guy down below. I don't even know where he ran to when we scored. Maybe he was even sent off by the referee?' (He wasn't, on this occasion.) 'It was all very, very special. But you have to say this: that was his birth. And then he was on his way.'

3. REVOLUTION 09

Dortmund 2008

It's a sharp winter's night in Marbella in January 2017, and the Don Pepe Gran Meliá Hotel lobby is a *Dynasty* set designer's dream: white marble, gold-cased pillars, potted palm trees. And a man playing the saxophone.

Borussia Dortmund staffers in shorts are pushing crates of dirty apparel from the evening's training session past the vacant hotel bar. Sitting on a cream-coloured sofa, Hans-Joachim Watzke takes in the scene with a contented nod. The 58-year-old BVB CEO is a successful entrepreneur; his workwear company, Watex, turns over €250m annually. He's the man who saved the club from bankruptcy in 2005, the man who brought back the good football, the excitement and the trophies to the Westfalenstadion by hiring Jürgen Klopp in 2008. But, like any true supporter, he seems to find the most happiness and pride in just being here, on a ten-day winter break trip to Andalusia with the team. He's wearing a training suit with his initials on the chest.

'Why Klopp? It's an easy question to answer,' he says, setting down his espresso cup. 'In 2007, it was clear that we would survive as a club, but also clear that we had no money to put into the team.'

Ballspielverein Borussia 09 e.V Dortmund, Bundesliga champions in 1995 and 1996, Champions League winners in 1997 and champions again in 2002, had done a 'Leeds'. A cash injection of €130m from floating the club on the Frankfurt stock exchange in 2000 had been spent on hugely expensive players in an unsustainable arms race with Bayern Munich. When the team failed to qualify for the Champions League in 2005 for the second time in a row, the club almost collapsed under the weight of €240m worth of debt. 'We were at the club HQ and didn't know whether we would still have a job the next day,' stadium announcer and former BVB striker Norbert 'Nobby' Dickel says. 'Awful times.'

'Dortmund is a city that lives with the club, that lives for the club,' Sebastian Kehl says. The former captain remembers the whole town being on edge, extremely worried that Borussia could be wound up. 'Taxi drivers, bakers, hotel employees – everybody feared for their livelihood. It was very tough to deal with for us players, knowing that winning or losing won't make much of a difference.'

It was Watzke, the former treasurer of the club (not the plc), who saved BVB, by wresting control from the quite literally discredited duo of sporting director Michael Meier and president Gerd Niebaum. He negotiated a loan from Morgan Stanley and a capital increase, enabling Dortmund to buy back their stadium and end a crippling lease-back arrangement. But the radical cost-cutting plan left no funds to buy star names.

Watzke: '[Sporting director] Michael Zorc and I had agreed that we wanted to build a young team. [Left-back] Marcel Schmelzer was already there, and [midfielder Kevin] Großkreutz. We wanted to play different football as well. Under Bert van Marwijk and Thomas Doll, the ball would go from one end of the back four to the other and back again, ten times in a row. We had 57 per cent possession but there was no action. You can't play like that in Dortmund. We wanted to promise people a team that ran so hard that bits would come off. That's what we had encountered at Mainz when we played there in the prior two years. You always felt they weren't that good but somehow made it very difficult for you and beat you sometimes. Because they had the mentality of murderers. And a very good set-up, tactically. That had to be down to their coach. Taking someone from the second division would have been difficult for Dortmund now. But back then, it was possible.'

Borussia weren't entirely sure Klopp could make the transition from patron saint at Mainz to reviving a Bundesliga giant that had fallen on hard times, Christian Heidel reveals. 'They had concerns,' he says. Watzke first approached the Mainz general manager in October 2007, ahead of the German FA annual general meeting. Heidel: 'He phoned and asked if we could go for a coffee. I didn't know him then. We sat down and the talk quickly turned to Jürgen Klopp. His contract was up at the end of the season. Watzke asked: "How good is Klopp?" I said: "If I now say that he's good, you'll pinch him off me. I could also lie and tell you that he's useless. But then you'll tell that to Kloppo and he'll be upset with me." Then I said: "This guy is a Bundesliga coach."' Watzke probed further, without explicitly mentioning

Dortmund. Was Klopp able to coach a big Bundesliga club? 'I told him that Kloppo could coach any club in the world,' Heidel says. 'That's because he's got an advantage [over his peers]: he's really intelligent. He will adjust at a big club. If you need someone in a suit and in a tie, don't get Jürgen Klopp. But if you want a top coach, you'll have to get him. It wasn't a case of making an immediate decision but I know that Dortmund were looking at him a bit more closely from that day on. But they still weren't entirely convinced. Watzke kept on calling me, I don't know how many times. I always said: "Go for it, go for it. You will never regret the day you sign Jürgen Klopp."'

Regrets over the hiring of Thomas Doll were growing all the time at Strobelallee. The former Germany midfielder, in the job since March 2007, failed to inspire the players or the public with the painfully dull brand of football his team played. Dortmund were closer to relegation than to the top of the table and ended up in thirteenth place, their worst league position in twenty years. A good run in the DFB Pokal, where in the final in April they were beaten only by Bayern Munich in extra-time (2-1), couldn't deflect from the shortcomings. 'Perhaps it was the most valuable final defeat in the club's history,' Sascha Fligge and Frank Fligge wrote in *Echte Liebe*, a chronicle of Dortmund's comeback over the past decade. 'In the case of a cup triumph, the club's leadership would have had a hard time firing coach Thomas Doll, in whose qualities they had stopped believing. Jürgen Klopp might never have gone to Dortmund. History would have taken a very different turn.' 'The defeat [in Berlin] was part of the strategic plan to clear the path for Jürgen Klopp,' Watzke joked later. Klopp, incidentally, had followed the match in Berlin as a TV pundit for state broadcaster ZDF and confided in programme editor Jan Doehling that he wanted to be 'down there on the touchline one day'. Back at their Berlin hotel, Dortmund fans were serenading him with 'Jürgen Klopp, you are the best man' in the lobby. They wanted him to take over.

Watzke says he always felt that Klopp's personality was big enough for the Herculean task: 'We had a sense from his TV work that he had the ability to present [a big project]. We didn't talk about any other manager. We only wanted Klopp.' A clandestine meeting at the offices of one of Watzke's friends not far from Mainz brought further certainty following Doll's resignation on 19 May. 'Once the employees were all gone, we got together,' says Watzke. 'It was a fantastic conversation. We told him our vision for the club, and it corresponded with his. Michael Zorc had gone to meet him separately the day before. We wanted to form an opinion independently of each other. We're often in agreement, but we were completely in agreement here. The chemistry was immediately very strong.'

Chemistry of a more synthetic kind exerted a pull on Klopp, too, however. Bayer 04 Leverkusen, owned by the eponymous pharmaceutical company, had also set their eye on the coach. They didn't have the cachet of the Black and Yellows, but were free from money problems as well as possessing a decent, well-balanced squad capable of challenging for Champions League qualification. 'Kloppo didn't want to go to Dortmund at first, he wanted to go to Leverkusen,' says Heidel. 'I said to him he had to go to Dortmund, because of the emotions there, and so on. He had a conversation with [Leverkusen CEO] Wolfgang Holzhäuser. They couldn't make up their minds . . . Then Dortmund's interest grew more concrete. But Klopp wasn't sure initially.'

His remuneration was another sticking point, Heidel adds, with a small chuckle. 'A funny story. Dortmund's first offer came in lower than his existing wages at Mainz in Bundesliga 2. They weren't that flush at the time. Kloppo said: "Listen, they offered me less than I'm making at Mainz." I said: "Don't worry, I'll help you." Dortmund couldn't get their head round the fact he was making that much already. Watzke called again: "How much does he earn at yours?" "He earns good money here, he's the most important man, I'd rather save money on a player," I told him. "I don't believe it," Watzke said. They revised his salary upwards.' Klopp signed a two-year deal at Dortmund's Lennhof hotel on the morning of Friday 23 May and was unveiled at 11 a.m. at the stadium.

Borussia, in truth, had more than pecuniary rewards to offer. In Josef Schneck, they employed a press officer that Klopp really liked, for starters. 'We first met in April 2004, at an event in Cologne,' Schneck, a kind, jovial man in his mid-sixties, says. That night, Klopp was receiving a Fair Play award from the association of German sports journalists for the way he had dealt with the heartbreaking finishes to the previous two Bundesliga 2 seasons. Matthias Sammer, then the Borussia Dortmund coach, was invited to give the laudatory speech. 'We went there with Matthias, and Karin, his wife, and we sat with Klopp at the same table. It was a very nice evening,' Schneck recalls. It's a touching little anecdote, considering that Sammer and Klopp would fall out spectacularly a few years later, at the height of the Bayern–Dortmund rivalry.

'I also knew Jürgen from press conferences [when Mainz had played in the Bundesliga between 2004 and 2007],' Schneck continues. 'Once, Mainz drew 1-1 with us, in Dortmund, and I congratulated him on winning a point. To draw at Dortmund was a success for Mainz, wasn't it? But he just looked at me and said: "Congratulations to you too." That was classic Klopp. And after he came here, in his first few weeks at the club, he joked to Michael Zorc: "I couldn't decide whether or not I should sign for Dortmund. But I knew you had a decent press officer, so you can't have been too bad a club."'

What's more, few clubs could count on such fervent support. The Signal Iduna Park's famous 'Yellow Wall', Europe's biggest terrace with 25,000 standing places, appealed to 'the football passion that burns inside of me', Klopp told reporters at his unveiling. 'Whoever has been down on the pitch here knows the [Yellow Wall] is something extra-special, one of the most impressive things you can find in football. It's an honour for me to be the coach of BVB and to be able to get the club back into the groove. It's a wonderful story. I'm incredibly excited to get to work here.' Was it a big step up for him, from the carnival club Mainz to one of the league's traditional heavyweights?, somebody enquired. 'We didn't stagger from one gala session to the next in Mainz,' he smiled. 'We worked with great discipline. I feel well prepared.'

There were rumours in the city that some of the sponsors and companies involved in Dortmund's debt restructuring had hoped for a more urbane coach, a big name with international pulling power.

Klopp, perhaps aware of these misgivings, wore a jacket in the press room. But no tie. 'Secretly, quietly, he has worked on the gentrification of his wardrobe over the last few months,' *Frankfurter Allgemeine Sonntags-Zeitung* noted. His fiery rhetoric, however, paid homage to the working-class region's deep-rooted love of football as wild entertainment, a source of identity and a quasi-religious experience.

'It's always about making the crowd happy, it's about producing games with a recognisable style,' he vowed. 'When matches are boring, they lose their rationale. My teams have never played chess on the pitch. I hope we will witness the odd full-throttle occasion here. The sun won't shine every day in Dortmund, but we have a chance to make it shine more often.' *Süddeutsche Zeitung*'s BVB reporter Freddie Röckenhaus was very impressed with so much solar-powered optimism. 'If Klopp trains the team as well as he does punch lines, Dortmund will soon be ready for the Champions League,' he wrote. 'It's only taken him forty-five minutes to sweep BVB supporters off their feet with his infectious sparkle and eloquence. If ever a coach's mentality fit right into the football-mad Ruhr area, then Klopp's does.'

The excitement was not confined to followers of Borussia. On Klopp's personal home page, a user stated his approval. 'It's great that you're going to BVB,' he wrote. 'That club isn't my team at all but I own plenty of their shares. Since I have great confidence in you and am aware of your abilities, I'm already looking forward to having more money in my pocket.' The anonymous investor's trust would prove justified. Dortmund's share price rose by 132 per cent: from €1.59 on 23 May 2008 to €3.70 on the day of Klopp's departure, precisely seven years later.

4. THE ROAD TO ANFIELD

2012–2015

On 11 April 2014 at 10 p.m., Jürgen Klopp met Hans-Joachim Watzke for a drink at Munich's Park Hilton Hotel and told him that he had made up his mind. He was staying put.

Earlier that day, ahead of the team's departure for an away game at Bayern's Allianz Arena, the Borussia Dortmund coach had still been undecided. He'd received a tempting, hugely lucrative offer from the north-west of England, a chance to take over and revolutionise one of the biggest clubs in the world. 'We first met in my kitchen,' says Watzke. 'Without going into details, it was an interesting talk. I think it made a difference because he said to me on the plane that we needed to talk again in the evening. I was due to have dinner with my daughter, who lived in Munich, so I could only see him at 10 p.m. He straightaway said: "I can't deal with this pressure any more. I've turned them down."'

Not long before, Manchester United executive vice chairman Ed Woodward had flown out to see Klopp in

Germany. David Moyes' short tenure at Old Trafford was coming to an end, and Klopp was United's favourite to replace him, to bring back a sense of adventure to the Red Devils' game. Woodward told Klopp that the Theatre of Dreams was 'like an adult version of Disneyland', a mythical place where, as the nickname suggested, the entertainment on show was world-class and dreams came true. Klopp wasn't entirely convinced by that sales pitch – he found it a bit 'unsexy', he told a friend – but he didn't dismiss the proposition out of hand either. After almost six years in the job at Dortmund, perhaps the time was ripe for a change of scenery.

Aware of United's interest, Watzke had intended to insist that Klopp honour his contract, which had been extended to 2018 only the preceding autumn. Sensing that the 46-year-old was quite conflicted, Watzke changed tack and opted for a very risky strategy. If Klopp wanted to go to Man Utd, he wouldn't stand in his way, he told him, playing on their mutual trust and a connection that had long since crossed from business into the territory of friendship. After some deliberation – and the conversation at Watzke's kitchen table – the BVB manager came to the conclusion that his work at the Signal Iduna Park was not yet done.

United, however, felt there was still a possibility of luring him away. When Moyes received his inevitable marching orders on 22 April, Klopp was quickly installed as the bookmakers' favourite to succeed the Scot. Incessant media speculation in the UK prompted the Swabian to release a statement via the *Guardian* the next day, to kill the rumour. 'Man Utd is a great club and I feel very familiar with their wonderful fans,' it read, 'but my commitment to Borussia Dortmund and the people is unbreakable.'

Klopp continued to attract interest from the Premier League, regardless. Six months after he had turned down Woodward, Manchester United's local rivals Manchester City made an approach. Tottenham Hotspur, too, enquired about his services. At the same time, Klopp used an interview with BT Sport ahead of Dortmund's Champions League game at Arsenal to make his long-term intentions known. Asked whether he would be coming to England once his time at Borussia was over, the answer was unequivocal. 'It's the only country, I think, where I should work, really, [after] Germany,' he nodded, 'because it's the only country I know the language a little bit. And I need the language for my work. So we will see. If somebody will call me, then we will talk about it.'

The writing was very much on the wall then, Watzke says. Dortmund were having their first – and only – poor domestic campaign with Klopp in charge, and an escape to rainier climes all of a sudden held more attraction than before. Watzke: 'Our season was already in the toilet, and you got that distinct feeling . . . For me it was clear that he wouldn't go anywhere else in Germany after Borussia, he wouldn't have been able to do that. He always said he didn't study English but I'm pretty sure he polished it a little bit. I could observe that he had. It was obvious that he'd go to the Premier League. That's his game.'

A football romanticist, Klopp had long been an avowed fan of the real, no-holds-barred version of the sport played across the channel. At a Spanish winter training camp as Mainz coach in 2007, he had devoured Nick Hornby's *Fever Pitch* (and chased a lizard around his hotel room with his toothbrush in front of a TV crew); much of the inspiration for his brand of muscular, passionate football, as well as the idea that his teams could feed off the electricity of a fanatical crowd, derived from the sport's motherland. Both at Mainz and at Dortmund, the crowds belted out passable versions of 'You'll Never Walk Alone', conjuring up fervent atmospheres that took conscious inspiration from (idealised) English traditions. 'I like what we in Germany call "*Englischer Fußball*": rainy day, heavy pitch, everybody is dirty in the face and they go home and can't play for the next four weeks,' he said to the *Guardian* in 2013. That year, his young Dortmund team had gatecrashed Europe's elite competition, bursting all the way to the final of the Champions League, while he was wearing a baseball cap that had the word 'Pöhler' imprinted on it – Ruhr area slang for somebody playing football the old-fashioned way, 'on a Sunday morning on a lawn, the basics, loving the game'.

Almost exactly one year after Klopp had said no to United, his bond with Dortmund turned out to be breakable after all. He announced he would resign at the end of the 2014–15 season, making sure to add that he didn't intend to take a sabbatical.

In an art nouveau villa in Bremen's leafy Schwachhausen quarter, the phone started ringing a few weeks into the new Premier League season. As Brendan Rodgers' time at Anfield came to a slow, drawn-out end, a number of people contacted Klopp's agent Marc Kosicke, promising to make an introduction to Liverpool. One, a German football agent, said he knew Kenny Dalglish really well. Kosicke preferred to wait. Eventually, somebody purporting to be Liverpool FC chief executive Ian Ayre called. Could they have a conversation about Klopp coming to Anfield? They could, Kosicke replied, but only via a video Skype call. While Ayre hung up, ahead of calling again over the app, Kosicke did a quick image search of the Liverpool official. Just to be sure. Too many pranksters and time wasters out there.

'Once you've been at Dortmund, where can you go as a coach?' Martin Quast, a friend of Klopp since the early nineties, asks. 'In Germany, there's only the national team left for Kloppo, everything else would be a step down, even Bayern. Kloppo gets off on emotions, on empathy, on rocking the house, on being a part of something really big. Compared with Dortmund, Bayern doesn't really give you that. I could only imagine him taking on a club abroad, a club like Liverpool.'

Christian Heidel says Klopp had only one reservation: his English. 'We talked about it for a long time. He asked me: "Should I do it?" I said: "The spoken word is your weapon, you know that. You have to decide if you can get across what's important in English. If you let others talk for you, it won't work. You're only 70 per cent Klopp then. You need to be sure." And then he said: "I'll manage it. I'll study now, and I'll get there." And since he's very intelligent, he got there, very quickly. I think at the time [of LFC's approach], no other club would have stood a chance with him. He'd always been keen on them, he was excited by the emotional dimension of the job. I don't think he'd have gone to Manchester City or a club like that – even though they really wanted him.'

Klopp's name had first cropped up at Anfield in the spring of 2012, as possible successors to Kenny Dalglish were being sounded out. A middle-man got in touch with the Dortmund coach but was told in no uncertain terms that Klopp had no intention of leaving. He was on the way to winning a historic double.

In September 2015, things got much more serious, rapidly. Brendan Rodgers' poor start to the season had prompted Boston-based Fenway Sports Group (FSG), Liverpool FC's owners, to scour the market for the next manager. 'We were thinking about someone who had experience and success at the highest level,' FSG president Mike Gordon, fifty-two, explains. 'Jürgen had done that domestically, obviously in the Bundesliga. He really had done that, apart from maybe one or two kicks, in the Champions League, too. I think his credentials as one of the best managers, if not the best, were apparent for all. And we liked the type of football he played. Both the energy and the emphasis on attacking: high-electricity, high-wattage football with an appeal. So from a football sense it was a relatively easy and straightforward decision.'

While there were 'obvious grounds for support' for Klopp, as Gordon puts it, FSG's point man for Liverpool conducted due diligence on the German to see whether the hype was borne out by reality. 'I tried to set aside his popularity in the football world and his charisma, for an unbiased analysis,' says the former hedge fund manager, who started out selling popcorn at baseball games as a kid. 'I did a fair amount of research along with the people inside the club, determining how he should be evaluated, purely in an analytical and football sense. The process was much the same you would undergo in the investment business before taking a big position. I am happy to say – and it is self-evident at this point – that however high and elevated his reputation was in the football world, the facts were actually more compelling and more persuasive still.'

Gordon's research pointed to Klopp having had 'a decidedly positive effect, in a quantifiable sense, relative to what you might otherwise expect' on Mainz and Dortmund. Put more simply, the Swabian had outperformed. The appeal to Liverpool, whose strategy is based on a smarter use of resources, in comparison with some of their more financially potent rivals in the Premier League, was clear. 'In a football sense, it was pretty straightforward,' says Gordon. 'But of course, I didn't know if philosophies and personalities, that of the club and Jürgen's, would mesh. It had to be a mutual fit. We also needed to know whether Jürgen wanted to lead the football programme and project of Liverpool. Those were very important pieces that needed to be determined.'

A meeting was scheduled in New York on 1 October. Klopp's and Kosicke's attempt at secrecy got off to a very bad start, however. In the Lufthansa lounge at Munich airport, one of the staff asked Klopp – whose baseball cap didn't make for much of a disguise – why he was going to JFK. 'We're watching a basketball game,' he replied. A plausible explanation, except for the fact that the start of the NBA season was another four weeks away.

An hour after their arrival in Manhattan, the two Germans were rumbled again. As luck would have it, the receptionist at the Plaza Hotel on 5th Avenue hailed from the coach's footballing hometown. 'My word, it's Kloppo!' he exclaimed in broad Mainz dialect. Somehow, news of the clandestine trip never leaked.

FSG's principal owner John W. Henry, LFC chairman Tom Werner, and Gordon met with Klopp and his agent at the offices of law firm Shearman & Sterling on Lexington Avenue, a few blocks to the east. 'My first impression was that he was very tall. And I am not,' Gordon laughs. 'It was very late but we had this very lengthy and substantive talk, and then we adjourned until the next day and met for more lengthy and substantive talks at the hotel. I want to emphasise: these were very much two-way conversations. This was about Jürgen being right for Liverpool FC and Liverpool FC, us as owners, being right for Jürgen.' Klopp's charisma, as suspected, was of a similar size to his frame ('he uses his personal skills, and his way of relating to people, to get across his message') but what Gordon was struck by most was 'the enormity of substance' he detected behind the toothy smile and super-sized persona. 'It wasn't about "boy, this guy is really charming, he is going to do wonderfully at press conferences and as a representative of a club". Very quickly, what came across was his breadth of talent: not just the personal side, but the level of intelligence, the kind of analytical thinking, the logic, the clarity and honesty, his ability to communicate so effectively even though English was not his first language. That side I think he doesn't always get full credit for because people are so taken with him as a person in the flesh.'

Klopp told the FSG executives that football was 'more than a system', that it was 'also rain, tackles flying in, the noise in the stadium'. Most of all, he said, the Anfield crowd had to be 'activated' by the style of performance, to spur on the team and vice versa in a self-amplifying cycle of exuberance.

Gordon: 'It was very hard to find anything that was in any way deficient and that is the honest truth. What I am saying is: it was clear that Jürgen, as a football manager, really was on the same level as a corporate leader or someone you would choose to run your company. I say this as someone who's spent twenty-seven years as an investor, engaging with some of the very top CEOs and leaders of business in America and Europe. At that point it was obvious to me that he was the right person. So we decided to discuss parameters and that's when Jürgen excused himself.'

While Kosicke continued to discuss remuneration, Klopp walked around Central Park. The stroll would last longer than anticipated. Both sides were initially rather far apart, financially, but the outline for an agreement was eventually found.

After Klopp had returned to Germany, Gordon sent him a text message. 'Words cannot express how excited we are,' it read. In his reply, Klopp apologised that he didn't have the right vocabulary either. But he did know one word that summed up his feelings: 'Wooooooooooooow!!!'

5. IN THE GAME OF THE FATHER

In the summer of 1940, school was out for Norbert Klopp. His father Karl, a hired hand at the farms and vineyards surrounding the city of Kirn in Rhineland-Palatinate, needed the six-year-old – the only son in a family of four kids – to join in the work.

Tending the fertile fields of the south-west kept the Klopps alive during Germany's darkest years. The region's most famous football team, 1. FC Kaiserslautern, too, relied on local produce for sustenance, once the sun started to shine again in 1945. The 'Red Devils', whose ranks included superstar and recently released POW Fritz Walter, played dozens of friendlies against village sides in exchange for potatoes and onions.

Norbert Klopp wanted to be a footballer. Who didn't? He had shot up to 1.91m in his teenage years, and grown into a strong, agile goalkeeper. He played for local side VfR Kirn, one of the best clubs in the region, and his early talent was such that he was invited to a trial with Kaiserslautern in 1952. 'I was awestruck,' the eighteen-year-old told family friend Ulrich Rath later, 'I was on the pitch with all these legendary players . . .' Lautern were royalty. They had won the German championship the previous season and would win it again in 1953. Four of their players – Fritz Walter, Ottmar Walter, Werner Liebrich and Werner Kohlmeyer – went on to lift the World Cup in Berne in 1954.

Klopp, for all his talent, wasn't quite at their level. Back at VfR Kirn, who had been promoted to the (regionally segmented) first division and took on the likes of Lautern and Mainz 05, he couldn't get past Alfred Hettfleisch, the number one between the posts. As Kirn's reserve goalkeeper, Klopp was briefly afforded the newly introduced *Vertragsamateur* (amateur under contract) status that introduced professionalism in all but name in West Germany. But monthly wages of DM40 to 75 made the players hugely dependent on points bonuses (between DM10 and 40). Klopp had little chance to share in these: since substitutions weren't permitted, he never made it into the line-up of the first team. He continued in the reserve team against other amateurs, for the fun of it.

Karl Klopp insisted the boy took on a 'proper job'. Norbert started an apprenticeship at Müller & Meirer, a manufacturer of small leather goods. About half of Kirn's population, 5,000 people, worked in the tanning and leather industry in the early 1950s, as Germany's economic miracle rapidly raised living standards. 'A leather craftsman earned between DM250 and 300 a month, it was a good job at the time,' says Horst Dietz, eighty, who worked in the same section as Norbert Klopp, sitting in the row behind him. A row consisted of three people: an apprentice, a 'gluer' (often a young girl) and a craftsman, and each room had about twenty rows, supervised by a master at the front. It was piecework: one row produced up to 100 wallets or similar goods a day, working from 7 a.m. to 5 p.m., with a one-hour lunch break.

The loft in Dietz's house in Kirn resembles a sports pub. Framed shirts and cups from his playing days for VfR Kirn line the walls, there's a photo of him and Franz Beckenbauer, a huge screen for live football and an actual bar. He used to live in the countryside as a youngster, Klopp's family were in the town centre. Norbert would often take him home for lunch during the working week. 'He was like a big brother for me. The Klopps were very well known, but they lived a normal life,' says Dietz. 'Working hard was one of their principles.' If articles remained unfinished at the end of a shift it was expected they would be completed at home. 'We tried to give them to our grandmas to do, because at fourteen, fifteen, we were interested in girls and going out in the evening,' he smiles. Unlike Klopp, who was three years his senior, he made it into Kirn's starting XI as a striker, playing for a few years in the second division before taking on a job with Coca-Cola. 'Norbert was very ambitious, he always wanted to go to the very top,' Dietz recalls. 'He was a daredevil, not only in sport. A charismatic guy who'd go somewhere and immediately own the room. He was full of energy and charm. A ladies' man, one might say. We often spent the whole day talking about football.'

In 1959, Norbert Klopp moved south to the Black Forest town of Dornhan, to work in the nearby Sola leather plant. He joined TSF Dornhan as player-manager, playing in a variety of positions. His shots from the edge of the box were much feared, Rath says. The neatly turned out septuagenarian – slick grey hair, lucid eyes – had been a promising footballer himself in his youth, playing for Württemberg's regional team before a treble leg break put paid to his playing career. He's now SV Glatten's honorary chairman.

At a wedding in Dornhan – 'they were public affairs then, you didn't have to have an invitation,' Dietz says – Norbert Klopp met Elisabeth 'Lisbeth' Reich. The daughter of a brewery owner was considered 'a good catch', Dietz adds. Following their wedding in the autumn of 1960, Norbert Klopp helped out in the Schwanen-Bräu family firm, run by his mother-in-law, Helene Reich. Elisabeth's father had come home from the war with a moving piece of shrapnel in his head and died soon after. Klopp's role at Schwanen-Bräu included being a *Festzeltmeister* – the person responsible for setting up beer tents for festivals. Elisabeth's brother Eugen took over the company until it closed down in 1992.

In his early thirties, Klopp retrained as a merchant, taking evening lessons in nearby Freudenstadt. His new job, as a sales representative for Fischer, a manufacturer of fixing systems, saw him travel all over the south of Germany during the week. Tall, smooth and handsome, Klopp was 'born to be a sales person', says Rath. 'He was likeable, sociable. A great entertainer who could tell the best stories. He could speak in the Swabian dialect to someone on the right and standard German to the left.' Her husband, Klopp's mother Elisabeth said, was a natural orator: 'He could just go.' 'An ace, rhetorically,' is how Isolde Reich describes her father.

Martin Quast's father, who also hails from Kirn, knew Norbert Klopp well. They played field handball together. 'He told me that Norbert was always at the centre of everything. "Where there was Norbert, there was laughter." Anyone who had the faintest interest in sport in Kirn knew and liked him. Sounds familiar, doesn't it?'

Norbert Klopp was a stickler for appearances. 'He needed more time in the bathroom in the morning than us three women,' Isolde smiles. 'He always looked his Sunday best. Jogging trousers were considered appropriate for sports but not acceptable inside the house. And under no circumstances outside!' One day, she recalls, Norbert drove one of his sons-in-law and a friend to see Jürgen play for Mainz 05. He wore a white shirt, a tie and yellow V-neck jumper, 'a bit like [the then German foreign secretary Hans-Dietrich] Genscher'. They stopped at a service station, and Norbert took the opportunity to lecture the critically underdressed state of his companions 'on the right attire for viewing a football game in Mainz'. Even at carnival, a dress code was strictly enforced: the whole family would go as clowns, with Jürgen riding in a handcart as a toddler. Klopp senior ironed his own shirts and cut the kids' hair. His son's eyebrows formed a natural border below which no strand of hair was allowed to fall. Stubble was also strictly *verboten*. 'Norbert, who dressed immaculately at all times, and Jürgen sometimes clashed about his casual outfits and sporty style,' says Rath. One of the first things her brother did upon moving out of the house was to 'throw away the shaver and hair brush', Isolde adds.

It was hugely important for Norbert that the kids witnessed historical events, such as the moon landing or Muhammad Ali's fights. The family huddled around a small, black-and-white television in the living room, fortified by tea and sandwiches. If one of the children fell asleep,

Norbert would poke them in the side to wake them up again.

Within a few years of coming to Glatten, Norbert Klopp had become one of its most important sportsmen. He played in SV Glatten's seniors' football team until he was forty (while his children picked up empties on the touchline to earn a few Pfennige), coached the first team for a season and served as a board member. As his legs tired, his passion for playing tennis grew. Norbert was instrumental in setting up SV Glatten's tennis section, and the building of a clay court. The club had initially hired a concrete court in an old quarry in Dornhan after Klopp had paid the reluctant owner DM50 to give the Glatteners access. In winter, he went skiing with Ulrich Rath. Isolde was named after Rath's sister.

Every Saturday, in honour of the father's return home, the house was tidied up. Little Jürgen, however, did his best to excuse himself from these chores, telling his older sisters that he had to study for school. 'In practice, he was lying comfortably in bed, his head buried in a book,' Isolde says. His roguish ways reminded her of Emil i Lönneberga, the blond, blue-eyed prankster in Astrid Lindgren children's book.

A photo from his first day at school shows him with a bandaged knee. He had run out of the house, traditional cone of candy in hand, and stumbled. 'You see,' his father gently admonished him, 'if you hadn't run so fast, you wouldn't have a Band-Aid on the picture.' On other occasions, he fell off his desk chair, lacerating an eyelid, and ran into a scooter, cutting his nose.

'Jürgen's birth was a huge moment for Norbert,' says Rath. 'He finally had a real sportsman to share his passions with.' Pressure on the girls to excel in sports ceased almost immediately after Jürgen's arrival. They were allowed to devote time to their own hobbies, like ballet and music. Elisabeth, a loving, even-tempered mum, who decided that the kids should become Protestants, like her (Norbert was Catholic), had a hard time fitting in all the children's activities.

Norbert was his son's personal football, tennis and skiing teacher, and he taught by subjecting him to an ultra-competitive regime. 'Early in the morning, come rain or shine, he would put me on the touchline on the pitch, let me start running for a bit and then ran himself, overtaking me,' Jürgen Klopp told *Abendblatt* in 2009. 'It was a far cry from being fun.' The exercise was repeated, week after week, until Klopp was faster than his dad. Norbert also registered him with the athletics club, to improve his pace. In addition, Jürgen would have to spend hours practising headers, just like Isolde had done before him.

Aged six, he joined the 'E' youth team (under-11) of SV Glatten, newly formed by coach Ulrich Rath in 1973. In his first game, Jürgen was tackled and did an involuntary somersault, breaking his collarbone on impact. 'The very next week he was back, his arm in a sling, staring longingly at his teammates from the sidelines and running to catch wayward balls, just to be involved somehow,' Rath says. 'That showed you what he was all about.'

He takes his visitor down a few steps, deeper into local history. Rath's basement is a shrine to all things SV Glatten. Naturally, it's the team of youngsters including his two sons and Jürgen Klopp, his third one, the son of all of Glatten, that takes pride of place. Rath still gets upset when the media refers to Klopp as a *Stuttgarter*: 'He was only there for one week, in the first few days after his birth!' he shakes his head and takes out a photo. Here they all are as nine-year-olds, celebrating a cup win in a regional tournament played on Pfingsten, Pentecost. Klopp, the team's striker, later self-mockingly joked that it was the only trophy he ever won as a footballer. Hundreds of hobby footballers have since won *the* Klopp trophy, but only a few of them know much about that fact. It had been Norbert Klopp's idea, Rath recalls, to cobble together a prize for the winners of Glatten's inaugural open tournament in 1977: he took one of his son's football boots, spray-painted it gold, and mounted it on a wooden box.

That same year, Stuttgarter Kicker's under-11s came to Glatten for a friendly game. The boys from the capital of Baden-Württemberg arrived with tents and slept in the nearby woods, where pigs were roasted on an open fire. The occasion is fondly remembered for a rafting trip down the Gumpen, where the Rivers Glatt and Lauter meet. Many of the Kickers lads fell into the water, among them an eventual European Cup winner. Robert Prosinečki, the future playmaker of Red Star Belgrade and Yugoslavia/Croatia, was playing for the Swabians at the time but was ultimately deemed not good enough. He returned to Zagreb two years later, aged ten.

Jürgen, like most boys from the region, supported Kickers' bigger, more successful, rivals, VfB Stuttgart. A trial as a youngster was unsuccessful but he did get a red tracksuit, which he proudly wore until Stefanie ruined it in an accident with a hot iron. Perhaps to make up for that tragic loss, his grandmother Anna famously knitted him a white jumper with a red hoop and a '4' on the back, the number of his favourite player, West Germany international Karl-Heinz

Förster. He wore it on trips to the Neckarstadion with friends and family.

Klopp admired the hard-nosed centre-back's calmness under pressure and utter dedication. 'We later found out that we had the same sporting idols,' says Martin Quast. 'Förster, a man with strategic vision, and Boris Becker, who lived off impulse and emotions. Kloppo once told me that he would be standing on the terraces as an ultra if football hadn't worked out for him, and that he had the red hoop implanted in his chest.' His love for VfB might have cooled a little in subsequent years. Ulrich Rath is moved to tears recalling the day when Klopp, as coach of Mainz 05, evaded officious stewards and jumped over an advertising board in Stuttgart's stadium to seek out a delegation of his old friends from Glatten, who were sitting in the Untertürckheimer Kurve section. 'I said to him, "Jürgen, I have a dilemma, two hearts are beating in my chest. One for VfB, one for you." He said: "Ulrich, that can't be true. A man only has one heart – and yours is beating for me." We all laughed but I think he was very serious.'

Norbert Klopp was one of those football dads who could barely contain his passion on the sidelines. 'Jürgen has his father's temperament and his mother's calmness,' Isolde Reich says. He felt the force of his father's uncompromising, exacting standards most acutely when it came to individual sports. Matches between the two Klopps were painfully one-sided affairs, with Norbert unwilling to cede a single point. Jürgen was frustrated, angry even, getting played off the court by a father who was either unable or disinclined to offer any words of support. Neither party enjoyed these early sessions, but Klopp senior considered them a necessary part of Jürgen's sporting education. They later paired up as a doubles team for Glatten's tennis club. His father was so obsessed with winning that he once refused to leave the pitch even though he was suffering from a bad sunstroke and was beset by violent chills. Klopp junior stopped the match of his own volition and put his father to bed.

On the piste, Norbert simply skied downhill, expecting the boy to catch up. '*Nix gschwätzt isch Lob gnuag*' – to say nothing is praise enough – a Swabian proverb goes. Norbert Klopp was its living embodiment. 'It was his way of getting me to perform,' Klopp said in an interview with *Der Tagesspiegel*. 'When I ran and did skips, he'd say it wasn't high enough, that there was still space for a whole sheet of paper! He didn't have the right text available. His tactic was quite obvious, I sussed it out early.' Klopp had to learn to 'read between the lines' to discover traces of his father's contentment, he added; seamless criticism smothered affirmation. 'When I scored four goals, he would say that I missed seven other chances, or talk about how well one of my teammates had done. Nevertheless, I knew that he was secretly very proud of me.'

Left to his own devices after school, Klopp would play more football with Rath's sons Hartmut and Ingo. Every patch of grass was transformed into a pitch, and after sunset Klopp would continue to play in the living room, throwing himself on a couch to save shots, or shooting at a small goal that Norbert had put up for him. 'The house was always full of kids. Jürgen was spoilt by our mum. Anything to make him happy,' says sister Isolde. A couple of glass panels of the cabinet had to break before the leather ball was replaced by one made from foam. 'He played and played until he fell asleep exhausted under the dining table.' Ulrich Rath laughs.

In the town's sports hall, blue mats had to serve as goals in lieu of the real thing. Rath had introduced a weekly 'sports hour' for boys in the seventies. 'We were doing gymnastics but the boys always wanted to play football,' he says. Jürgen Klopp, nicknamed 'Klopple' (little Klopp), was often sent forward to ask Herr Rath on behalf of his friends. 'Jürgen was a decent tennis player, but in his head he was always a footballer. He was quick, dynamic and explosive. He had to kick every ball, even if one or two flew wide and high over the goal. Heading was his speciality. For a few games, I played him as a sweeper but that wasn't his position. Attack was his calling.'

'It was totally idyllic,' Klopp told *SWR* in 2005. 'There were only five or six boys [of our age] in that little village, and we were the football team, the tennis team and the ski team. It was wonderful, I had a great childhood.'

Jürgen found going to school easy. At least in the literal sense. He only had to cross the street from his family home to get to Glatten's primary school. For third and fourth grade, the Rath brothers and him took a bus south to the village of Neuneck. Local legend had it that there was an illegal brothel there at the time, run privately in the back room of a pub. All attempts by the curious schoolboys to find that secretive place of rural sin proved futile, however.

'Jürgen was not a guy to be 100 per cent punctual, but you could rely on him 1000 per cent as a mate,' says Hartmut Rath, the godfather of Klopp's son Marc, born in 1988. When the boys weren't kicking a ball around, they built models and solved puzzles. Klopp had an 'arty streak', he adds. 'He had a huge interest in culture, and listened to many records and tapes of Kabarett artists.' His favourite was Fips Asmussen, a one-hundred-jokes-a-minute comedian whose early work was more political and satirical (and no doubt funnier, too). 'Jürgen was a genius in telling jokes, he made everyone in class laugh. He was extremely popular, the life and soul of the classroom,' Hartmut Rath says.

Jürgen Klopp has credited 'Hardy' for helping him pass his Abitur (A levels). That might be pushing the truth a little bit, but Hartmut admits that his friend – who excelled in languages and sports but was rather less proficient in sciences – did benefit from sitting next to him in class during exams. 'Copying was easier in those days,' the younger of the Rath brothers laughs. They both went to the Pro Gymnasium (grammar school) in Dorfstetten and shared a classroom from eighth grade onwards. Klopp had been in a class with Ingo Rath the first two years but went on 'a lap of honour' – repeating a year, in German schoolkid parlance – on the advice of his teachers. 'School wasn't the most important thing to him,' Hartmut Rath smiles. 'He was more into football and girls.' But he was a good kid, somebody who respected his teachers and rarely got into trouble. 'Hardy' estimates that the two of them were only given detention a couple of times per year.

Other transgressions came with their own, swift, punishment. Aged fourteen, Klopp and his friends took part in an open football tournament. Entrants were supposed to be at least sixteen but, as one of the organisers, Norbert Klopp looked the other way. The boys played badly but still took home the first prize – a bottle of whisky – when the victorious side didn't show at the winner's ceremony. Jürgen and the Raths imbibed their ill-gotten spoils outside the marquee and came home feeling much the worse for wear.

The 'Klopple' moniker was soon ditched for 'Der Lange', the long one, as he started towering over class and teammates. After tenth grade, Hardy and Klopp went to the Eduard-Spranger Wirtschaftsgymnasium in Freudenstadt to prepare for their Abitur. Jürgen had a scooter from the age of fifteen, then drove a couple of 2CVs – '*Ente*', duck, Germans called it – one of which was the colour of Bordeaux red. Robert Mongiatti, one of Norbert Klopp's best friends, serviced the car outside the family residence. Jürgen later inherited a bright yellow VW Golf from sister Stefanie.

A school friend often invited class members to study in a secluded garden shed. The curriculum wasn't always strictly adhered to, by any means. In Rath's basement and Norbert Klopp's garage, the teenagers threw parties, playing spin the bottle. If somebody's parents were away, bedrooms were made available to couples. Although details are sketchy, French kissing was very probably on the syllabus: Klopp's class went to the city of Port-sur-Saône on a school exchange, speaking exclusively French for two weeks. The boys enjoyed their time in Burgundy so much they returned for a camping holiday the following summer.

'Jürgen was the leader as far as social activities were concerned,' Hartmut Rath says. 'He was outgoing, he was part of the school's theatre group. He was interested in loads of different things, people used to say he had an eye for the bigger picture.' There were often heated political discussions between Jürgen and his more conservatively minded father.

In 1998, three weeks before his planned retirement, Norbert Klopp fell ill. Cancer of the liver. Doctors gave him three weeks to three months to live. The diagnosis came as a total shock to the family. Norbert had led a healthy, sporty life. He didn't smoke. 'The cancer won't get me,' he vowed. He resolved to stay upbeat and found encouragement in Lance Armstrong's book on beating testicular cancer. The children took him to many different clinics. His liver was surgically removed, frozen and re-implanted. He lived for over two more years, determined to enjoy every single day. 'His traditional view of men and women changed, he was more understanding of my rebellious streak and my quest for freedom,' Isolde Reich says. Shortly before his death in 2000, a weak Norbert pushed himself to the limit and beyond to once more play a tennis match with the club. His testimonial. His victory. The Klopps found solace in Norbert fulfilling his very last wish.

For the last two weeks of his life, the family took him home to Glatten. The two sisters were by his side, taking turns to hold his hand day and night. Jürgen suffered a lot, Isolde says, being unable to be with his father as much as he wanted due to his playing commitments with Mainz. He came home one night after a game and spent the night in Norbert's room, then drove off to train with 05, having slept very little.

'It was the first great fortune of my life to do exactly what my father had wanted to do,' Jürgen Klopp said later. 'I live the life he had dreamt about. Any other job [for me] would have caused friction, I think. My father wouldn't have understood if I wanted to become – let's say – a florist. He wouldn't have said: "No problem, I'll buy the first bouquet." No, he would have thought I was crazy.'

After Norbert's death Jürgen wanted answers, but eventually determined that 'somebody up there surely had a plan'. The sadness Klopp feels about his father having not lived long enough to witness his success as a coach is tempered by his religious outlook. 'I'm pretty certain – or I at least believe very strongly – that he can see me, looking down in a relaxed manner,' he said.

Being constantly told to do better on the pitch, on the court, on the piste, was perhaps not a young boy's idea of paternal devotion. Forty years later, however, Jürgen Klopp has certainly come to realise that spending all those weekends pushing his son further along an infinitely demanding scale was Norbert's 'way of being affectionate'. For a father's love is not measured in words, nor kisses, but in time.

6. WOLFGANG FRANK: THE MASTER

'Our father was brutally self-disciplined, some might say he was a little obsessed,' says Benjamin Frank, thirty-six, sitting alongside his older brother Sebastian, thirty-nine, over a lunch of pasta and bittersweet memories in a Mainz hotel.

The Franks work as agents and as scouts for Jürgen Klopp's Liverpool FC. Before that, they were consulting for Leicester City, the surprise Premier League champions of 2015–16. They grew up in Glarus, a slow-paced Swiss valley town of 12,000 people who revered their father Wolfgang as a hero. The former Bundesliga striker (215 games, 89 goals for VfB Stuttgart, Eintracht Braunschweig, Borussia Dortmund and 1. FC Nürnberg) had taken local minnows FC Glarus to Nationalliga B, the Swiss second division, for the first time in their history as player-manager in 1988.

Frank senior, the brothers recall, saw no difference between being a coach and being a father. Both roles came down to the same thing: a duty to educate. 'He was a freak, in a positive sense,' says Sebastian – an immensely ambitious man for whom football wasn't just games and tactics, but everything. A school of life.

During his last season as a pro, Wolfgang Frank had qualified as a teacher, specialising in sport and religion. Both subjects instilled in him the belief that there was 'no such thing as coincidence, that everything – injuries, defeats – happened for a reason,' Benjamin Frank says. He was consumed with passing on that one, central article of faith to anyone who would listen.

The young boys had to go on regular endurance runs through ice and snow around the town. A few years later in Greece, on one of the very few family holidays Wolfgang's busy schedule allowed, the teenage brothers woke up at 5 a.m. every day for a run along the beach, followed by breakfast with vitamin pills. Then a second session with weights before lunch.

Late at night or early in the morning, the fax machine in their home in Glarus would start bleeping. Frank was sending through pages with motivational phrases and advice, or intricate training schedules, paired with best wishes and greetings, from hundreds of kilometres away, at one of the fifteen clubs he coached during his career. 'Every time we had a problem in school or in sport, a long fax would arrive, cheering us up and showing us that he had thought long and hard about the problem, from a distance, in his own way,' says Benjamin.

As a player, Wolfgang had been fascinated by the playing style of Arrigo Sacchi's AC Milan, a team that dominated European football in the late 1980s and early nineties thanks to their revolutionary collective tactics, a synchronicity of movement that suffocated opponents by depriving them of space and time. He would study the players' unified manoeuvres on videos late into the night, and also mull over the importance of regeneration, nutrition and mental training at a time when such topics were considered esoteric in Germany. In Switzerland, by contrast, a lack of funds and the much smaller player pool had facilitated a more open-minded approach. Zonal marking, a system that replaced the defending team's focus on the opposition forwards with a primary concern to defend the space in front of goal and attack the ball, had been adopted as early as 1986, under the auspices of Swiss national coach Daniel Jeandupeux. Internationals brought knowledge of the system back to their clubs, where some continued to work on it of their own volition, as former defender Andy Egli recalled. Jeandupeux, Egli believed, had first encountered the playing style as a pro and coach in France.

Frank understood that tactical innovation could be a small club's weapon in their battle with bigger and better sides; that the right ideas could markedly increase the quality of your own performances.

His miraculous success with FC Glarus saw him appointed at FC Aarau, a provincial first division side that had experienced unexpected triumphs themselves under the guidance of German coach Ottmar Hitzfeld. Hitzfeld, who would go on to win the Champions League with Borussia Dortmund and Bayern Munich, had done so well at the unfashionable club that his side had become known as 'FC Wunder' in the media in 1985. They were runners-up in the league and won the Swiss Cup.

Frank, too, took Aarau all the way to the Swiss Cup final, in his first half-season in charge (1989–90) but the miracle ran short. The Argovians were beaten 2-1 by Hitzfeld's Grasshoppers Zürich in Berne; Frank departed a year later. He subsequently failed to make a mark in positions at relegation battlers FC Wettingen (1991–92) and second division FC Winterthur (1992–93). (The key player and captain at Winterthur, incidentally, was a veteran German striker called Joachim Löw. The Germany manager, then in his early thirties, once stood up in the dressing room to defend the team against Frank's criticism. Löw also tried his hand at fashion: he sold novelty ties out of his car boot to Winterthur teammates.)

At last Frank got a chance, of sorts, to prove himself back in his home country, in January 1994. Rot-Weiss Essen, a well-supported second division side from Germany's industrial and football heartland, the Ruhr, needed a new manager after Jürgen Röber had been poached by VfB Stuttgart during the winter break. However, before he'd even taken charge at Georg-Melches-Stadion, Frank and his team had been doomed to relegation. The German FA had withdrawn the club's professional licence in the wake of financial irregularities. On top of that, Frank had a dressing-room revolt on his hands on his first day in the job: captain Ingo Pickenäcker and his deputy Frank Kurth had resigned in protest as they had not been consulted about Röber's successor despite a promise from the board.

RWE were hopeful the German FA might show some leniency on appeal. The club's astute lawyer, Reinhard Rauball (now president of Borussia Dortmund), unearthed many procedural mistakes on the behalf of the football authority. Sensationally, Frank's men won the DFB Pokal semi-final against Tennis Borussia (2-0) in March to reach the cup final in Berlin, but the enforced drop to division three was confirmed by an arbitration panel a few days later. All of their goals and points were chalked off.

In May 35,000 Essen supporters travelled to the German capital in a mood of defiance. There were many banners decrying the unfairness of the German FA's decision. 'If there's justice in the heavens, we will win,' said Frank. Down on the Olympic stadium pitch, however, odds-on favourites Werder Bremen, coached by Otto Rehhagel, were indifferent to the prospect of divine retribution. The northerners, who had lifted the Cup Winners' Cup courtesy of a 2-0 defeat of Arsène Wenger's AS Monaco two years earlier, ran out easy winners in Berlin. Final score: 3-1.

Decades later, it emerged that an ugly political intrigue had played its part in the defeat. RWE's Frank Kontny still hesitates to reveal a story he calls the 'darkest moment of my playing career'. The 52-year-old was captain at the time and destined to start the final in defence. 'But on the morning of the game, Frank told me that I was out of the squad, and that I had to find a new employer if I wanted to play again,' he says. 'My world came crashing down that day. The greatest-ever game was taken away from me.'

Like most RWE players, Kontny was working part-time away from football to support his family during the club's insolvency. Board member Wolfgang Thulius had arranged a job for him as a property agent. After the club had reached the DFB Pokal final in March, new people had come in and won control of the board. They seemed to put pressure on Frank to cut all ties with the old regime. Kontny: 'I was on the wrong side of the divide and unfortunately Frank took a decision that had no basis in football.' In Kontny's place, the manager started Pickenäcker, who had suffered a serious groin injury just a few weeks before and wasn't quite ready. Pickenäcker was at fault for Werder's first two goals and was subbed off seven minutes before half-time. Essen rallied after the break, pulled one back through Daoud Bangoura but Wynton Rufer secured Werder's 3-1 win with a late penalty. 'I'm convinced it would have been a different game with me on the pitch,' says Kontny with a heavy heart. 'I was very disappointed in Frank, I cursed him. He was a good coach – he always said we had to keep learning and expand our horizons, training sessions lasted two hours – but I think today he would recognise that he made a big mistake.'

Three weeks after the final, Rot-Weiss travelled to Mainz for the penultimate game of the season. A tumultuous match at Bruchwegstadion (attendance: 3,000) with three red cards, two for the away team, ended with a ninetieth-minute equaliser by 05 midfielder Zeljko Buvac that made it 1-1 and mathematically confirmed the home side's safety from relegation.

In September 1995, perennial strugglers Mainz were once again bottom of the table in Bundesliga 2 and on the lookout for a new man on the bench. General manager Christian Heidel contacted Frank. 'The last-straw man,' *Rhein-Zeitung* called him.

'He came and said a lot of things that sounded very nice and lovely,' Heidel says with playful irony. 'He had the demeanour of a teacher. I'm always careful with teacher types, they're sometimes not easy to deal with. But after a while, I said: "Okay, why don't you do it." In hindsight, that was a momentous day for Mainz 05. I'd like to tell you that I knew straightaway that he was a good coach. But the truth is, nobody else wanted to coach us.'

The team were impressed by training methods they perceived as 'quite sophisticated' (Heidel), but they kept losing their games regardless. Mainz went into the winter break as the worst team in the division, with twelve points on the board, five adrift of safety. Heidel: '*Kicker* magazine wrote: "Mainz's chance of relegation: 100 per cent." Not 99 per cent, 100 per cent. I'll never forget that.'

Frank knocked on Heidel's door. 'He said: "We have to make a change." I thought, yes, you can say that again. He told me he had thought things through and decided that we would go into the winter training camp and play without a sweeper in future. I said to myself: "What? He can't be serious."'

A professional football team without a *libero* or sweeper, a 'last man' behind the defence, was largely inconceivable in mid-nineties Germany. The clubs and the national team had won all their big trophies with a *libero* since Franz Beckenbauer's heyday in the 1970s. 'We all believed that you needed somebody as a safeguard in case the opposition got behind your lines,' says Heidel. 'How could you get rid of the sweeper? Impossible. I had played as a sweeper myself, so it felt to me as if he was attempting to get rid of me as well, in a way.'

Former Germany international Hans Bongartz had employed a version of a sweeper-less flat back four as early as 1986 at 1. FC Kaiserslautern – he had been inspired by a defeat at the hands of Sven-Göran Eriksson's tactically ahead-of-the-curve team IFK Göteborg in the 1982 UEFA Cup semi-final – but hadn't made a lasting impression in the German top flight with his innovation. As president at FC Bayern, Beckenbauer expressly forbade Erich Ribbeck from continuing his (admittedly rather amateurish) experiments with four at the back in 1993–94. A few weeks after Frank's appointment at Mainz, national team manager Berti Vogts told Swiss tabloid *Blick* that a system without a sweeper was 'fundamentally destructive' and thus not destined to find acceptance in the Bundesliga.

Heidel: 'I thought we'd be a laughing stock, I was very fatalistic. During the training camp, I vowed that I would take a closer look. There were all these poles on the pitch. And the players thought "this guy has lost his mind". For hours, they ran around without the ball, they practised moving from side to side in formation. Today, it's obvious that one flank is left open as the back four move towards the side of the pitch where the ball is. But when we played the first game at home that way, the whole stadium was shouting at us. An opposition striker was by himself all the way to the left but the whole of our team was on the right. Nobody realised then that the ball couldn't get to the left that quickly, that the defence had enough time to shift back over. Ball-orientated zonal marking, that was called, and it was a completely new thing in Germany. Witchcraft, basically. So we trained and trained and trained. And I was certain we'd get relegated.'

In the mid nineties, practice sessions essentially came in two flavours. There was work (lots of running), and there was fun (playing). Exercises in collective movement or theoretical study were unheard of. Frank, by contrast, was 'possessed by tactics'. Heidel says. 'I had never seen anything like that before.' The coach spent hours watching football, especially Italian football. And Sacchi was still his idol. 'He showed us all of his matches on video tapes, I was always there. "A general manager has to be there," Frank said. So I had to watch all that crap, too. There was no editing then. He would pause the picture, rewind, play and rewind again, for hours on end. He was crazy for Sacchi's tactics.'

Frank also travelled to Italy to see the master's training in person. 'Sacchi didn't take him seriously, but he was allowed to watch from the sidelines,' says Heidel. 'That's where he got his ideas from. We weren't nearly as advanced in Germany.'

In sports science professor Dr Dieter Augustin from Mainz University, located a short walk from the stadium, Frank had met a fellow football theorist. Augustin preferred acutely structured positional play to FSV's verticality but differences in taste notwithstanding, they both agreed that players needed visual aides to further their footballing education. Students from Augustin's course were asked to put together short video clips of Mainz and their opponents to help with match preparation. A simple but original idea: German teams had neither the staff nor the knowhow to work with video analysts then. One of the young sports scientists who volunteered for the experiment was Peter Krawietz. He would later become Mainz chief scout and Klopp's trusted assistant.

'Frank's video sessions at 7.30 in the morning were much feared,' former 05 player Torsten Lieberknecht said. 'We sat on these garden chairs made from steel in a tiny room and had breakfast, while Wolfgang Frank was pushing buttons on the video player. It took for ever.'

Frank also found inspiration from his playing days. A year at AZ of Alkmaar in the Dutch Eredivisie in 1973–74 had seen him marvel at Ajax's total football. Upon his return to Germany, the slender forward nicknamed 'Floh' (flea) had reunited with his former Stuttgart coach Branco Zebec at newly promoted Eintracht Braunschweig. Zebec, a Yugoslavian who had led Bayern Munich to their first-ever Bundesliga title in 1969 with a punishing fitness regime and strong tactical discipline, was the first manager to experiment with zonal marking in the German top flight in the mid-seventies. Everybody was still strictly man-marking then. 'We no longer stupidly ran after our [individual] opponents under Zebec, he was ahead of his time,' Frank later recalled.

Twenty-one years later, Mainz were craving similarly futuristic impulses. 'We were practically dead as a team during the winter break,' Mainz defender Klopp told *Süddeutsche Zeitung* in 1999. 'We were open for new ideas. We would have even climbed up a tree fifteen times for the promise of some points in return.' Frank estimated that it took 150 hours of theoretical training before the new system was internalised. Instead of the usual fun-packed training German pros were accustomed to, they spent entire days without the ball. 'But we thought: if Gullit and Van Basten had to learn that at Milan, we could put up with it as well,' Klopp later said in an interview alongside his mentor with *Frankfurter Rundschau* in 2007. 'You have to realise how courageous that was. In football, it takes a long time to put new things into place. Wolfgang introduced four at the back in the middle of a raging relegation battle. We had basically been in the jungle before he came. We had chased after everyone in an opposition shirt.' Frank, he remembered thinking, might as well have told the team 'to take an exam in quantum physics for all we knew about four at the back.'

'The football at Mainz had been quite conservative, but something had to happen. The time was ripe for it,' Frank explained. The team, Heidel says, were not entirely convinced from the start. 'They didn't know what was happening to them. All this running around without the ball. To the left, to the right. Frank explained to me over many hours in an Italian restaurant that one fewer guy at the back would mean we had an extra guy in midfield. And I would say: "Yes, but what if one guy just runs straight through on goal?" Then he said: "There won't be anyone running through, there mustn't be." Up front, we were pressing, to force the opposition into playing long balls. At the back we had giants like Klopp, 1.93m, who won all the headers. That was our new game. That's how we left the training camp.'

A first friendly with the new set-up pitted them against third division 1. FC Saarbrücken, 'a "money team" who led their league by miles and were certain to go up,' Heidel remembers. 'It was in Frauenlautern, near the French border, and I was pretty sure we'd concede five goals. But at half-time, we were 6-0 up. I thought I was dreaming. They had their best XI out but no idea how to play against us. They were completely overwhelmed. That was the birth . . . the rebirth of Mainz 05 and the birth of the back four [in the second division]. We were the first to play it this way, in conjunction with a ball-orientated, zonal marking. Ralf Rangnick [at Ulm] and Uwe Rapolder [at Waldhof Mannheim] came afterwards.'

Former Mainz defender Jürgen Kramny played for Saarbrücken in that game. 'I was there when Mainz's four at the back came into life,' he says. 'We were a pretty decent side in the third division and Mainz were up against relegation in Bundesliga 2. But we had no chance. They killed us. They played us off the park.'

Jürgen Klopp, Peter Neustädter, Michael Müller and Uwe Stöver were the four defenders that day. 'It worked so well that we didn't change at all for the next eighteen months,' Klopp said.

Frank described his tactics as a sophisticated version of children's football: 'Everybody had to go where the ball was. The aim was to create numerical superiority to win the ball, then to sprawl out, like a fist that opens.' These novel methods turned Mainz into the best team of the Bundesliga 2 *Rückrunde* (second half of the season). They won thirty-two points, more than any other team in the top two divisions. 'It was nuts, unheard of in German professional football,' Heidel smiles.

For Klopp, it was 'an epiphany: I realised that our system made us beat teams that had better players. He made our results independent of our talent, to an extent. Up until then, we thought that as the worse team, we would lose. Frank's great strength was to have a concise match plan.' It was widely accepted that hard work or 'wanting it more' than your opponent could make up, a little, for inferior quality. But a collective concept, based on the utilisation of space? Nobody in Germany had thought it possible that it could make such a difference. 'I fell in love with tactics for the first time,' Heidel says. 'Suddenly we could beat teams that were individually better than us, simply because we had an idea that worked.' The team practised 'until they passed out', he adds. 'Eventually everybody got it. Today, it's commonplace to have smart, adaptable players, but back then, you needed a few heads who could lead the others. Kloppo, of course, was the tactical head of the team, even if his game didn't look like that. He relied on his power, on his emotions, on his physicality as a player, he wasn't one for playing nice stuff. But he was the team's brain.'

'At Mainz, I came into contact with tactics for the first time,' said former FSV midfielder Christian Hock, who had played at Eintracht Frankfurt in his youth and for Borussia Mönchengladbach's first team. 'Tactics were never coached at Borussia. It took a long time to learn the system, it was very unfamiliar: you had to watch the ball and the men at the same time, constantly. Years later, when I was doing my coaching badges, many former players had real problems understanding the back four theoretically. Thanks to Wolfgang Frank, I was already very used to it.'

'Wolfgang's aim was always for us players to learn new things,' Klopp said. 'We were not just supposed to meet up to play a bit of football at the weekend. Of course we sometimes complained when we spent four hours on shape work on the pitch but we always understood why we were doing that.' Klopp remembered Frank telling local journalists not to write too much about the back four because he knew he would have a lot of explaining to do in the case of defeats. The break with tradition was viewed with plenty of suspicion.

Despite the marked upswing in results, the disastrous opening half of the 1995–96 campaign had left survival still in grave doubt ahead of the last game of the season, at home to VfL Bochum. Mainz had to win.

TV reporter Martin Quast remembers covering the game: 'There were 12,000 people at the Bruchweg, nearly sold out at the time. Marco Weißhaupt scored early on. Eighty-three incredibly tense minutes later, Mainz were safe. Everyone went wild celebrating with their hands in the air but Wolfgang Frank had a serious face on and walked up and down, like a caged tiger. He didn't know what to do. The situation was totally alien to him. Thousands were partying like there's no tomorrow. And Wolfgang Frank staggered around the pitch, totally withdrawn, as if somebody was controlling him remotely.'

'Everyone celebrated but my father was totally exhausted, unable to say a single word and suffering from a terrible headache,' Sebastian Frank says. He had left it all out there. Wolfgang Frank was one of those coaches who'd do 100 miles an hour stuck in neutral gear on the sideline, ablaze on the inside but unable to find an outlet for all that energy. 'He didn't want to be the centre of attention,' Sebastian says, 'bathing in adulation was not his thing.'

'The next season, we all stayed together. And no one knew how to handle us,' Heidel reminisces. 'For the first time in Mainz's history, we were all of a sudden challenging for promotion to the Bundesliga.' 'No one's ever taken this club seriously, they've been marooned in no-man's-land for years,' *Süddeutsche Zeitung* wrote in October 1996. 'But now, they are the only team in the second division who play (and understand) four at the back.' The self-styled 'carnival club' suddenly commanded respect and admiration for its radical ways. 'We've suddenly been gripped by euphoria,' 05 president Harald Strutz was quoted as saying. The whole city stirred with excitement as never before.

And 05 kept on winning. Frank's team went into the 1996–97 winter break second in the table, only behind Otto Rehhagel's 1. FC Kaiserslautern, who would claim the *Meisterschaft* a year later.

Yet for Frank, progress couldn't come quickly enough. At the same time as he had introduced the fundamental changes to the team's tactics, in January 1996, he had surprised the board with demands for a bigger, modernised stadium and better training facilities. The Bruchwegstadion had only just had floodlights and an electronic scoreboard installed a few months earlier.

'He taught us that we needed to have "a vision" if we wanted to achieve things, that was decisive,' says Strutz. 'He asked us straight up: "Do you want to play in the Bundesliga one day?" I'm not sure anyone had really thought about that here before. We were still bottom of Bundesliga 2 then. Frank's vision was to renovate the Bruchweg – the name (literal translation: broken path) 'was very fitting then', Strutz concedes – and he demanded the installation of a plunge bath and a sauna, as well as better pitches. 'Wolfgang Frank was a unique person, very distinctive. A wonderful man. But overly intellectual, spiritualised. He drove the Mainz board nuts with his demands to make success sustainable. I remember he insisted on the plunge bath. All Mainz had at the time was a grubby bath tub, where the kit man washed the boots sometimes. After a game, the team captain would be in there, so nobody else could cool down. Frank was adamant. New pitches, new changing rooms, 'the press room can't be here, in the centre of the building, where the players are,' he said. Slow progress was regression to him. Everything had to change at turbo pace.'

The tiny VIP area in one of the containers that also housed administration was converted into a chill-out room replete with loungers for the players to use during the week; there was talk of hiring of a nutritionist. 'He wanted to show prospective players that we had the facilities to train them well. That was very important to him,' Strutz says. 'And he was always surprised that the bulldozers didn't turn up the very next day to start the renovations.' 'The board must have thought I was bananas,' Frank admitted years later.

In the club anthology *Karneval am Bruchweg* local football reporters Reinhard Rehberg and Christian Karn write that negotiations with the stadium owners, the Mainz city council, were fraught. The politicians didn't see the justification for spending serious money on a club that got only 3,000–5,000 regulars through the turnstiles.

Undeterred by such niceties, Frank kept pushing internally until Mainz had funding in place for a modest stadium extension. 'He was not an easy coach, nor an easy person,' says Strutz. 'He was a complicated personality to deal with, for me as president of the club. He had so much drive. He wanted the club to develop rapidly.'

In January 1997, the unlikely promotion contenders went to Cyprus to prepare for the second half of the season. The Frank brothers were there as well, as youth players. 'Some of the pros were in tears laughing at us, because we had to join in with the team's core-stability exercises on the adjoining pitch,' Benjamin recalls. 'Our father said, "Don't worry what others think, just do your thing."' (Seven years later, German tabloids and battle-hardened pundits laughed, too, when Jürgen Klinsmann had the national team practising similar drills under the auspices of American fitness coaches. Those exercises became standard practice at club level after the 2006 World Cup.)

When reports of fresh snowfall in Mainz reached Cyprus at the end of a ten-day training camp, Frank decreed that he and the team should stay for another fortnight, to take advantage of the perfect training conditions on the island.

The players were less than pleased. They wanted to get home to their families. But the club were so in thrall to the first coach that had ever brought them a semblance of success that they bowed to his every wish. 'We were second in the table. Mainz 05: *second* in the table,' Heidel exclaims for effect. 'If Frank had said: tomorrow, the church tower should be knocked down, then we would have gone up there and knocked the church tower down. We had never been at the top before. Everything he said was immediately put into practice.'

After what must have been the longest training camp in the history of German professional football, Mainz came back and lost the first game at home to Hertha BSC 1-0. They also lost the second game, 3-0 away to VfB Leipzig. And then they lost their coach.

Heidel: 'I stayed behind in Leipzig because of an event. The next day, I'm sitting in a taxi and Frank calls me. "Christian," he says, "I just wanted to tell you that you'll have to find a new coach." So I'm thinking, ah, for the summer. Because his contract was up after the season. But then it dawned on me that he meant now, straightaway. I flew back to Mainz, and four journalists were waiting at the stadium. That was a lot, by our standards. He had already told all of them that he was leaving. Just like that.'

Frank had spent the entire journey back from Leipzig brooding over the reasons for the two defeats. Somehow, he had concluded that he himself was the reason. Heidel describes Frank resigning as a *Kurzschlussreaktion*, a short-circuiting. Not even Jürgen Klopp, the coach's confidant in the dressing room, was able to change his mind.

Frank's successor was a man called Reinhard Saftig. A seasoned, moustachioed operator with experience in the

Bundesliga (Dortmund, Leverkusen) and Turkey (Kocaelispor, Galatasaray), a safe pair of hands. Or so Heidel thought. 'Signing him truly was one of my finest hours,' he winces. 'Saftig didn't have the faintest idea. I have to be honest. He didn't have a clue about the game. Of course we didn't get promoted. We messed up on the last day of the season, in Wolfsburg. We lost 4-5 there, so Wolfsburg went up in our place. A legendary game, with a grandiose Jürgen Klopp.' Playing as a right-back, Klopp scored a goal as the away team battled back from being 3-1 and one man down to equalise but also made a calamitous mistake to seal Mainz's defeat. The game had effectively been a promotion play-off.

Frank, in the meantime, had moved on to coach FK Austria Wien. Benjamin remembers being in the car with his father on the way to the airport. 'He hardly said anything. All he did was memorise the names of the Austria players by heart. He wanted to know them all ahead of the first training session.'

The Viennese side, a modest collection of journeymen that included the impossibly hirsute Bulgarian international Trifon Ivanov, was as bewildered by Frank's system as Saftig was at Mainz, where the team still believed in his predecessor's system. Attempts to switch back to a three-man defence with the newly signed Kramny as a sweeper proved disastrous.

Saftig apparently liked taking nightcaps with the players before games. 'Key figures such as Jürgen Klopp feared these invitations. Saftig was thirsty and had stamina.'

After five months at the Bruchweg, Saftig was replaced by the Austrian Dietmar Constantini. He had worked as an assistant to the legendary Ernst Happel and explained to bemused local journalists that Mainz's pressing game followed 'the shape of a bagpipe'. In practice, that meant the introduction of Frank's back four, with an important difference: there was a sweeper behind them, too, in Kramny. Heidel: 'So we had four in a line in defence plus a sweeper behind them. Kloppo was driven to distraction by that. We always had a relationship built on trust. He would come into my office and say: "The coach hasn't got any idea of tactics. We can't play like that. A back four with a sweeper . . ." That's when I sensed he might become a coach himself one day.'

Constantini didn't lose many games. But he didn't win many either, only four out of eighteen. 'The king of draws,' *Allgemeine Zeitung* proclaimed him. Constantini's last game, a 3-1 home defeat to SG Wattenscheid 09 (with Souleyman Sané, the father of Germany international Leroy Sané, in attack) in early April 1998, saw Mainz slip into the relegation zone again. 'The guys that came after Frank didn't trust in the back four,' says Kramny. 'They said the players were too slow to play that system and instead came up with all sorts of crazy schemes. But the team didn't buy into them, they fundamentally still believed in Frank's formation. That's why none of the other tactics worked for us.'

Constantini admitted to Heidel that he couldn't connect with the dressing room. The Mainz general manager swallowed his pride and called on the only coach he could think of who might be able to return the team to winning ways: Frank. His engagement at Vienna had run its course, both sides had already agreed to part ways at the end of the season. After getting a call from Heidel, who sweet-talked him until 3 a.m., Frank left his post immediately to turn back the clock and save Mainz from the drop a second time. He won his first game 2-1 away to Stuttgarter Kickers, thanks to a quick injection of hope. 'This guy burns so brightly with excitement,' Klopp told the cameras after the final whistle. 'If anyone can ring in the changes after only three days, it's him.' Mainz finished in tenth position.

The team were happily playing the system they were most comfortable with again. Having restored them to a flat back four and zonal marking, Frank shifted his focus to the conquest of an altogether different space: the one between the players' ears.

'He made it his mission to work on the team's mental strength,' Strutz says. 'He went very far in that, with the introduction of psychological and autogenic training, a type of relaxation technique. He also employed an autogenic coach, who – as we later found out – was a former train driver. He had changed jobs.'

Strutz, a former triple-jumper and silver medalist in the German championships in 1969 and 1970, feels he's partly to blame for Frank's journey down the rabbit hole of the inner mind. 'I gave him a book as a gift, *Die Macht der Motivation* (the power of motivation), by Nikolaus B. Enkelmann, that I had myself been given as a Christmas present, because I thought he might like it. But he adopted that psychological approach to the extent that it changed his life altogether. It went as far as breathing exercises and the repetition of mantras. It got very esoteric.'

Frank's home was filled with Enkelmann's books and videos, his sons say. Each morning, he'd wake up and conduct elocution lessons. Little notes with autosuggestive phrases were stuck to the bathroom mirror: 'I will get stronger and stronger every day,' and such like. 'Those who didn't know him well thought he was sometimes a little odd or cranky,' Benjamin concedes. In the winter training camp of 1998, again held in Cyprus, Mainz's players were instructed in speech therapy, training their vocal cords by repeatedly shouting out vowel sounds, much to the amusement of the Greuther Fürth team, who happened to be at the same hotel and heard them scream out 'aaaaaa' and 'oooooo' from the dining hall. Austrian goalkeeper Herbert Ilsanker once noticed that Frank was conducting an interview in the team sauna. A strange place for it, he thought. But even stranger still, Frank sat in the sauna alone, interviewing himself – to practise the way he addressed the team. 'His tone of voice was never monotonous. When he spoke to you, you were alert,' Ilsanker told *Allgemeine Zeitung*. And Frank spoke a lot. Team meetings lasted an hour on average, and they were scheduled every single day. 'Things got a little out of hand, some thought,' Klopp said. 'Players who had left school relatively early were suddenly reading books on the bus with titles I didn't even comprehend.'

Strutz: 'Our priorities shifted a little bit. Frank wanted to improve the players by giving them that "personality stability", he wanted to show them that there was more to it than tactics and running, that you could beat your opponent through the power of the mind.' Later, at Kickers Offenbach, Frank would place a table-tennis ball on a bottleneck and asked his players to concentrate on flicking it away in full flight. 'How can I maximise my mental potential? That will be one of the decisive questions,' he told *Frankfurter Rundschau*. (Few believed him then, but many top coaches are today convinced that cognitive training and work on the shortening of reaction times is vital if players' minds are to keep up with an increasingly rapid game. 'To get better translates into taking things in more quickly, analysing them more quickly, deciding more quickly, acting more quickly,' Ralf Rangnick says.)

He was a disciplinarian but also a communicator, remembers Sebastian, very different to the martinet-type coaches dominating the sport at the time. 'The way he dealt with us players made us go: Ah, look here, there is a different way,' Klopp told *Frankfurter Rundschau* in 2007. 'He would also put the human being centre circle. We really liked him. When we lost, we had two problems. Firstly, that we lost. Secondly, that we had disappointed Wolfgang. That was pretty important to us. It was remarkable how he got the whole team behind him.'

Klopp and Frank sometimes argued, but they only once fell out with each other. Klopp had confessed to the coach during another training camp that he felt as if the coach was 'chucking a bucket of water over a glass that was already full and overflowing', and that many players felt the same way. Frank was insulted and Klopp worried about getting fired ('I didn't sleep all night') but the next day, things carried on as normal. 'I talked to players the way I would have liked coaches to talk to me,' Frank said about his management style.

Perhaps he didn't always hit the right note. 'Frank was a man with a very special character,' says Strutz. 'He could have been a fantastic coach if he'd been a bit more relaxed. Unlike Jürgen Klopp later, he was simply too serious. And he didn't really understand that young players sometimes want to have fun and drink the odd beer, that they don't want to be boxed in.'

His sons paint a more nuanced picture. At home, they say, Frank could be very funny, very warm. But he didn't like the limelight; he wasn't the type of guy who climbs the fence in front of the home section. 'My father,' Sebastian Frank says, 'lost himself in the life of being a football coach. I'm not sure he knew the price of a bread roll. He sometimes found it hard to deal with normal life. His working days started at seven in the morning with breakfast at the club and finished after midnight. Dad pushed himself to the very limit; he wanted to demonstrate that level of commitment to his players.'

Frank collected anything he considered useful for his job. He cut out articles, archived his training regime and schedule in big files. 'He soaked up everything,' says Benjamin Frank. Like many obsessives, he found it impossible to delegate. He wanted total control or at least needed to know everything that went on, down to the last detail. Often, there'd be arguments at home, because he had again given his winning bonus, which was meant to supplement his modest wages, to the groundsman or somebody else at the club, insisting that they were just as important as the strikers or defenders. Frank regarded a football club as one large organism, not a company made up of different departments that had little to do with each other.

His emotions as a coach were directed inwards. Once, he got so disappointed and angry that he moved all the furniture out of his office at the club. Mainz pretended to everybody they were renovating and re-painting the room. The reason for Frank's anger had nothing to do with an argument with club officials or the players. No, his team had lost a cup game. Away to Bayern Munich. 'That was him,' Sebastian Frank nods. 'He was certain that little old Mainz could win in Munich if they played at their very limit and perhaps caught Bayern on a bad day.' (Klopp, incidentally, had watched the 3-0 defeat at the Olympic stadium in the stands, having been sent off in the previous round for scything down Hertha BSC's Iranian striker Ali Daei. After the defender's dismissal, another Mainz player, Marcio Rodriguez, was shown the red card for an excessive goal-scoring celebration. The Brazilian didn't notice that Klopp was in the toilets in the dressing room and accidentally locked his teammate in once the match was over.)

With Frank in charge, 05 once again overachieved in relation to their minuscule budget. They finished seventh in 1998–99 and ninth a year later. But the man who had 'woken Mainz from their deep slumber', as *Süddeutsche Zeitung* years later acknowledged, was again impatient. He wanted to coach in the Bundesliga, and believed that MSV Duisburg, the Zebras, offered a better chance to earn his stripes at the highest level. But the move to the traditional, mid-sized club from the Ruhr area backfired. Frank was axed four months into the next Bundesliga 2 season, with the team hovering near the relegation zone. 'His methods were met with rejection by large parts of the team from the start,' *Rhein-Post* noted. He had, amongst other things, instructed his players to hug trees during an endurance run through the woods.

His next stint, at SpVgg Unterhaching, was more successful – he led the former top-flight side, based in a suburb of Munich, from the third division to Bundesliga 2 – but was sacked a year later. A campaign with SSC Farul Constanţa in Romania proved another dead end. The roll call of his subsequent employers reads like a who's who of lower-division basket cases and clubs that specialised in racking up thwarted dreams and false dawns in lieu of points: FC Sachsen Leipzig (now defunct), Kickers Offenbach, Wuppertaler SV, SV Wehen Wiesbaden, FC Carl Zeiss Jena, KAS Eupen (Belgium). It didn't really work out for him at any of them.

Frank later admitted that he had perhaps taken on a few too many clubs in his career. 'It would have been much better for him to wait for the right offer. But to be out of a job, not able to put everything he had into his work, scared him,' Sebastian Frank says. 'There was also the fear of getting forgotten and overlooked if he were to stay off the radar for too long. Our father often thought about what could have happened, where the journey could have taken him.' Once, Werder Bremen had contacted him, but Frank had been sure he would find happiness in Austria at the time. The same happened again with Hansa Rostock a couple of years later.

'Our father had a huge knowledge base and visionary ideas,' Benjamin Frank adds. 'He came across as confident, but also secretly doubted himself all the time, as far as his work and his effect on the team was concerned. As a coach, he remained unfulfilled.'

'He never quite made it into the big time because he was a difficult character,' Heidel says. 'I was the only one he got along with. We were quite close, until we fell out very badly. After he left us the second time, for Duisburg, we didn't talk to each other for two years. He always thought he could find something better.'

But neither party did. At the turn of the millennium, Frank's groundbreaking system was still so advanced by the standards of German football that subsequent Mainz coaches had little idea how to make it work. 'Tactically, the side were better than their coaches,' Klopp said. The national team and the vast majority of club sides were still firmly wedded to a sweeper system. Heidel: 'At Mainz, half the players knew how to play with four at the back, and the other half didn't. And the coaches had no clue. We put anyone on the bench who happened to have a tracksuit in his wardrobe. But no one was able to explain to the players what they had already been taught by Wolfgang. We were basically dead in the winter of 2001. Finished. I said to Kloppo: 'You're smart, you're eloquent, you understand the game. Do you want to see if you can make it work?' Within two weeks, he had it sorted.'

Klopp and Frank had had long discussions about football and the art of coaching, Benjamin Frank says. 'Klopp always asked questions, he wanted to know the purpose of specific drills. Dad advised him to write everything down: team talks, tactics, training sessions, playing ideas. He had a sense that Klopp would make good use of it one day. Our father was certainly the inspiration behind him turning into a manager.'

On the day of the lanky defender's promotion to player-coach, Mainz became the first club of note in Germany to put the cart before the horse. Starting with Klopp, coaches would now be picked to fit the squad and a certain playing style, not the other way around. 'We don't want a coach that explains his concept to us, we want to formulate a concept and then find the right man for that,' Heidel says. 'That became the way we did things, until I left in 2016. And it all goes back to that first year with Wolfgang Frank, our first year of any success. We understood then that tactics could get us somewhere, even with individually inferior players. It's like that at Mainz today.'

What's prudent for FSV, he adds, should also be right for more financially potent sides. 'You can't change your whole set-up and team every time you change coach, you'll never find stability that way.' He namechecks Hamburger SV, giants of the Bundesliga in the seventies and eighties, who've been stuck in a rut due to a lack of joined-up thinking.

Like another restless, highly-strung prophet before him, Frank was allowed only glimpses of the promised land: impatience barred his admission, too. But he was at least able to witness his people – his protégé Jürgen Klopp, and a host of other former players such as Joachim Löw, Torsten Lieberknecht, Jürgen Kramny, Peter Neustädter, Christian Hock, Stephan Kuhnert, Lars Schmidt, Sandro Schwarz, Sven Demandt and Uwe Stöver – help bring German football tactics in from the wilderness as coaches.

'He would tell us, "when you've all become managers, please come back and tell me about your heroic deeds,"' Klopp said. On the day of the Champions League final in May 2013, the BVB coach sent his old friend a text message: 'Without you, I wouldn't be here today, in London at Wembley.' Klopp also kept in touch with the sons, inviting them to visit Dortmund's summer training camps at Bad Ragaz, Austria.

Frank's most prominent apprentice, along with another Swabian tactics-obsessive, Ralf Rangnick, went on to establish The Flea's maverick blueprint of zonal marking, a back four and hard pressing as the new orthodoxy in the Bundesliga in the mid to late noughties. But it took another few years before the scale of Frank's impact was more widely appreciated. 'When great things happen, the rewards often come too late,' Klopp said a few days after Frank's death on 7 September 2013. He had been diagnosed with a malignant brain tumour only four months earlier.

Frank had worked as an opposition scout for Mainz in the last year of his life. He had looked after himself, been careful to eat well. Both the diagnosis and the speed with which the cancer took him came as a huge shock to everybody. 'One week before he had surgery, when it was already quite clear that he wouldn't live much longer, he told me again that leaving Mainz had been the one grave mistake of his life,' Heidel says. 'It was very hard to deal with his death . . .'

'But maybe it was meant to be that he got sick,' Sebastian wonders. His sons were with him until the end. Mainz 05 supporters honoured Frank with a tribute ahead of the Bundesliga game against Schalke 04 a few days after his death. '*Mainz ist deins*', Mainz is yours, read the banner. Plenty of coaches win trophies, but only a few can make a club and a city their own. Fewer still leave behind a legacy that far outlasts their time on the bench.

'There is not a single person in football at Mainz who's not 100 per cent convinced that everything started with Wolfgang Frank,' Klopp said about his *Lehrmeister*, his teacher and role model.

Klopp also made sure many former players came to pay their respects at the funeral at Mainz's main cemetery on 19 September. 'Everyone showed up,' says Martin Quast. 'Players from the clubs he coached, representatives from the German FA, from the Bundesliga, from the coaching academy. I get goosebumps thinking about it. Most people have no idea. But those who work in football, the insiders, they all know. They know that Wolfgang Frank didn't just have a huge hand in the development of football in Mainz but on modern football. Fundamentally. He thought about things no one had ever thought about.'

'You were a Bundesliga coach, even if you didn't work there,' Klopp said, holding back the tears. 'I have told more than a thousand players that Wolfgang influenced a whole generation of footballers and still continues to do so. He was the coach who has influenced me most. He was an extraordinary human being.'

Quast has known Klopp for twenty-five years but Frank's funeral was the first time his friend was struggling for words. 'He spoke, of course, but he'll probably say that was his toughest job ever. Giving a eulogy for his great mentor. I got the sense that this wasn't just a farewell: many turned up to pick up a spiritual message, or to deliver one. It was more than a funeral. It was a recognition.'

It's through the work of Klopp, Frank's most studious disciple, that the pivotal importance of this introverted, complicated man in the renaissance of German football has since been more widely realised. There's no greater honour an apprentice can bestow on his master.

7. 'SCHÖNEN GUTEN TAG. HIER IST JÜRGEN KLOPP.'

Dortmund 2008–2010

Strangely enough, there's no German equivalent for 'sell the sizzle, not the sausage'. But that's the classic marketing trick Borussia employed in June 2008, the month after Jürgen Klopp signed his contract. Six weeks before any balls would be kicked, huge posters with Jürgen Klopp's head went up next to the B1 Schnellstraße that runs past the Signal Iduna Park and through the city's more genteel southern quarters. His face was the message, a promise: the new man in the driving seat would transform the 'sleeper carriage football' (*Tagesspiegel*) from the past few seasons into a roaring, rumbling express train.

'Dortmund weren't stupid,' says former press officer Josef Schneck over a glass of mineral water in a business hotel a short walk from the BVB stadium. 'They used him to push the sale of season tickets. And they went through the roof. People were camping outside the club offices the night before.' *Süddeutsche Zeitung*'s Freddie Röckenhaus, one of two reporters who had revealed the shocking levels of debt and financial mismanagement in the early noughties, compares the posters to election advertising. 'They might have said: "Vote Merkel". But they said: "Vote Klopp!" People did.' Dortmund had to cap sales at 49,300 to ensure that a few thousand day-tickets were kept available for employees and fan clubs.

From the outset, says Schneck, Klopp was happy to talk to anybody: 'He wanted to meet with the ultras and with fan club representatives to get them on board.' Jan-Henrik Gruszecki, one of the founding members of BVB ultra group The Unity, remembers being distinctly underwhelmed by his club's choice of manager at the beginning. 'We thought Mainz, that "La La" club, always in a good mood – not cool. Klopp was one of the faces of the 2006 World Cup – also not cool. And what had he done as a coach? Not a lot. We were worried he wouldn't be able to arrest the slide. The football was dull. There was no money. Aki Watzke had to get every transfer over €500,000 signed off. We were well on our way to becoming a nothing mid-table team. But Klopp . . . I don't think I've ever been so impressed with somebody in my life. We taught him how to play "Schotten", a card game, and he talked to us. It was crystal clear that Klopp and his wife Ulla, who'd come with him, were 100 per cent committed to Borussia. They wanted to know everything about the club and its people. He told us how excited he was to get going, and that we had a huge role to play as the twelfth or thirteenth man, that we had to develop this feeling of "we". He had us, from that moment on. No coach had ever done all of that.'

Schneck: 'When somebody in marketing told Klopp that a few corporate customers had given up their VIP seats, he said he would call them to see if they changed their mind. He went into the office, picked up the phone and said: *"Schönen guten Tag, hier ist Jürgen Klopp.* I am the new coach of Borussia Dortmund. I've been told you want to cancel your tickets. Don't you think you should reconsider?" Some of them were so gobsmacked, they said: "Okay, we'll think it over." He reeled them back in. Can you imagine any other coach doing that? That was Jürgen. He stole everybody's hearts.'

'We've had successful coaches at Dortmund who were also class acts in their dealings with people before,' says Fritz Lünschermann, a bespectacled, cheerful, bear-like man in his early sixties, who has been looking after the first-team's organisational needs as 'team manager' since 1988. 'Ottmar Hitzfeld, Matthias Sammer. But Jürgen Klopp is unrivalled. He had the whole staff eating out of his hand, by treating them seriously and valuing their efforts. Jürgen asked people how they felt, if they had any problems and so on. I remember I was wearing very colourful shirts at the time. Jürgen went up to me and said: "Ey, listen, are you always wearing such wallpaper?" I said: "I'll have to see if I've got anything else in my cupboard." And then I put those wallpaper shirts in the bin. I listened to his advice. You couldn't be upset with him.'

His freelance work as a personal stylist aside, Klopp used the summer break to immerse himself in the club's traditions and heritage. Lünschermann, 'a walking lexicon' (Schneck), explained to him the importance of the 'Drei Alfredos', the attacking trio of Alfred 'Ady' Preißler, Alfred Kelbassa and Alfred Niepieklo who won back-to-back championships in the mid 1950s. He and Klopp immediately hit it off, Lünschermann says. 'He is a guy always having fun, and I'm of a positive disposition, too. I had to coordinate the football schedule with him for the season but there was another matter in those early weeks. Every year, our Council of Elders, made up of former players and long-standing members, have their summer party. I said to Jürgen: "It would be good if you came." They all gathered in a restaurant in Wickede and were straightaway smitten with Jürgen. He sat down with everyone and talked to all these elderly gentlemen and their wives, who didn't have a clue about football. But he made them feel appreciated and took their concerns seriously. He stayed much longer than he initially planned, a few hours, and left a lasting impression on that generation. They will still say today: "Jürgen was a one-off."' Legendary players such as Aki Schmidt and Hoppy Kurrat loved Klopp, Schneck adds. 'Other coaches treated these meetings like an unwelcome chore. Jürgen, on the other hand, acknowledged that the club wouldn't be there without them. His interest was genuine. He treasured the history.'

Klopp won over the club even when he lost, and lost badly. On a staff day years later, employees were put into mixed groups to compete in physical games and a quiz. Schneck: 'I was in a group with Jürgen, a groundsman and a woman from accounts. There was an egg-and-spoon race, you had to shoot on goal, that sort of thing. And there were questions about Dortmund's history. We were sure we were in the lead but in fact we came last. Everybody else was cheering! As losers, we had to wash the team bus. You could do these things with Jürgen. He was there, he was approachable. You felt: this is the perfect fit.'

Klopp's force of personality, he recounts, smashed through the barriers between work and private life. 'One day, I mentioned in passing to him that my mum would soon turn ninety, and that she was still very sharp. Klopp replied: "Shouldn't I come and congratulate her?" That would be a dream, of course, but I didn't take him seriously at first. I never mentioned it again. But a few weeks later he asked me: "Tell me, isn't it her birthday soon? Please write down the address, I'll come and visit." And then he rang the doorbell. They had coffee and cake, and all the guests who came to the party couldn't believe that Klopp was sitting there, chatting with my mum. To him, it was the most natural thing.'

The pre-season started with a training camp in Donaueschingen, in the Black Forest, and a canoe ride down a river. 'That was the first thing we did, all get together and have a good time,' Dortmund defender Neven Subotić says. 'Kloppo is the kind of guy who leans over and flips somebody else's canoe. That's when the fun starts. You know, aha, this is not about him showing who's boss and us doing a serious race. I don't think Klopp ever thinks: "How can I be funny?" It comes naturally to him.'

'Jürgen is a born entertainer. Straightaway he had this huge presence, this aura, in Donaueschingen,' Watzke says. 'The team went with him immediately.' They didn't have much choice, of course. 'He knew what he wanted, there was only one way for him,' says Subotić. 'His strategy was basically to run the opponents into the ground. That's not for everyone. Some thought: "I just want to play. Give me the ball." Especially some of the older, more experienced players, they had their own views. Winning them over to such an intense way of playing was a challenge he mastered really well, I think. It was a new situation for him, because at Mainz he had had a team that was put together to play his way. At Dortmund, he had to find out who was with him and who wasn't.'

Sebastian Kehl, twenty-eight at the time, was appointed captain by Klopp during the training camp. Kehl makes the point that getting the players to run in pre-season was only half the job. The new system, a radical departure from Borussia's methodical, possession-based game under Doll and Van Marwijk, needed not just more running but a different way of thinking about football.

'Klopp worked tirelessly to implant his philosophy in our heads,' Kehl says. 'I remember that he called me during my holidays to talk at length about his ideas and concepts. It was a completely new path we ventured on.' Some smaller Bundesliga sides, notably Klopp's Mainz, had played such an extreme style before. But there was an unspoken consensus that better teams, with more quality, didn't have to work and think as hard. 'Tactics is for bad players,' the former VfB Stuttgart and FC Bayern manager Felix Magath had memorably proclaimed a couple of years earlier.

Klopp's brand of pressing and *Gegenpressing* necessitated both strong theoretical underpinnings and a selfless attitude. The groundwork for the former was laid via 'many, many video sessions' (Kehl). Some of the clips came from other leagues and clubs, including Barcelona, but the analysis centred on Dortmund's games. Klopp drew arrows on the screen, outlining where the players should be, or move to, to overload the zone near the ball. Kehl: 'All of that was combined with incredibly intense work on the training pitch, with many stops, corrections, moving across. It's good to look at videos, but you have to feel it on the pitch. You have to get a sense for the right moment, begin to understand the game in a new way. You have to switch between attack and defence much quicker, you have to adapt to a different impulse in your head. These things won't happen overnight.'

A holding midfielder, Kehl was used to protecting the defence and calmly distributing the ball to the players ahead of him. Effectively, he functioned as a human speed bump. But Klopp's way was the highway, *Autobahn* football. Kehl's game had to change more than others' to adjust to the acceleration all around him. Instead of instantly falling back into his own half as soon as Borussia lost the ball upfield, he and his teammates were asked to flood forward, in an effort to win the ball back immediately. 'Other coaches said: "Let them have the ball in their own half. We'll only attack once they get closer,"' Kehl says. 'Jürgen's instructions were to press and move up in unison if we lost the ball in their half, or if they turned their back on us. We also laid traps on the pitch, by not going for the first ball out and making sure the opponents played into an area where we wanted it to be, to the flanks, for example, where we could double up. That was the match plan, paired with a firm willingness to run and tolerate pain. "Even if it looks stupid": that was one of his mottos. If the first guy pressed and missed, the next one had to be ready to join in. It was very, very wild running [towards the ball]. "Wild" was one of the words Klopp used. He wanted to make it a wild game, to pose problems for the opponents and put them into difficult situations. Many players in the Bundesliga were used to calmly controlling the ball and then coming up with a good idea. With time and space, all players are good but if you step on their toes as soon as they get the ball, even the best ones struggle. If you double- or triple-up on them, it's even more difficult.'

Subotić was used to the drill from two previous seasons under Klopp at Mainz but at Dortmund the coach had to go back to the basics. 'The team was much better but the system was completely new for them. There were many sessions that really weren't much fun. Klopp explaining things while twenty guys are standing around. Or tactical, synchronised running. No fun at all. But it was important. In time, Zeljko [Buvac] got involved more and more. He's very silent outside the training ground – nobody asks the assistant, do they? – but he struck up a super relationship with the players. He played football with us as well. That earned him a lot of respect. The players saw: "Ah, he can play." '

The same could soon be said of BVB's new defensive partnership of Subotić and Bayern Munich loanee Mats Hummels, both nineteen. Dubbed *Kinderriegel* by *Bild* – best translated as 'child lock' – the two untried teenagers (at Bundesliga level) were picked ahead of the far more experienced Croatian international Robert Kovač, to the astonishment of many experts. The make-up of the BVB defence became younger still when crowd favourite left-back Dédé ruptured his cruciate ligament in the first game of the season, a 3-2 win at Bayer 04 Leverkusen. Klopp had described the Brazilian as 'the best player I've ever worked with' to a friend only two weeks earlier, and he was devastated. Fortunately, twenty-year-old Marcel Schmelzer, a product of BVB's youth system, turned out to be a more than able replacement. 'He was a machine,' Klopp told Fligge and Fligge in *Echte Liebe*.

'None of the four centre-backs in the squad were confirmed starters at the outset, that very much worked in my and Neven's favour,' says Hummels, who'd been deemed surplus to requirements by 'the other Jürgen' – Klinsmann, the new coach at FC Bayern. 'We quickly managed to put ourselves into contention, and Jürgen could see that we had good personalities. We were only nineteen, yes, but Klopp fully trusted us, perhaps because he saw that we were mentally a bit further on than your regular nineteen-year-olds, due to our backgrounds.' Hummels had been a supremely confident star performer at academy level for Bayern, whereas Subotić's personal story was reflected by an air of determination and maturity. A child of Bosnian Serb refugees who had moved from the Black Forest to the US to avoid deportation, he had joined Mainz as a seventeen-year-old from the University of South Florida in the summer of 2006. (He and FSV striker Conor Casey shared the same agent, Steve Kelly. Kelly had arranged for the teenager's successful trial.)

As a former defender, one might have expected the coach to micro-manage the young duo. But to Hummels' mild surprise, Klopp was open about his own limitations with his protégés. 'He said: "I have never played at your level, therefore I will never pretend to you that I know everything. But I will always try to help you."' The obvious lack of experience in the back four, Hummels adds, was mitigated by a strategy that shifted a huge part of the defensive responsibilities 40 metres further forward, onto the strikers and midfielders. 'The opponents were rarely able to play out the ball without pressure, that led to many long balls that lacked precision and direction. Those passes, played under duress, often went too far or out of touch. It was easier to play for us at the back. It was new but hugely enjoyable. We were so young that we hadn't yet developed our own routine, we could totally devote ourselves to that way of playing.' It all came down to the amount of pressure that could be applied 'against the ball', as Klopp would stress to his players over and over again. A tracksuit missionary, preaching gospel to the tactically unbaptised.

Not all ears were sympathetic to his dogma. Croatian striker Mladen Petrić, the leading goal-scorer of the previous season (thirteen goals) and arguably the squad's most talented player, found it hard to accept the new regime. The day after the Leverkusen match, he was sold to Hamburger SV in a €5m part-exchange deal that brought one of Klopp's old Mainz favourites, Egyptian Mohamed Zidan, to the Signal Iduna Park.

Klopp's move to get rid of the widely popular Petrić was interpreted as a high-risk manoeuvre, a powerplay by a hard-nosed coach eager to lay down the law. But Watzke implies that there were firm financial and footballing reasons that made the transfer advisable from the club's perspective as well. 'We all wanted it,' he says, grimacing a little as the hotel lobby saxophonist shuffles closer to his sofa. 'Jürgen was keen to get Zidan in, that was key. And the offer [from Hamburg] was good. Petrić and [Alexander] Frei didn't really fit well up front.' Frei, a Swiss centre-forward and orthodox poacher, wasn't a natural Klopp player, either, but Borussia felt that he could combine well enough with the more mercurial Zidan behind him. The partnership of Frei and Petrić, the elegant shadow striker, would not have produced the required work-rate.

'The strategy was to play all-action football with *Gegenpressing*,' says Watzke. 'They were very good players, but not the right ones for that.' Dortmund's high-pressing game worked even better as a consequence. 'You could quickly see that the team was more stable at the back,' Watzke says about an encouraging start to the campaign that brought a win in the Supercup against Bayern (2-1), a win in the DFB Pokal (3-1 v RW Essen) and seven points from the first three league games. 'Jürgen brought a defensive balance to the side, and the *Gegenpressing* was his trademark. Today, everyone's at it, more or less. Back then, you could see from the very first day that something was happening. But we honestly didn't think it would get that big.'

As destiny would have it, Klopp's fourth Bundesliga appointment with Dortmund was the most important game of the season: the *Revierderby* at home to despised neighbours Schalke 04. The Blues – Dortmund supporters never use their rivals' official name – were 3-0 up after sixty-six minutes. Borussia's young team looked totally out of their depth, Schalke's players were arrogantly strutting around the pitch in the knowledge that the fortress Signal Iduna Park had fallen. Kevin Kuranyi had nearly made it 4-0, hitting the crossbar with a header from close range. Klopp was horrified. '[My wife] Ulla sat in the stands and thought about packing our suitcases,' he said later. But, somehow, the impossible happened. Riled by S04's over-confidence, Subotić scored a goal that set fire to the stadium. Both the visitors' and referee's control over proceedings melted away in the furnace. Substitute Alex Frei scored from an offside position. In the eighty-ninth minute of the game, Dortmund were awarded an extremely dubious penalty. Klopp couldn't bear to watch. He turned his back to Frei, who calmly stepped up and converted: 3-3. 'Possibly one of the best derbies of all time,' *Frankfurter Rundschau* cheered. 'An epic,

worthy of a 1000-page novel. A resurrection.' 'If it stinks of
sweat here, that's me,' a relieved, exhausted, overwhelmed
Klopp said in the press conference. 'The game was so thrilling.
I've seen wins that haven't felt this good.' Dortmund's best
start to a campaign in five years got the whole city excited.
'Everywhere we went, people were giving us thumbs up, I
had never seen anything like it in ten years in the job,' says
Schneck. 'If you ask me how he managed to wake up the
sleeping giant: with a kiss. And an attitude that chimed with
the Ruhr area. That's him. He didn't go on a course, he didn't
ask anyone how the people here were. He sensed it,
instinctively, and behaved in a way that connected with them.
He got them going. People kept asking: "Are you sure you
don't have any ancestors from here? A grandfather who
worked in the mines or in the steel factories?" They were
certain he was one of them. No one could believe he hailed
from the Black Forest, that he was Swabian. He himself didn't
see himself that way. He always said: "I knew very early on
that I had to leave. I couldn't imagine myself sweeping the
driveway to make sure my neighbour saw me and said: Ah
good, he's swept his driveway." He never had that kind of
small-minded attitude the Swabians are known for. It's his
openness. He approaches people. My lord, in the beginning, he
fulfilled every supporter's wish. If somebody wanted him to
go somewhere and say hello, he went there. I never felt as
if he was doing that in a calculated way. He simply is that
kind of guy: he likes people. I believe I once heard him say:
"A coach who doesn't love his players can't be a good coach."'

Bild pundit Mario Basler hailed Klopp as 'the white
Barack Obama'. Both had 'an excessive amount of
intelligence and know-how', the former Bayern Munich

midfielder wrote, 'both are bearers of hope, both are idols. At Dortmund, they're so fired-up that him cleaning his glasses on the bench in a semi-competent manner brings out the cheers on the south stand.'

Klopp warned that he was 'not a messiah, only a coach', and that it was too early to contemplate Dortmund getting into the top third of the table: 'If we will be able to show commitment and readiness to battle for ninety minutes, something might grow here.'

His scepticism was vindicated, much more than he would have wished for, when Dortmund crashed to a 2-0 home defeat against Udinese in the first round of the UEFA Cup. (They had qualified for the competition by reaching the DFB Pokal final under predecessor Thomas Doll.) BVB's first game in Europe in five years revealed how far the young team and their roughcast tactics still had to travel to compete with the elite. The Italians, unfazed by the hurly-burly, coolly bypassed Dortmund's pressing game and hit them hard on the break. 'I've never seen a team I was involved with play this badly, it was embarrassing in parts,' Klopp said, shaking his head in disgust. Two early, enforced, substitutions – Zidan and Hummels both got injured – had only heightened the confusion. The hosts had been 'helpless like a beached whale', *Gazzetta dello Sport* reported gleefully. Worst of all, the manner of the loss raised questions about the club's transfer policy. 'Is this squad, put together by [sporting director] Michael Zorc over the years, good enough to play top-level football in the long run?' *Süddeutsche* wondered.

Those questions only got bigger in the wake of a 4-1 defeat against newly promoted Hoffenheim, the season's surprise title contenders. 'It was a drubbing,' says Watzke.

Ralf Rangnick's men were playing a very similar style to Dortmund's, only much better. 'That was systematic football, the way it should be,' Klopp conceded. 'We need to get where they are now. Tactical behaviour is not like riding a bike, unfortunately. You have to practise, again and again.'

Re-programming the team's operating system simply took time, Subotić stresses. 'Three v three or five v five, it's quite easy. But during the game, you're tired and you say to yourself: "Do I really have to press again?" Then you press and the guy simply lays off the ball because your teammate hasn't pressed with you and it's all a waste. Getting used to that wasn't easy. It's mentally and physically very demanding. You were used to running 105km per game as a team. Suddenly, you were up to 115km, and the target was to hit 120km or more. Klopp knew that couldn't happen overnight. He knew everybody had played twenty years of football and never been asked to work to such a plan before. More work, and more time, was the answer.'

If the early weeks were shaped by an *Aufbruchsstimmung* – a sense of departure, to a glorious black-and-yellow future – Dortmund had suddenly arrived at a very unwanted destination in the autumn. This was crisis territory, a deeply troubling concoction of a leaky defence – ('a shooting gallery', *Süddeutsche* sneered), a half-baked concept and a coach struggling to find the best starting XI. There were six changes in the line-up for Hoffenheim, and another six for the subsequent cup game against Hertha BSC that Klopp could not afford to lose. 'These are black days, a black week,' he lamented.

'You can be the nicest guy as a manager but everything depends on success,' Schneck says, raising an eyebrow.

Subotić hints that confidence in the dressing room in the new coach and his ways was fragile in that period. 'I knew him, I trusted him,' he says, 'but for every team, it's really important to see that all the stuff the guy in front of you is going on about actually works. They might all really like him. But his methods working is the most important benchmark.'

'He had to talk people round, it didn't all come off on day one,' says Kehl. 'We had some difficult moments at the beginning, thinking: "How's that ever going to work?" There were discussions. Nevertheless, he made it clear from the first minute that there was only his way of playing because he was absolutely convinced it was the right way.'

Against Berlin, raw luck came to Klopp's rescue. Dortmund scraped a 2-1 win in extra-time, playing a slightly more defensive diamond in midfield to provide an extra layer of security. Next up, VfB Stuttgart were trounced 3-0 at the Mercedes Benz-Arena, with Borussia showing just how good their well-executed match plan could be.

'By now, the very last person in Dortmund should have realised that we're on the right path,' Watzke said after the second leg against Udinese. His team had lost the match on penalties, having won 2-0 at the Stadio Friuli in regular time. But the quality and courage of the performance had made this a knockout of the inverse kind: it put the team firmly on their feet. Dortmund's progress under the new man in charge had become self-evident. Dismissed by some as merely a motivational coach, shadow-boxing, jumping up and down on the touchline like a hyperactive six-year-old at Disneyland on a sugar rush, Klopp showed that he couldn't just read a game. He could write one, too.

Klopp also won over the local press corps by intervening on their behalf in an altercation that night. Stewards in the stadium had blocked the journalists' access to the BVB players after the final whistle, until the Dortmund coach personally muscled in and cleared a path. One of the Italians cursed Klopp, shouting *cazzo* at him – polite translation: prick – but he just smiled, and, ahem, stood tall. 'Not to worry – I don't speak Italian,' he said.

Dortmund went on to lose just once more before Christmas – against Hamburger SV, a team that would inexplicably become Klopp's bête noire in the Bundesliga – and hibernated during the winter break in sixth spot, ahead of Schalke. The improvement was real.

'We all know that money gets you goals in football,' says Norbert Dickel, perched on a wobbly plastic table outside a hole-in-the-wall café in Marbella in January 2017. Across the road, inside the red-bricked Estadio Municipal de Marbella, Dortmund's first team is training this evening. 'But we didn't have money then. It was a divine blessing to get Jürgen in. The team we had then started playing really well in that first year, we all saw that. The whole style of playing changed. Leaving aside the fact that we underwent an incredible development in terms of our football, Jürgen also ensured that the popularity of the club rose beyond belief. Simply because he was there, twenty-four hours a day, bringing people together. He never complained about players being injured or sick. He'd say: 'We have enough good players.' He wasn't a moaner; he thought there was no point worrying about things you couldn't influence. We all sensed that things were moving forward, towards a point where you could believe in success.' Lünschermann: 'It was a transformation. We had seen plenty of games that had been rather unwatchable. Suddenly, these young guys were dashing about like hares, going after every ball. They started combining, too, after a while. It was superb. All of us said: "Oh boy, this could turn into an era." And it did – into an unforgettable one. That's his doing.'

The first half of Klopp's debut Bundesliga season in North Rhine-Westphalia had BVB sitting pretty with seven wins, eight draws and two defeats. An almost identical record (eight wins, seven draws, three defeats) after the winter break, despite a serious ankle injury for Hummels and a poor start to the calendar year, steered the team towards UEFA Cup qualification. Klopp's contract was prematurely extended until 2012. 'Not one person in the club was against Jürgen Klopp, everybody supported the decision,' Watzke declared that March.

The team missed out on Europe, however, in classic, painfully dramatic Klopp style: in the last minute on the final day of the season. Fifth-placed Hamburger SV, 2-0 down to Eintracht Frankfurt after an hour, rallied to win 3-2, thanks to a Piotr Trochowski goal scored from an offside position. Dortmund, who had drawn their match 1-1 at the other Borussia (from Mönchengladbach), were left empty-handed. Missing out on the 5 to 7 million euros the club could have made in the re-branded Europa League group stage left a hole in the budget.

'There'll be a little less money,' Klopp said after the frustration had receded. 'But we've had some incredibly powerful experiences and have become much more of a unit with the fans. I'm hoping that some sponsors will say: "Something's happening here, that's cool, we want to be part of that." Everyone can jump on the bandwagon. But it's much more rewarding to be a part of getting something started.'

'On the whole, it was a great season,' Watzke says. 'Unfortunately the icing on the cake was missing. The way it ended was a huge disappointment to all of us. We hadn't exactly been spoilt before; an improvement of seven places was pretty good. There were other disappointments over the years, and they always brought us closer together. At the end of the day it's a fact that the three of us – Jürgen, Michael Zorc and me – were an extraordinarily good fit. That was key.'

Somewhere, half-buried underneath the relentless, contagious positivity Klopp was projecting, there had also been anxiety and trepidation about a coach who'd only ever worked on German football's periphery. Too many managers had come and failed since the departure of Matthias Sammer in 2004. 'There was a bit of fear inside the club, due to the recent history. "Please not another failure," they said,' says Subotić. 'We managed to allay those fears in the first year. Finishing sixth after coming thirteenth the season before was a success. We won games, we drew games, we also lost games of course but on the whole, you could see that the plan was working. We learned that we could trust him and each other. The whole club could take a deep breath.' Kehl agrees. 'It was palpable that the mood had changed completely,' he says.

But not everyone was deemed suitable to continue the journey. Swiss striker Alex Frei was offloaded to FC Basel for €4.25m in the off-season. Dortmund spent all the money bringing in a replacement, Argentinian striker Lucas 'The

Panther' Barrios, who would be happier to toil selflessly on the frontline, as Klopp's system demanded. Hummels' loan deal was made permanent in a €4.2m deal that Bayern Munich would come to regret. Two more crucial signings cost almost nothing. All-rounders Sven Bender (twenty, TSV 1860, €1.5m) and Kevin Großkreutz (twenty-one, Ahlen, free transfer) added youthful dynamism in midfield.

Munich-born Bender remembers Klopp phoning to sell Dortmund to him during that summer. 'I was in the car. The connection dropped four times but he kept on trying. I knew that Dortmund were interested, but the moment a coach calls you and tells you why and how much they want you is really decisive. First of all, it was cool for me to speak to him. I only knew him from television, so to have him on the phone was very nice. He came across exactly like the guy on the box. The conversation was very pleasant. He told me about all the things he had encountered in his first year there, that Dortmund was a fantastic club that he could wholeheartedly recommend to me and that I should do it. And he said he'd be "brutally" happy if I chose him as my coach and Borussia as my club. Of course I wanted in. Dortmund are a big club, with a huge aura, and Klopp was the perfect man at the helm from the very start.' Bender was even more impressed once he met his new coach in person. 'The guy was huge! Astonishing. He didn't look that tall on TV, I had to do a double-take. He was a superb motivator. As a young player, he really hit the spot for me.'

Klopp had a talent for hitting the spot with everyone, Lünschermann says. 'He didn't have a routine in the dressing room before a game, or a particular superstition but away from home, he always looked for a quiet, secret place to

have a smoke. That made him extremely likeable in my
eyes. He didn't pretend to be ascetic, he had the odd beer,
he was unashamedly human – unlike many coaches who try
to hide anything others could perceive as a weakness. It was
that human side of his, above everything else, that got the
whole club going.'

At Dortmund, sporting director Michael Zorc and chief
scout Sven Mislintat were responsible for finding player
solutions in line with Dortmund's relatively narrow budget,
a few Mainz players (Zidan, Subotić, Markus Feulner) who
Klopp had personally put on the shopping list excluded.
There was little choice but to plump for exotic nobodies
such as Barrios and unknown Polish striker Robert
Lewandowski, who was signed from Lech Poznan in 2010.
The €4.25m outlay was so significant that Lewandowski
was scouted about thirty times. Klopp himself travelled to
Poland to cast an eye on the forward, disguising himself
with a hoodie and baseball cap.

Empty coffers made playing the youth card a must.
Fortunately for Dortmund, Klopp developed an appetite
beyond coaching, as Subotić noted. He enjoyed building a
new team. 'At Dortmund, he had a chance to change the
squad, almost from scratch, to put his vision in place. I think
that really appealed to him. My guess is that it was similar
at Liverpool.'

Klopp regularly proclaimed that his young side 'were hot
like frying fat', but his second season started off rather
lukewarm. Two heavy defeats, at Hamburg (1-4) and Bayern
(1-5), three draws and a troublesome 1-0 home defeat in the
derby against Schalke in the first seven games made for the
club's worst start in twenty-four years. One month ahead of

the club's hundredth anniversary, the team had crashed to fifteenth place. 'The supporters got a little antsy,' Watzke says. One hundred angry ultras turned up at the training ground after the Schalke defeat, demanding answers from players and officials. Klopp defused the situation by engaging with the dissenters head-on. Schneck: 'He got out of the team bus and said: "Okay, tell me." They complained that the team hadn't fought enough, that they weren't true Borussia, that sort of thing. Jürgen explained to them over fifteen or twenty minutes why that wasn't the case at all, and assured them that he took their concerns and ideas very seriously. They went home peacefully, thanking him for his time. That was no mean feat. Other coaches don't want anything to do with these types of situations.'

Klopp had a great knack for hitting the right note with supporters, he spoke their language, says Dickel. 'We had plenty of coaches who would say: "Today, our game between the lines, between defence and midfield, and between midfield and attack, hasn't quite worked out." Or: "The transition game was a little off." Nobody wants to hear that in the Ruhr area. Jürgen said: "We played some real crap today, that's why we deserved to lose." Everybody can live with that.'

The media were less easily placated. When Dortmund got knocked out of the DFB Pokal by third division VfL Osnabrück in November, *Berliner Zeitung* fundamentally questioned Klopp's ability to take Borussia forward. 'It's a regression,' wrote the broadsheet. 'Klopp has impressively shown at FSV Mainz that he can make a small club bigger. Whether he can make a not-so-big club big again remains unclear. This season can already be seen as a lost one in that respect.'

The Dortmund coach professed himself disappointed about the sharp change in perception ('everything is a crisis these days, people's competence gets doubted far too quickly') and promised improvement. 'We will pull ourselves out of it, I'm quite certain of that.' Watzke maintains the club 'had no doubt that he would come good. Zero point zero.'

Klopp's aptitude for keeping the internal mood upbeat was vital at the time, says Bender. Some coaches take out their frustrations on players or lose faith in their own footballing principles. Not so Klopp. 'Naturally, he would tell somebody in no uncertain terms if they didn't run in the right direction or paused at the wrong moment,' Bender says. 'But he never made a player feel that they were dead to him, that they had blown it. On the contrary, he always made sure the player was given another chance if they wanted to take it. You could prove to him that you were still there, ready to step on the gas.'

The BVB boss, too, treated every game as a new chance to get things right. Dortmund's poor run in the autumn of 2009, he felt, was but an unavoidable by-product of a very young side adapting to a system that needed full-blooded commitment and detailed execution to work. Growing pains.

The answer was simple: more work. 'We held a brief training camp and told the boys they would be getting an extra three days off over the festive season if they – as a team – could cover more than 118 kilometres in each of those ten games,' he told *FourFourTwo* years later. They didn't quite manage it, but Klopp granted them their extra holiday regardless. 'I did that because the extra effort the team put in immediately translated into more liveliness on the pitch. We were instantly more assertive, we created superiority in numbers – all the things you associate with additional effort.'

'He would stand on the sidelines and shout his head off that we should push forward,' says Subotić. 'As a player, especially as a defender, you're often thinking: "Safety first, let's stay back." He had to make a lot of adjustments during matches in those early days. It was still a completely new system for almost everybody. Hoffenheim had played that way, but only in the first half [of 2008–09]. They couldn't keep it up. For us, it was a continuous process, and we couldn't look at any other team in the league as a role model for what we wanted to do.'

Dortmund had to set their own example. With each passing week, an 'absurdly youthful team' (*Süddeutsche Zeitung*), often with an average age of less than twenty-three years old, got a little closer to reconciling high-tempo 'wildness' with stability. By mid-December, they were in fifth place. Lucas Barrios' goals, nineteen in total, kept them in touch with the Champions League places in the New Year, all the way to the penultimate game. The 2009 champions VfL Wolfsburg, who had just lost their title to Louis van Gaal's Bayern, were the opponents on a day that ended in celebrations leaving even the former Mainz coach Klopp flummoxed. 'I have never experienced such support in my life,' he said, after the Yellow Wall and the rest of the stadium had saluted the team with chants and standing ovations that wouldn't stop. It was impossible to tell from the across-the-board exaltation that Dortmund had only drawn the game 1-1. The result, coupled with Werder Bremen's 2-0 away win at Schalke, meant that they could no longer finish in the top three and qualify for European club football's most lucrative competition. But the supporters didn't care. Their joy had its source in neighbours Schalke's defeat – which ensured the Royal Blues would not, heaven forbid, win the league – and centred on fifth-placed Dortmund's first direct qualification for the Europa League in seven years. Germany's most passionate and most knowledgeable crowd were all too aware of how far the club had come in its first two seasons under Klopp to bemoan them falling a couple of points short of Champions League access. 'Bombastic party: the team were hailed as if they had pulled off the biggest coup imaginable,' *Frankfurter Allgemeine Zeitung* reported incredulously.

Ahead of Klopp's first day in office, Watzke and Zorc had given him a small winged rhinoceros figurine as a good-luck charm. Devised as a mascot for the newly opened concert hall in 2002, the chimera had become a symbol for the city, the embodiment of its thick-skinned pride and aspirations. In May, the Signal Iduna Park allowed itself to believe that this fantastical beast might actually . . . fly? The BVB rhino was pawing the ground, primed for take-off.

8. PUMP UP THE VOLUME

Liverpool 2015–16

It's a beautiful early summer's day in Liverpool, best enjoyed on the players' terrace that stretches the entire length of Liverpool's Melwood training complex, from Jürgen Klopp's multiple-bay-window command centre on one corner past the dining hall to the other end, where club nutritionist Mona Nemmer, and Andreas Kornmayer, the head of fitness, have their glass-panelled offices.

You'd never know from the lazy afternoon vibes, the silence of the deserted training pitch and the laughter of Jordan Henderson on the next table, that Liverpool are due to play Southampton in a must-win game in three days, that THE PRESSURE IS ON! to come fourth. Adam Lallana, smiling and squinting in the sunlight like a tourist on the first day of his holiday, couldn't look much more relaxed if he were sipping a pink cocktail with a paper umbrella instead of bottled mineral water.

The conversation is all about how hard it is to play Klopp's brand of football, but the England midfielder is not doing a good job of conveying his and the team's suffering. There's a simple reason for that: he finds the pain pleasurable.

'I was on international duty [when Klopp was appointed on 9 October 2015] and I remember how I couldn't wait to get back,' he says. 'I looked up his history and the way his teams played. I saw the word '*Gegenpressing*' everywhere, *Gegenpressing* style. 'Heavy metal' style. Ever since day one really, our first game against Tottenham, it was a very physically demanding game. But you embrace it, it's a challenge to become fitter. You get fit, so you can do it. I look at [Philippe] Coutinho sometimes and how hard he works. He wants the ball back and he still has the ability and the strength to take a man on and put it in the top corner.'

Motion and motivation have the same Latin root. One cannot exist without the other. Klopp's very first message to Liverpool supporters, that they had to turn 'from doubters into believers', was repeated to the players at Melwood ahead of the debut training session. 'He talked a lot about the team trusting itself, about belief, and not fearing any other team,' Lallana says. 'He definitely had that confidence himself, that aura and belief that he is a top manager. He walked through the door and you could feel it. And I think that automatically filters through to his players.'

Before the German could have the players' legs, he would have to get into their heads. There was no point joining in the public lament about the team's poor defenders and general lack of quality in relation to the title contenders; Klopp had to work with the squad at his disposal and talk up its strengths instead. His trick was to stress the link between performance and effort, rather than with ability. Lallana: 'He said, "Work hard for me." That's all he wants.

He can handle mistakes, he can handle bad games. "Work hard for me and give me everything." He's convinced that technical ability and quality will come out as a result. That is what the boss has done for me since the Tottenham game.'

Two months into the 2015–16 season, there was no time to practise the new pressing style on the pitch, nor did the fixture list allow for additional fitness exercises. Klopp's notorious double-training sessions, criticised as excessive and counter-productive by some pundits and experts as the odd muscle injury beset the team after Christmas, never took place. The ad-hoc introduction of pressing and *Gegenpressing* necessitated a firm collective commitment. 'It's an agreement a team makes with itself,' says coaching assistant and chief scout Peter Krawietz. 'A social contract. "Yes, we want to do that together." One guy doing it by himself is nothing. He'll try once, he'll try again, but then he'll turn around and say: "Where is everybody else? Come on. I'm running my socks off and you're sitting back and enjoying the spectacle." That's why you need an agreement that's binding for everybody. "We will do it together, as soon as we lose the ball in the final third, we will try to win it back." There are a huge amount of advantages to doing that. You disrupt the opposition attack. You might catch out a team in the very moment they're preparing an attack and change their positioning accordingly. The left-back might have started running up the pitch. You save energy that way, too. If you track back to protect yourself from the counter-attack with eight men, then eight men have to run a combined 80 metres, 640 in total. Or you play a proper *Gegenpressing*, with the right trigger and the right intensity, then you run 5 or 10 quick metres with three or four players. That's why it's not so much a question of your legs but of the mind. You have that moment where you have to overcome your inertia. Don't switch off. Don't be disappointed. The attack isn't over yet. It takes some work to drum that into players. There are special sessions and ways of training to make that happen. Video analysis. We showed the team: "Look, these guys are very compact, it's terribly difficult [to get behind them] but winning the ball back from them is the one moment they're vulnerable." We tried to make that idea stick. Once you do that, and do it orderly, you save yourself a lot of metres [tracking back], too.'

Lallana, who had been exposed to a similar regime under Mauricio Pochettino at Southampton, reveals that concerted action comes with a feel-good factor that offsets any complaints: 'It is mentally very demanding, but when you have ten other lads all operating like that, it is easy. You enjoy feeling that pain, because everyone else is feeling it. You want to keep going for your mate. He's hurting, and you're hurting, but it's all right. That's what the manager likes, that's what he is like. He celebrates tackles like goals sometimes. Because he knows it hurts.' He adds that Klopp's tactics can't really accommodate dissidents and egotists who won't submit to the collective dictate. 'Maybe you can carry one player, but that's not how he wants to play. You can't operate like that.'

How difficult was it for Klopp and his staff to get his players to think and play that way? Krawietz considers the question for a moment. 'I believe that the team we encountered has been incredibly ready to take on things,' he says. 'They were ready and willing to try something new; they knew that there were reasons why things hadn't worked out so well before and why we stood there now, wearing red-and-black tracksuits. We felt it from day one. They want to understand what we're trying to get across to them.' Complications didn't stem so much from a lack of willingness as they did from the initial language barrier. Tactics brain Zeljko Buvac was reluctant to speak much English at first, Klopp translated for him. 'A lot of the time, mainly when he's angry, Klopp says: "I fucking wish I could speak German to you," ' Lallana laughs. 'His English is tremendous, actually. I understand whatever he needs and wants to say. But it does frustrate him at times.'

'I'm muddling through with my English at a low level, and the team listen,' Klopp said with classic self-deprecation in an interview with German *Focus* magazine a month into his tenure. 'Everyone's cool at the club and eager to develop, we take time to do it properly.' He was having so much fun and working so hard that he didn't quite have the time to appreciate his luck just yet, he revealed. 'It's passed us by a little bit but, of course, there has been a moment where you think: "It's so great being the coach of Liverpool." I never thought I'd be here one day.'

Nevertheless, it took a little while before cultural footballing differences were fully reconciled on the training pitch. 'The odd misunderstanding was inevitable,' Krawietz says. 'Everybody throws in their twenty years of footballing experience; you think you're all talking about the same things but in the end you realise they're two wholly different things.'

Pressing and tackling, the way the coaching staff understand it, expressly forbids fouling the opponent. A foul immediately renders your own ball-winning attempts futile. But during the very first tactical exercise, meant to be a light session, the Liverpool players flew into the challenges with abandon, believing that they had to interrupt the opposition build-up by any means necessary. Klopp had to stop them and tell them to slow down. Krawietz remembers the episode with a content smile. 'It was cool to see that the lads were absolutely ready to implement new ideas and immerse themselves in them completely. That made life a lot easier for us.'

Lallana says that the players responded to the manager's 'honesty': 'He can give you a bollocking, he can really praise you. The hugs, they are really genuine as well. He will tell you when he is happy with you. He will tell you when he is not happy with you. He is just genuine, straight-up. He can't hide his emotions, can he? If he wants to say something he will end up saying it. He says he can be your friend, but not your best friend, because he has to have those difficult conversations with you at times.'

Belgian striker Christian Benteke, for example, found the team's new direction a bit tricky to adjust to. Klopp quickly realised that the 6ft 3in forward was not best-suited to a high-energy pressing and counter-pressing game. Divock Origi and former Hoffenheim forward Roberto Firmino (as a false 9) were preferred instead. The Klopp–Benteke partnership failed to get off the ground. The German had years ago decided for himself that there is no point explaining to players why they aren't being picked, that all he can do is tell them about the areas of their game that they can improve. But Benteke couldn't reconcile the coach's silent stance with his keenness to sign him for Borussia Dortmund a couple of years earlier. Klopp had met the former Aston Villa striker in a hotel in Germany, enthusiastically talked about the prospect of working together, and thrown in a few text messages subsequently for good measure. But the move had never materialised. (Like his peers Antonio Conte and José Mourinho, Klopp is a voracious texter. On the day of Dortmund's Champions League final, no less, he sent a message to Kevin De Bruyne, then at Chelsea, expressing his excitement at the prospect of coaching the Belgian at Dortmund in 2013–14. The prospective move was eventually vetoed at the last minute by the Blues.)

Benteke, on as a substitute at Stamford Bridge, did score Liverpool's third goal to secure a 3-1 win over Chelsea, Klopp's first win in the league after two draws (0-0 at Spurs, 1-1 v Southampton), a frustrating 1-1 in his debut home game, against Russian outfit Rubin Kazan in the Europa League, and a League Cup win over Bournemouth (1-0). Beating Mourinho's champions in west London with cleverly executed counter-attacking football served as a crucial marker of early progress. Maybe the wall-to-wall hype on sports television and in the back pages since Klopp's arrival on Merseyside was justified, after all.

'Can you win the league?' a reporter asked Klopp after the final whistle. 'Are you crazy?' he barked back incredulously. 'At first, I thought I didn't understand the question. I've been here for three weeks. The last time Liverpool won an away game, I was still on holiday.' Later, in a separate briefing in the tunnel, he was bombarded with questions about Liverpool's targets in the January transfer window and their chances of qualifying for the Champions League. They were eighth at this point. 'I can't believe the impatience,' he said. 'They want to know whether I'll finish fourth,' he shouted at referee Mark Clattenburg. 'Welcome to England,' he nodded.

The flight of Klopp's private plane from Germany to Liverpool had been monitored on the Internet by 35,500

Reds supporters, before the club had put him up in a boutique hotel on Hope Street ahead of his unveiling. The heavy symbolism was not accidental: in the minds of many fans, the Swabian wasn't so much the new coach but a harbinger of dreams, the man who would shake the club out of its mid-table stupor and ring in a return to glorious days past. 'His appointment feels so instinctively right because the 48-year-old's extra-large personality will immediately cut through much of the befuddled silence that has befallen Anfield since the club almost won the championship in 2014 and ensure the volume is from now on turned all the way up,' wrote the *Guardian*. Former Liverpool player Mark Lawrenson, not a man prone to emotional outbreaks, predicted that Klopp would 'bring back excitement to Anfield'. With his 'over-sized personality and 1,000-megawatt smile, he's box office,' Lawrenson added during a break from doing a show for lfc.tv in a city-centre high-rise. 'People hope that he will bring back the good times. That's already worth something.'

No other footballing country believes as much in the transformative powers of a manager as England, and Liverpool is the city that believes it most – thanks to Bill Shankly. The club's past greatness and a much more complicated present, in which they've been forced to play catch-up with richer rivals and upstarts, has created an unsteady climate, swinging wildly from overblown expectation to deep depression. Many prospective saviours have come and gone, unable to navigate the maelstrom of volatility.

Klopp (dark jeans, black blazer, Chelsea boots) presented himself as a supremely relaxed football electrician at his unveiling, confident that a bit of re-wiring could get the current flowing again, but also acknowledged the complexity of the overall challenge. 'We must not carry 20kg of history on our backs,' he warned, nor should the club bemoan its relative lack of funds. 'We should not think about money, only football.' Amen. Liverpool's situation, he added, was 'not that bad. It's a good time to make changes, a restart.' He promised 'full-throttle football' to cook up an emotional storm in the stadium but was at pains to play down his own importance. He was neither 'an idiot' nor 'a genius', 'a know-it-all' or 'a dreamer', he ventured, before landing the killer line. 'I'm just a normal guy from the Black Forest. I'm the Normal One.' Cue laughter all around. It takes huge amounts of self-assuredness to proclaim yourself ordinary in front of the world's media ahead of the first day in a big job. *Süddeutsche Zeitung* was reminded of the famous scene in *Monty Python's Life of Brian*, where the eponymous hero tries – and fails – to convince a crowd of disciples that he's wholly unworthy of their adulation. 'Only the true messiah denies his own divinity,' one woman exclaims. Liverpool, not slow to recognise the marketing potential of the new man in charge, duly trademarked 'The Normal One' as a phrase and produced a range of official merchandise bearing the slogan.

FSG president Mike Gordon says he was not surprised by the huge hype that greeted Klopp's appointment. 'Jürgen Klopp and Liverpool FC really are a match made in heaven. The passion of our fans, the authenticity of our fans and our supporters, the way that they feel about our football and their intelligence as football fans, meant that they understood right away that this was an extraordinary person to lead something that was so important to them. While I keep mentioning that the substance of Jürgen actually surpasses the style, the style is still very compelling. We all can agree on that. It is not surprising that the people took to him immediately and so powerfully. That started at the very first press conference. That is among the least surprising things that have happened so far.'

Gordon predicted to the LFC press department that they would be 'getting a Ferrari' in the new manager. Kenny Dalglish, too, anticipated a white-knuckle ride. 'I just heard Klopp's press conference and he sounds very, very impressive,' the former coach said. 'I think the supporters will need to fasten their seat belts – I'm sure they will really enjoy him.'

Acquaintances from Germany who visited Klopp in Liverpool during his first season in England noted that everybody at Anfield and Melwood happily opened doors for them as soon as they announced that they were there to see the manager. TV reporter Martin Quast sat in Klopp's office one day, waiting to shoot an interview, and could already hear his friend's laughter echoing through the corridors. 'I took a peek outside and saw Liverpool employees running about, all with huge smiles on their faces. And of course Kloppo's there among them, making jokes and making them feel good. That's his style, that kind of openness. I remember in his place in Mainz, all the doors to the various apartments were always open, and the guy who rented the flat above him would just pop in for breakfast in the morning. He just loves having people around him.' Klopp's so approachable that he's unofficially been serving as Melwood's resident agony aunt. At least one LFC employee with relationship troubles has turned to him for advice.

Before the Swabian's arrival, goalkeeper Simon Mignolet had taken it upon himself to organise get-togethers and team events. Klopp sought him out and told him that there would be much more of that in the coming months. 'We are one team and one family,' the manager announced. That ethos expressly stretched to non-playing staff, Klopp made clear. He learned the names of all eighty employees at Melwood, lined them up in the dining hall and introduced them to the players, explaining that the squad and the staff had 'a responsibility' to help each other achieve their best.

In Klopp's mind, the match-going public, too, had an important role to play even though he was reluctant to make any overt demands. At Mainz and Dortmund, he had seen players regularly tap into the stadium's energy, but Anfield, the crucible of football, didn't quite live up to its billing as a cauldron. Supporters left in droves eight minutes before the end in the 2-1 loss against Crystal Palace in November 2015, Klopp's first defeat as Liverpool coach. 'I felt pretty alone at that moment,' he said afterwards, visibly disappointed with the crowd's premature capitulation. But as a new immigrant member of the LFC community, he had to be careful not to blame the audience for the paucity of the show. The supporters' reaction was understandable and amounted to a silent but powerful commandment: he and the team had a duty to produce football that would thrill and hold the prospect of success until the very last second, he conceded. 'We should be responsible that nobody can leave the stadium a minute before [the end] because everything can happen,' Klopp said. 'We have to show that and we didn't.'

The Etihad proved a much more hospitable environment in the next league game. Klopp's Reds tore through the shaky Manchester City defence to win 4-1 and offer more evidence of an upturn in fortune. A year and a half later, Lallana believes that trip along the M62 marked 'the best game' of the Klopp era so far. 'I really enjoyed it, it was a real team performance,' he says. A subsequent meeting with the same opponents in the final of the League Cup was altogether less pleasant for Lallana and the rest of the squad. Liverpool did well to come back for a 1-1 draw at Wembley, against a City team boasting more individual quality, but lost the penalty shoot-out after extra-time had come and gone without further goals. 'We feel down but now we have to stand up. Only silly idiots stay on the floor and wait for the next defeat,' Klopp said. His frustration about losing out on his first piece of English silverware was tempered by the knowledge that Liverpool had fought valiantly with little left in the tank.

The league campaign failed to take off, however. Big wins were followed by draws and defeats against the lesser lights, in an unnerving pattern that would become familiar. Six months after he'd started managing on Merseyside, the team was still treading water in the table outside the European places.

'Jürgen has done a lot of things right,' Steve McManaman told *Süddeutsche Zeitung* in April 2016. 'He's very popular, even fans of other clubs like him. Over the last few months, I have had plenty of Manchester United, Arsenal or Chelsea supporters come up to me and say: "I'd love him to be our manager." He's very charismatic, he says the right things, people love his passion on the touchline. Jürgen's won over the fans, they believe in him. But there's an obvious lack of consistency, as far as results are concerned. Jürgen's squad doesn't have enough depth and quality to deliver five, six really good matches in a row.'

Progress didn't so much register in points as in decibels. The Kop was beginning to suspend its doubts, amassed over a near-decade without a significant trophy, and find its voice again. In mid-December, Belgian striker Divock Origi scored a dramatic, very late equaliser to rescue a point for Liverpool at home to West Brom (2-2). Klopp took the players in front of the Kop after the final whistle to show his and the team's appreciation for the unwavering support to the very end. 'It was the best atmosphere since I came here,' he said. 'Of course people are disappointed but they didn't let us feel that. They saw that the lads tried everything and played football.' The gesture was – predictably – belittled in some quarters as an overblown celebration of a mediocre result against mediocre opposition, but Klopp didn't care about the view from the outside. The players' tribute was a piece of clever crowd management, meant to remind Anfield of its extraordinary power to influence a result.

You sow the wind to reap the storm. And harvest-time came quickly. The last-16 draw in the Europa League pitted Liverpool against their hated rivals Manchester United. Europe's second competition, previously an unloved consolation prize for teams who had failed to break into the top four, offered a backdoor entrance into the Champions League for the winner, and, almost as importantly, a chance to ruin United's season. Anfield, crackling with the excitement befitting a big European tie, played its assigned role in pushing the home side to a devastating 2-0 win in the first leg. A cool, controlled 1-1 draw in the return at Old Trafford sealed qualification for the quarter-finals. Klopp knew the next opponents quite well: Borussia Dortmund.

'These two games were certainly challenging for the both of us, and also for our friendship,' says Borussia CEO Hans-Joachim Watzke, relieved that the saxophonist in the

Marbella hotel lobby has finally concluded his medley of Kenny G's greatest hits. 'We had to do some things we usually wouldn't have done.' Watzke had implored the players to get into 'competitive mode, out of the hugging mode' ahead of the emotional reunion with their former manager. 'He wants to kill our team and the fans with kindness,' the BVB boss had warned. 'But we aren't playing against our friend Kloppo. We mustn't lose our aggression.'

Watzke emphasises that he hadn't said anything disrespectful. 'All I said was: these games cannot turn into the Jürgen Klopp festival. I had heard that he was a little miffed about that and from the way his family greeted me ahead of the return leg in Liverpool, I could tell he had indeed taken it badly. It also annoyed him that it worked.' It had only worked up to point, however, as Watzke is quick to admit. The crowd at the Signal Iduna Park were ready for battle but the players found it hard to come to terms with Klopp sitting on the opposition bench. 'In a normal game, we would beat them,' says Watzke. 'But this wasn't a normal game. At the beginning, the team were completely inhibited, you could feel that we lacked bite in the first half. It probably would have been worse if I hadn't talked so much to the players and the people around the club beforehand.'

Klopp could not hide that the return to Westphalia had touched him, too. 'I lied if I told you all that stuff going on didn't somehow knock me sideways,' he said after the 1-1 draw. The ice-cool facade he had put on the day before, he now confessed, had been just that. 'I prefer being here than in North Korea,' he had joked on the eve of the game. 'But I don't think there will be a big emotional effect on me. We will change, get out there and play. That's it.'

For Dortmund, it certainly wasn't. Unable to play to the incredibly high standards of their season thus far, the Thomas Tuchel-coached side only truly got going well into the second half. Due to the away goals rule, the advantage lay with Liverpool. 'Anfield will burn,' Klopp threatened. His competitive streak trumped all emotional connections to former comrades-in-arms, temporarily at least. 'I bumped into him outside the changing rooms – they're very close together at Anfield – and wished him "a good game",' says BVB team manager Fritz Lünschermann. 'He went: "Listen, you arse. I don't want to see a good game. I want to win."'

At first, it was Dortmund that laid fire to Liverpool's home. The Bundesliga side's mazy, cutting runs in the final third completely overwhelmed the flat-footed defence of the Merseysiders to give the Black and Yellows a 2-0 lead within nine minutes. The Premier League team needed three goals to advance against vastly superior opposition. The game was over.

Klopp thought otherwise. In the dressing room at half-time, he showed his team clips of three Liverpool attacking moves that had nearly paid off, assuring them that more chances were bound to come. He also reminded the players of their club's capacity to triumph in the most unlikely circumstances, mentioning the comeback of all comebacks, Liverpool's Champions League win over AC Milan in Istanbul 2005, after going 3-0 down in the first forty-five minutes. 'He told us we should create something that we could tell our grandchildren about one day,' said Origi.

The Belgian striker's goal shortly after the restart did bring some hope but Dortmund struck back to win the tie a second time when Marco Reus completed another fine combination on fifty-seven minutes. Liverpool's heads dropped. Anfield was ready to accept the inevitable.

One man, dressed in all white, was not. Klopp said he could 'smell, hear and sense the sensation'. He egged on the crowd to scream until the hopelessness was drowned out by defiance. 'It felt as if he had brought himself on, as a twelfth factor, as an instigator and motivator for the players and the fans,' wrote *Die Welt*.

'He cooked up a storm on the touchline, he's good like that,' says Watzke. 'Using the power of the crowd against us was legitimate, it was his job in retrospect, just as it had been my job in the first leg. But it was nevertheless strange for us. I have rarely seen something like that, at that level of severity.' Norbert Dickel, too, felt somehow hurt that Klopp turned the stadium against them. 'I didn't like the fact he whipped up the fans like that,' says the former BVB striker. 'It was professional, from his point of view; it was the right thing in his eyes, but not in ours. He could have done without doing that. I know he'll never admit that. But I'm not upset with him any more.'

Philippe Coutinho scored to make it 2-3 on sixty-six minutes. Liverpool had clawed their way back to a two-goal deficit. The Germans continued to play really impressively, technically far ahead of their hosts. But this was one of those nights when the noise at Anfield becomes a weapon and opposition hearts wilt in the floodlight. A mythical force grabbed hold of the contest and pulled it into the realm of fantasy, or nightmares, depending on your viewpoint. 'We started shitting ourselves,' Mats Hummels said later. Dortmund were so shaken that 'different parts of the teams were playing different systems.'

As soon as Mamadou Sakho headed in the Reds' third goal twelve minutes from time, Watzke knew it was all over. 'I resigned myself to losing at that point,' he says. 'We knew how much power Jürgen could generate on the touchline. It's no coincidence we scored many goals in the eighty-ninth minute. Against Malaga, he had been the only guy in the stadium believing we could still do it and we did it. At 3-3, it was only a question of time before we would concede again. And then the whole stadium . . .' He doesn't finish the sentence, overcome by horror and admiration. 'Karl-Heinz Riedle and Nuri Şahin had both played at Anfield. But they told me, they had never seen anything like that. That's Jürgen's doing.'

Dejan Lovren made the madness a reality, two minutes into injury-time. Klopp could not believe the ball had actually crossed the line at first. Anfield was shouting his name at the final whistle, over and over again. 'The German manager departed the arena like a gladiator exiting the Coliseum following the slaying of a formidable beast,' wrote the *Independent*. His vanquished opponent, Tuchel, found it impossible to come to terms with the result. 'I can't explain it because there are no logical explanations. Emotions won the day,' he said, staring into the middle distance in utter desolation. Unlike the experienced miracle-worker Klopp, he hadn't been able to anticipate the approaching insanity. Such an irrational turn of events was beyond the realms of his imagination. He had no means to intervene effectively.

'It was one of the worst defeats during my twelve years at Dortmund,' says Watzke. 'Not because of Jürgen – I was even pleased for him at the end. No. We were so close to winning an international trophy. I think we would have won it. We got knocked out in Liverpool. But actually, we had already lost the tie in Dortmund, I feel.' It took a month before his relationship with the former Borussia coach recovered, he adds. 'I don't think I'll ever experience something similar. But our friendship is strong enough to endure.'

'I know it might sound funny but if I'm being completely honest, I thought he deserved it,' says former BVB midfielder Ilkay Gündoğan, now at Manchester City. 'Even though we got knocked out and were really hurt, I was pleased for him.' Lünschermann had noticed the same signs of involuntary fraternisation. 'His former players still feel a strong emotional bond with him. You could see it when Sven Bender went to high-five him while warming up. I don't think everybody liked it. But it's understandable.'

Liverpool's owners FSG had seen enough. That April, they approached him and his staff with an offer to extend their contracts to 2022. 'When you have an individual of Jürgen's quality in the building it makes perfect sense to secure that person for the long term,' principal owner John Henry, chairman Tom Werner and FSG president Mike Gordon declared after the new deal was signed in July. 'To not do so would be irresponsible.' In exchange for the board's commitment to him, Klopp pledged eternal loyalty. 'I will never go to another Premier League club,' he assured the Americans.

Both FSG and the coaching staff agreed that the team's limited resources were best focused on winning the Europa League during the last two months of the season. Liverpool still tried to make headway in the league, of course, but the emphasis had firmly shifted to winning the final in Basel.

Villarreal were duly brushed aside without too much trouble in the penultimate round but holders Seville were made from sterner stuff. Unai Emery's team were unimpressed by Daniel Sturridge's wonderful angled opening goal (thirty-five minutes) and staged a powerful comeback after the break, scoring three times to claim the trophy for a third consecutive time.

Reflecting on the defeat, Krawietz puts Liverpool's second-half collapse down to 'a mixture of physical exhaustion and getting it in the neck, mentally' – by conceding Kevin Gameiro's equaliser one minute after the restart. 'The stability was missing. The first half was all right, without being all that good. In retrospect, I feel that the spell after the break was Seville's last chance. They went for it in a clever way. They picked up momentum and managed the turnaround. We were mentally prepared that they would go for it and that we would get chances to counter-attack, on the basis of being 1-0 up, the plan was to wait for them to lose their nerve. But they kick off and the ball's in the net. They were like: hurrah. We were like: aargh. We couldn't come back from that and also had nothing left in the tank, physically.'

'I know from my own experience how difficult it is to win a European trophy,' says former LFC defender Jamie Carragher. 'That's why losing the final was a big disappointment. But you think of the journey and the legendary nights along the way: Manchester, Villarreal. Borussia Dortmund – the big one . . .'

Happy memories can never quite fill up that empty space in the trophy cabinet. But if you're lucky, they'll stay with you for ever, just like the silverware would have done.

9. STARTS AND STOPS

Ergenzingen, Frankfurt, Mainz 1983–2001

Word of the fifteen-year-old village *Wunderkind* swept through the region like the cool Black Forest mountain wind. Gracious under pressure, always ahead of the game by about two seconds, blessed with silky feet, he was evidently special, and Jürgen was his name. Jürgen Haug.

The teenage prodigy played in Ulrich Rath's SV Glatten youth team with Hartmut 'Hardy' Rath and Jürgen Klopp, and he was so good that TuS Ergenzingen, the area's most renowned club for budding footballers, agreed to take him on. But Haug's parents were reluctant to drive the 60km round-trip to take their son to training and games in the suburb of Rottenburg. Walter Baur, the much-respected Ergenzingen coach, had to think on his feet. He extended his offer to Klopp, on the understanding that his mother Lisbeth would give Haug a lift three times a week.

That's how Klopp, ever eager to belittle his own football abilities in retrospect, told the story. The late Baur (he passed away in 2012) admitted to *Die Zeit* that Haug was 'clearly the greater talent' but Klopp and Rath, who also made the move east, must have been able to play a bit too. 'Ergenzingen was as far away as FC Barcelona for us,' Klopp said in an interview with *Der Tagesspiegel* in 2012. 'If you were considered good enough by Walter Baur, you had made it.' Ulrich Rath says some people in Glatten are still upset with him, over thirty years later, for letting the three boys go. 'They don't realise that Ergenzingen was a huge opportunity for them, a real chance to get ahead,' he says. His son Hartmut ultimately proved too slow to make it into professional football, and Haug's progress, too, came to a halt. 'We had at least five players with similar basic skills,' Baur said. 'But that's not everything. If Klopp put his mind to something, he made it happen.'

Supported by his parents, who thought nothing of getting up well before six in the morning to drive him to games, Klopp duly established himself as Ergenzingen's captain and a regular goal-scorer. Baur's approach – far ahead of its time – was key for the youngster's development. The Ergenzingen coach wanted his players to spend as much time with the ball as possible rather than clock up hours on endurance runs around the pitch. He had travelled to Brazil, met Pelé there, and been inspired by Futsal, a five-a-side version of the game that forced players to hone their skills and creativity. 'We had to juggle the ball for thirty minutes before every training session,' Klopp recalled. 'After six months, we could have starred as performing seals at Christmas parties.'

Baur had been diagnosed with cancer of the stomach in 1977 but refused to give up. He was one of those men whose limitless love for football makes it possible for six million registered players to kick a ball around in Germany.

Hermann Bauer (no relation), the team's general manager, has a fine collection of photos and press clippings from TuS Ergenzingen under-19s' exploits in 1984–85. They only finished third in the league but picked up a number of other trophies. Ergenzingen came third in an indoor tournament with teams from the Soviet bloc in Katowice, Poland, in March 1985. The Germans, hailed as 'great ambassadors for their country' in a local newspaper report, visited Auschwitz ('It was very moving,' Klopp was quoted as saying) and gave their hosts a set of football kits and five balls. They received a vase made from coal in return. 'It was a real coming together of East and West,' said the article. The cold war was still ongoing.

Later that year, Klopp, Haug and teammate Ralf Scheurenbrand travelled to Hamburg to pick up the second prize in a competition sponsored by aftershave brand Hattric. Ergenzingen's strike force had notched up ten hat-tricks at under-19 level that season; only Chemie Wirges had done better, with thirteen. In Hamburg, a selection of the competition winners, including 1990 World Cup winner Bodo Illgner in goal, lined up against an HSV legends team featuring Uwe Seeler. The iconic striker handed Klopp the second-place award at the festive banquet at the Plaza hotel. Klopp had scored the winner in the exhibition match.

Walter Baur's team went on to win the annual International Pentecost Day tournament he had been organising in his hometown since the early seventies. Vítkovice Ostrava of Czechoslovakia had been the better side in the final and Baur was minded to let them win on penalties after the 120 minutes had ended goalless. Klopp told his coach he was mad. 'We will convert every single kick now,' he vowed. The home side won 3-2.

Klopp admired Baur so much that he threatened the club he would leave if the coach wasn't allowed to take over the first team, where he would be playing in the 1986–87 season. Ergenzingen relented. In one of his first games with the seniors, the nineteen-year-old Klopp came up against Bundesliga club Eintracht Frankfurt, who had decamped to the Black Forest for their pre-season training. 'Die launische Diva' (the temperamental diva), as they were colloquially known, weren't in a forgiving mood. Dietrich Weise's side hammered their hosts, despite missing seven regulars and not trying too hard.

Being on the wrong end of a humiliating 9-1 scoreline might have persuaded one or two of the Ergenzingen amateurs to try their hand at a different sport, but for TuS forward Jürgen Klopp, the match on 21 July 1986 was a breakthrough of sorts. 'That summer day, when Dietrich Weise visited the Black Forest, many decisive things for my life were set in motion,' he acknowledged in an interview with *Tagesspiegel* in 2012. 'He took me to the Frankfurt region – a much bigger stage for football than the Black Forest.'

Klopp had scored Ergenzingen's consolation goal and, the story goes, nearly added a second, sprinting past elegant Frankfurt defender Thomas Berthold, the Germany international who had just come back a runner-up from the World Cup in Mexico. Weise was impressed. As a former national youth team coach, he had an expert's eye for up-and-coming talent and would play a key role in the reformation of Germany's grassroots system at the turn of the millennium.

Berthold can still vividly remember the training camp in the Black Forest ('it was very beautiful') and how he had gone back into full training with barely a break after the final against Diego Maradona's Argentina at the Azteca stadium. But the former AS Roma and Bayern Munich defender admits he has no recollection of the game versus Ergenzingen itself, let alone Klopp as an opponent. He finds the suggestion that he was outrun by a lanky amateur incongruous, verging on offensive. 'He did what? He dashed past me? Never!' he laughs. 'I ran 100m in less than 11 seconds at that time. Maybe I let him go [to gift them a goal]?'

What is certain is that Weise approached Klopp about a move to Frankfurt after the game. 'I was so excited that I broke my *Spezi* glass,' Klopp said. (A *Spezi* is a mixture of Coke and Fanta, the non-alcoholic cocktail of choice in mid-1980s West Germany.) Nevertheless, he had to politely turn down the offer. 'Jürgen told me that he had to finish his Abitur [A levels] first,' Weise, eighty-two, says. 'We agreed that we would speak again in a year's time.' Weise's friend Walter Baur promised to send regular updates about the forward's progress.

Frankfurt, almost three hours away by car from Glatten, was not a viable destination as long as Klopp was still in school. But Oberliga (fourth division) club 1. FC Pforzheim were a different proposition. Situated in a 120,000-inhabitant town seventy minutes to the north of the Black Forest, the side coached by Bernd Hoffmann, a former Bundesliga 2 striker for Heilbronn and Karlsruhe (no relation to the Hamburger SV CEO), offered a useful step up for Klopp. 'He was well known in the area as a young and dangerous attacker,' says Hoffmann. 'I had watched him in many games for Ergenzingen and saw how many goals he scored. His presence in the box, due to his height, and also his pace, was impressive.'

Pforzheim and Ergenzingen officials met at a service station halfway, where DM12,000 (€6,000) in cash was handed over in exchange for Klopp's signature. He spent six months driving there and back for games and training, in his sister Stefanie's yellow Golf.

Between 3,000 and 5,000 people turned up at the Stadion im Brötzinger Tal for the games. Klopp was largely a spectator, too. He featured only four times and drew blanks in front of goal. 'He couldn't make the transition to Oberliga,' Hoffmann says. 'He was frustrated, as you can imagine. But he respected that there were people in the team that were tough to displace. His attitude in training, apart from the odd, quick outburst, was always spot on.'

Pforzheim was a dead end. But Eintracht Frankfurt hadn't forgotten about him.

'Jürgen, me and a few schoolmates were on a post-Abitur trip, travelling around southern Europe by train in the summer of 1987,' says Hartmut Rath. 'About ten days in, we had reached a very remote spot on the island of Crete. Jürgen hadn't spoken with his parents in a while but there were no mobile phones then. A tiny fisherman's boat took him to a post station. "Good of you to call," his mother Lisbeth said. "You have to go to Frankfurt for a trial." Jürgen thought about it for a couple of days, then took a train by himself from Athens – a 48-hour ride to Stuttgart.'

Norbert Klopp, Isolde Reich adds, agreed for Klopp to move to Frankfurt only if they arranged a place at the Goethe University in Frankfurt for him to study sports science.

Klopp did well enough at the footballing casting session with the Eagles to get a contract, but it was with Eintracht Frankfurt Amateure, the B team made up of reserves and

young talents who played competitive football in the regional
third division (Oberliga Hessen) and weren't allowed to be
promoted into the proper professional football of the
Bundesliga and Bundesliga 2. Klopp's mentor Weise had
been relieved of his duties six months earlier. Karl-Heinz
Feldkamp, an altogether more old-fashioned coach, had no
use for the teenage prospect in the first team.

'This blond, tall, very tanned guy with a moustache and
steel-framed glasses showed up, speaking in a very strong
Swabian dialect,' says Eintracht Amateure striker Sven
Müller. 'He was supposed to be my partner in attack, so I
thought I'd better take a closer look. Jürgen told me he had
just been on holiday in Greece and that it had been so hot that
he'd sweated driving a scooter.' He imitates the Swabian
inflection, a high-pitched melody composed of 'sh' sounds
that grates a little in the ear of non-locals: 'You shhit on the
shcooter and shweat.' ('*Da schitscht auf der Veschpa und schwitscht.*')

Müller, two years Klopp's senior, was technically more
accomplished and a much better finisher. Klopp hardly got
any starts under coach Hubert Neu, who – perhaps
predictably – disliked the fact the twenty-year-old was
working late shifts in a bar in Frankfurt's nightlife district,
Sachsenhausen, to supplement his meagre income.

His substitute appearances for Amateure didn't leave the
best of impressions either. Klopp's most noticeable moment in
a barren season, Müller says, came in a game against SG
Hoechst. 'The match was tied 1-1 or 0-0 with only a couple of
minutes to go. Klopp was brought on. We were awarded a
free-kick. One of our players stepped up . . . and smashed it
into the corner! We started celebrating wildly but then the
referee blew his whistle and chalked it off. Klopp had pushed

over two opponents in the wall. The team were not best pleased.'

Football aside, the Black Forest lad had a very good time in the big city. Müller had been instructed by Norbert Neu, the general manager of the Oberliga Hessen side, to look after Klopp and teammate Armin Bohn, who were both new in town and living in student digs. He took his task very seriously. 'We went out in Sachsenhausen at night, drinking cider. Never the night before games – we were too professional for that – but after, and during the week sometimes. We were rivals but we bonded due to a similar love for life and sense of humour. We rocked the city, we went everywhere they had some nice, shining lights. Luckily, there were no camera phones then. Nobody caught us out.'

Müller is convinced that those days – or rather nights – prepared Klopp for dealing with young players as a manager later on. 'He knows exactly what young men are like at that age. You're still a child, really. You go off the rails sometimes. You have to. He can relate to that, because he was the same.'

At Frankfurt, Klopp got his first taste of coaching. Together with Amateure teammate Michael Gabriel, he took charge of the under-11s – 'for DM400, a winter coat and an Eintracht season ticket', as he told the *Sunday Times'* Jonathan Northcroft in January 2017. 'We, the two coaches and the players, had a lot of fun together,' Gabriel said. Klopp enjoyed the experience so much that he continued coaching the same squad of players in the following season, after he had left to play for Viktoria Sindlingen in the city's periphery. 'It was my first real decision as a coach to keep all of these guys,' he said, 'the club wanted to change them for younger kids.' Klopp won that particular battle but eventually found he had too much on his plate to keep instructing the youngsters. Right-sided midfielder Patrick Glöckner was the only one of Kloppo's kids to make it into the Bundesliga (fourteen games for Eintracht Frankfurt and Stuttgarter Kickers in 1997–98).

The friendship between Müller and Klopp lasted well beyond that one year at Frankfurt's second team. Müller, an event organiser and PR expert, arranged the festivities for Klopp's beach wedding to Ulla, his second wife, in 2006. (They had earlier married civilly at the registrar's office in Mainz-Gonsenheim. Klopp wore bleached-out jeans, a striped blazer and an untucked striped shirt, and Christian Heidel had arranged for singer Thomas Neger and his band to perform 'Im Schatten des Doms', 'In the shadow of the cathedral', a Mainz anthem that had become part of the stadium DJ's repertoire on direct orders of the FSV coach.) 'Jürgen is just a great guy,' Müller says. 'Funny, authentic, and a good man who knows what's important in life, hasn't forgotten where he came from and values a good friendship. He's the cool boy next door.'

Unless he's involved in any kind of football game. Then all coolness goes out of the window. On a family holiday in Turkey a couple of years ago, Müller was playing in a five-a-side team with Klopp's sons, Marc and Dennis. Klopp himself was injured but coached the team with real passion, giving detailed instructions from the sidelines. 'I had to go off because it was extremely hot and I'm quite old,' Müller recalls. 'I think we were narrowly in the lead. Kloppo, in his inimitable style, came up to me and slapped me softly across the face. 'You will score one more goal, you'll score one more!' he told me. I went back on and did indeed score one more. He's got this doggedness when it comes to winning football games. Even when it's just for fun on a beach somewhere. He cannot help himself.'

But as far as his Eintracht Frankfurt career was concerned, no help from the men in charge was forthcoming. Hubert Neu's designated successor as Amateure coach, Jürgen Sparwasser – the famous goal-scorer in East Germany's 1-0 win over World Cup winners West Germany in 1974 – told Klopp in the spring of 1988 that he didn't feature in his plans for the subsequent season. 'Jürgen was basically pushed out,' says Müller.

Dietrich Weise still felt the young Swabian had potential, however. Weise was by now coaching Al Ahly in Cairo, Egypt and had set up the first regional training centre for talented youngsters in the Frankfurt area, ten years before the German FA would accept his blueprint for youth development and roll out these 'Stützpunkte' all across the nation. Weise, too, acted as a consultant for Viktoria Sindlingen, a third division part-timer team unglamorously situated right next to the Hoechst chemical plant in a westerly suburb of Frankfurt. Norbert Neuhaus remembers Weise's sales pitch. 'He came up to me and said: "I have brought in this player from Pforzheim – he doesn't really get on at Eintracht. But I believe he's got something, I believe that he has something to give to football. Maybe it'll work if he takes a detour via Sindlingen . . ."'

Neuhaus' diary shows that he met Klopp at the ground of FC Homburg on 16 April 1988 for a first talk. By May, they had an agreement. Sindlingen bought the striker from Eintracht for DM8,000 (€4,000), and he was paid DM1,200 (€600) per month, in cash – but only during the season. Little more than pocket money.

Sindlingen were in the relegation zone for most of the campaign. Teammate Axel Schubert sensed Klopp's frustration. 'He hadn't made the sort of progress as a player he had hoped for. He probably found it hard concentrating on football in those days, what with his sports science studies in Frankfurt and a heavily pregnant girlfriend.' (His son Marc was born in December 1988.) The year wasn't without some sweet moments, however. Away to his former team Eintracht Amateure, Klopp scored four goals in a 6-0 win. 'It was horrible for us and great for him,' says Müller. 'He sent a nice message to Sparwasser that day: look at what you're missing.'

Neuhaus, seventy-one, has proudly kept a match report of Sindlingen's 2-0 defeat away to Rot-Weiß Frankfurt from November 1988. He was in charge of the team as caretaker that day, after coach Günter Dutiné (an ex-Mainz 05 captain) had been fired. 'I've told my grandchildren that I managed the great Jürgen Klopp for one game,' he laughs. 'He wasn't a *Rakete* [rocket], to be honest, but always involved and present for every training session.'

Sindlingen's new boss, Ramon Berndroth, had the team play a game in his first training session, to learn about his players' strengths and weaknesses. Less than thirty minutes in, Berndroth stopped the session and singled out one player for a bollocking: Klopp. 'Klopp enjoyed revisiting that story in front of everyone in the VIP room of Dortmund's youth team stadium, Rote Erde, when he spotted Berndroth watching a game there years later,' says Neuhaus. Berndroth, who has been working as a youth team coach in recent years, told Neuhaus that he had never before come across a Bundesliga coach who didn't just know all his youth team players, down to the reserves, but also all of their backgrounds and biographical information.

As a player, 'Klopp was ambitious and knew how to look after himself on the pitch, he was no snowflake,' Schubert reports. 'He also had no qualms telling his older teammates how they could improve technically. After the game, he would think about the team's performance. I'd say there were small hints that he could read a game.'

Klopp's aerial prowess saw Berndroth devise a set-play routine. It came off at the crucial moment of Sindlingen's season. They were playing FC Erbach in a one-game relegation play-off at a neutral ground, and were tied 2-2 with twenty minutes to go when Walter Braun floated in a corner towards the near post. Schubert headed the ball on towards the second post, where Klopp rose to power it into the net. Sindlingen won 4-2.

In 2009, Neuhaus sent Klopp a DVD with shaky home video footage of the game. 'You don't make a bad impression at all,' he wrote, adding that he had seen the trick replicated by Klopp's Mainz team. Klopp phoned and thanked him profusely. He and Schubert met on the pitch at Mainz again, but not as players. 'I was working as a groundsman for the city of Mainz and looked after the pitch of the Bruchwegstadion [which was owned by the municipality then],' Schubert says. 'The first day on the job, Mainz were training in the stadium. Klopp was very surprised to see me. He was on the other side of the pitch, where his team were stretching, and ran across to hug me, full of joy. "What are you doing here?" and so on. We spoke for a long time and the stretching exercises lasted a little longer . . . He has always had time for former players and coaches. For their coach Helmut Jakob's birthday, the

Sindlingen team organised for him to do a coaching session with Klopp in Mainz. He agreed straightaway. Jakob came back buzzing, with a poster showing him and Klopp next to each other on the training pitch.'

Klopp's total of fourteen goals in 1987–88 had played a part in saving Sindlingen from the drop but the club had 'expected more', Neuhaus says. 'By our standards, the wages were very high.' Fortunately for Klopp, another team, stuck in the same lowly division but with deeper pockets and much bigger ambitions, had shown an interest: Rot-Weiss Frankfurt.

'A friend of mine had told me: there's this right-winger at Sindlingen that you'll like,' Dragoslav 'Stepi' Stepanović says. Stepanović, a former international for Yugoslavia, had moved to Germany in the late seventies, playing for Eintracht Frankfurt before an outing at Manchester City (1979–1981). After retirement, he opened a well-frequented pub (Stepi's Treff) in Frankfurt city centre and became friends with many of the city's influential people. Eintracht Frankfurt's general manager Bernd Hölzenbein, his former teammate, appointed Stepanović as coach in 1991 and his young side – featuring luminaries such as Uwe Bein, Andy Möller and Anthony Yeboah – very nearly won the Bundesliga with football so fast and exciting that it was dubbed 'Fußball 2000' by the German media. Stepanović, a cigar-smoking natural showman with a Mexican bandit's moustache, an idiomatic Hessian-Serbian dialect and a liking for salmon-coloured blazers, was the nascent commercial TV stations' darling. He once sang Frank Sinatra's 'My Way' on a football programme.

A couple of years earlier Stepi had been entrusted to take Eintracht's much smaller neighbours Rot-Weiss

Frankfurt from the semi-amateur division three into Bundesliga 2. RW had a bit of money courtesy of benefactor Wolfgang Steubing. 'The champagne club,' the local media dubbed them. 'We were the Bayern Munich of the Hessenliga,' Stepanović says.

Stepanović went to see a Sindlingen game to check out that tip-off. The right-winger turned out to be Jürgen Klopp. 'In that match, he played like a god,' the 68-year-old says. 'He went past his man on the flank a thousand times and put in great crosses. I would have never guessed from watching him that he had technical deficiencies. I liked players who were fast and wanted to have very attacking players on the flanks.' RW Frankfurt paid a transfer fee of DM8,000 (€4,000) to Sindlingen.

Klopp was 'perhaps himself surprised' to get a contract with RW, Stepanović says. Pre-season brought disillusion for both men. Klopp clearly wasn't the player Stepanović thought he'd bought. 'After three, four league games, I sent him to the second team. I got into trouble with people at the club; they wondered why I had got him in the first place and called him a failure. He even sat on the bench in the second team. He simply didn't have enough to play in the starting eleven. I thought, is it possible that I got it so wrong?'

'Stepi told me that I was his wife and daughter's favourite player but that he could not play me, regardless,' Klopp said in a talk with *Ruhrnachrichten* in 2014. 'I think I could have sat in my jeans on the bench for half a year, he wouldn't have noticed it at all.'

The RW coach resolved to give the forward another chance after the winter break. He brought him back into the fold with the first team, and changed his role to a '9'. As a target man, Klopp suddenly started scoring goals in industrial quantities. 'Three, six, ten – he hit the net in every training session. In the air, nobody got near him. His headers were sensational. He got fourteen in the second half of the season for us, to take us to the Hessenliga title in 1989–90. His goals won us the championship.'

Stepanović believed that Klopp was predestined for a career in football without boots. 'I always thought, this guy is such a good talker at such a young age; he'll probably become a general manager or sporting director one day. I never thought he'd be a coach. That came as a great surprise to me. He always spoke his mind, never hid his thoughts. After the ups and downs we had, we weren't the best of friends, but I liked that he never gave up.'

Legend has it that Mainz coach Robert Jung signed Klopp after Rot-Weiss Frankfurt twice played (and lost) against Mainz in the Bundesliga 2 play-off round in the summer of 1990, but Stepanović reveals that the striker had already signed for FSV at the end of the regular season, a few weeks earlier. 'When we celebrated winning the division, I saw Jürgen sit in the dressing room, smoking a cigarette. I was a smoker myself and had to laugh. I said to him: "If I had known you smoked, I would have played you more often." That day, he told us that he was off to Mainz. We were disappointed but for him it was a logical step.'

Aged twenty-three, Jürgen Klopp had become a real professional at last.

On the other end of the phone line, you can hear Hermann Hummels chuckle before he's even started the sentence.

'With Kloppo, it was hard to tell,' he says, pausing for effect. 'Was it a first touch or a shot at goal?'

Jürgen Klopp, by his own admission, was not a short-trousered magician. He described himself as 'an aggressive arsehole on the pitch' (*taz*, 2004), as 'a mentality and fighting machine, extremely good in the air and very fast' (*Der Tagesspiegel*, 2012). But 'technically', he conceded, he 'wasn't good enough'; 'I realised my own limits before others did. To sum it up: in my head, I was Bundesliga, and my feet were Landesliga [fourth division]. The result was Bundesliga 2. I quickly accepted it. To be upset would have been a waste of time.' He was far too thrilled to dwell on his deficits. 'I couldn't believe that I was a professional footballer,' he said. 'I would have paid for being allowed to play football at the time!'

At Christian Heidel's twentieth anniversary party as Mainz sporting director in 2012, Klopp recalled the time Heidel saw a Homburg player mis-control the ball horribly in a game and exclaim: 'Look, they also have a Kloppo!'

His ineptitude as a player might have become exaggerated a bit, by himself and others, for good effect. His former Mainz 05 teammate Guido Schäfer, now a football journalist based in Leipzig, has a more nuanced take. 'Jürgen was well aware of his strengths and weaknesses,' he says. 'He didn't attempt to dribble, because he couldn't. But he was incredibly fast. He didn't look that quick over the first few metres but once he got going, you could hardly keep up with him. His time over 100m was very good. He certainly wasn't a total disaster. You don't get to play 325 league games in the second division if you can't kick a ball. He was a very important player for the team for many years, due to his performances and his exemplary attitude.'

Starting out as a centre-forward, Klopp scored a respectable ten goals in his first season at the Bruchweg (1990–91) and notched up another eight by February in his second campaign, which included his most glorious moment as a professional: a four-goal outing away to RW Erfurt. (Mainz won 5-0). 'That was his shining hour,' says Martin Quast, who reported on the match for a local paper. 'Kloppo mounted the fence to celebrate with the two-dozen Mainz supporters who had made the trip. The photo I took has been printed hundreds of times since. Klopp, times four. In a white shirt with a big four on the back. Fantastic.'

Soon after that feat, the lanky but mobile forward was contacted by a veritable Bundesliga giant: Hamburger SV. 'They had the hots for him,' says Schäfer. 'But they couldn't get him, for whatever reason. Years later, they missed out on appointing him as their coach, too. One club, two dramatic mistakes.' Klopp was understandably desperate for the switch, trading the tough second division slog for a much more financially rewarding shot at the big time. But according to Mainz president Harald Strutz, FSV coach Robert Jung vetoed the move. He threatened to resign if the club let his first-choice attacker go.

'Klopp was very angry at the time. You don't get a chance like that every day,' Strutz says. 'But he accepted it. He understood that we were struggling to stay up with the players we had and couldn't afford anyone leaving. You have to say, we got very lucky that it panned out this way.'

At first, however, the effect was entirely negative. In the wake of HSV's failed attempt to take him north, Klopp scored only three more times over the course of the next eighteen months. He was moved back into defence, and Mainz's goals dried up altogether as their relative illiquidity began to bite. 'Year after year, the only aim was to somehow stay up,' says Hummels, who coached the team for a six-month spell in 1994–95 after a couple of years as assistant manager. 'Come April and May, the bosses would go and light a candle in church, praying for salvation.'

'We had been promoted in 1988 after twelve years as amateurs, then gone down and come up again. In truth, we didn't really belong in the second division at all,' says Christian Heidel. 'When I arrived in 1992, we were in the relegation zone and went into the last game of the season, at Darmstadt, knowing we could only afford to lose by one goal. And we lost by one goal. We had no training ground, no proper stadium, and no money. In 1994, our budget was DM3.5m (€1.75m). That included all the youth teams as well.'

It wasn't until 1998 that FSV had their first player, Michael Müller, on DM10,000 (€5,000). Per month, not per week. Klopp's salary was significantly smaller, in the low thousands, as was Schäfer's. 'In 1988–89, our first Bundesliga 2 season, we had three basic tiers,' he says. 'DM1,500 [€750] a month for the blind; DM2,500 [€1,250] a month for the one-eyed; and DM3,500 [€1,750] for those who could see. I was with the one-eyed. Harald Strutz, the president, said to me: "Guido, it'll be great, because you'll get DM2,000 for every win as a bonus on top." The problem was: we never won.'

Klopp jokingly said to his wife Ulla that Heidel didn't warrant a present for his twentieth anniversary in charge at Mainz: 'I already played for free for him for ten years.'

Signing his player contracts at Heidel's BMW car dealership, the de-facto club offices at the time, had brought his modest wages into sharp focus early on. 'With the money he paid me, I could never afford the cars he was selling,' Klopp laughed later.

The club's only employee, an administrator, was a part-timer, showing up every other day to sort through the mail in a container. Mainz stadium announcer Klaus Hafner worked for free as the club's CEO. He sold tickets to the games at weekends, and another volunteer provided the stadium catering: homemade butter sandwiches. Quast remembers Hafner stalking fans in the city centre with a collection box at Christmas time, asking for funds to pay for tracksuits for the under-17s. Their old set was worn out.

'The only club merchandising they sold in 1995 were towels,' Hummels says. 'I think they sold four. I still have mine. If anyone had said to me Mainz would be in the Bundesliga in five, seven or eight years' time, I would have bet everything I had against that. I even would have taken out a loan to bet more. It was simply unforeseeable.'

Mainz's reserve team (the under-21s), who Heidel had agreed to look after, were the worst in all of German professional football, playing in Kreisklasse C, at the lowest level of the organised game. 'They didn't even have a complete set of shirts, and came up against teams who couldn't actually play football at all,' he smiles.

Training for the first team, who were split up into VW mini vans, was only possible if the groundsman of the publicly owned playing field agreed. The changing room inside the stadium was a mould-ridden 'wetland biotope', Schäfer bristles. 'You were afraid to hang your towel up in there. There was one rusty big bathtub in there, with room for four or five players, and if you spent too much time in there you contracted all sorts of diseases. To never get relegated, at that club, with those players, really was a tremendous achievement.'

Mainz's perma-desperation chewed up coaches. In Klopp's eleven years as an 05 player, he was managed by fourteen different men. The instability at the top bred a certain lawlessness in the dressing room. 'It was a horde of pretty wild players,' says Hummels. 'The police had to be called in a couple of times.'

Attacking midfielder Ansgar Brinkmann (nickname: the White Brazilian), for example, had a well-deserved reputation for partying. Playing for Osnabrück, he had once been stopped for driving under the influence in his Porsche Boxster but managed to break out of the police car and run away on foot before they had checked his levels. He was let off. 'Heidel and Strutz put me up with Kloppo in hotels for away games, for him to keep an eye on me,' he says. 'He always had his head in a book and I always watched a lot of television. He was like: "Turn that thing off, we have a game tomorrow." "Kloppo," I replied, "there's a stop sign for you at the halfway line tomorrow. Just give me the ball, I'll do the rest. Because you can't play." He'd chuck a pillow or other things at me. One night, I threw the TV out of the window from the eighth floor. He woke up from the bang. "Where's the TV, Ansgar?" "I threw it out of the window." "Why?" "The film had a shit ending."'

Schäfer, still rocking a marvellous peroxide mane at fifty-two, was a free spirit, too. He'd sometimes come late to training, or miss it altogether. 'I had to pay a lot of fines thanks to Kloppo, who was on the players' council. The coaches would usually let the council decide on the size of the fees, and Kloppo showed no mercy. Thank you, Kloppo. I once paid DM500 [€250]. I hadn't overslept or been to a pub. I was late because my cat had gone missing. Obviously nobody believed me. Kloppo laughed: "Your cat? Pull the other one. DM500 it is for you." Three days later, we lost a game at Chemnitz. Hermann Hummels said: "That was the first time a second division team has lost because of a cat." Another time, they took DM1,000 [€500] off me for being out too long during a training camp.'

In his early twenties, Klopp was a saint by comparison: a good-natured, pretty quiet, moustachioed lad, a husband and young father who prayed underneath a towel before matches. On the way home from away games, he and others would gather around the flamboyant Schäfer in the last row of the bus and listen to tales of his rowdy pub crawls and women. Schäfer: 'He was the first one to sit there, he laughed as soon as I said the first sentence, and he was the last one to stop laughing. He caught fire easily. He always liked to listen, he wasn't a loudmouth then. He once told me that he picked up some of the quick wit and charm from all those rides in the last row of the bus.'

Klopp, Schäfer recalls, didn't eat like a top athlete – 'grilled sausage and chips were his thing' – and he smoked the odd cigarette underneath the extractor fan in a hotel bathroom; but Brinkmann's recollection of Klopp's hotel rooms 'being so full of smoke that you needed to hang up a disco globe to see anything' are in all likelihood a little embellished. Both agree that Klopp very rarely drank any alcohol. Schäfer: 'He always went straight home to Frankfurt after training;

he didn't have a chance to paint the town red with us. On the few occasions he did have a drink, on a team night during training camp, it didn't much agree with him. He would have two long drinks and then throw up. He wasn't capable of going the distance at all.'

During the game, it was the opposite. Klopp's passion and commitment took him far in the rough-hewn environs of Bundesliga 2, possibly too far at times. 'No opponent has ever insulted me as much as he did, as my teammate,' says Brinkmann. 'That's a fact. I played right in front of him. He constantly screamed at me: "Ansgar, you idiot, get back into the formation!" Or: "If you don't come back right now, I'll do you, you donkey! Get a move on!" I was more afraid of him than I was of my opponent. He was always the first pick in training games because nobody wanted to play against him. When his team was down, he started bending the coach's ear until he forgot that the game should have already been over. Every one of those games lasted until Kloppo had won. You always wanted to be on his side. He wouldn't and couldn't lose.'

Klopp's desire to win, Schäfer concurs, was literally frightening. 'It got uncomfortable at times. He was very impulsive, hysterical, you might say. Choleric. At one game, in Saarbrücken, he came right up to me and screamed in my face for half a minute. I had conceded a corner, I think. One minute later, it was forgotten again, and he was your mate again. He's not always that smiling and hugging guy; he can be wild and he can be unfair. But he doesn't bear a grudge. Which is just as well.'

Jürgen Kramny, another Mainz alumni who had the pleasure – or misfortune – of playing directly in front of the highly-strung right-back, has similar tales to tell. 'I was a good footballer, and it wasn't easy for me to have Kloppo behind me. He was loud. If I didn't help out enough, he moaned. Boy, could he moan. He used to lose it on the pitch. We would, shall we say, exchange frank views. I got in the odd bit of repartee. Things like: "If you played better passes, I wouldn't have to run so much." But using different language.' He laughs. 'We could both handle it. By and large, it worked well for the two of us.' Striker Sven Demandt, too, had a good working relationship with Klopp, aided by a bit of distance: 'Luckily, he was far away from me back in defence, I couldn't hear him scream that much.'

Kramny remembers one training ground incident that left Klopp a little angry, however. 'He sat on a movable, small goal, and I stood before him over a ball. I pretended to take a shot. He jumped up, the goal toppled over and he fell badly on his lower back. He got up and chased me around the pitch until he had to give up because the pain was too bad. He might still feel it today.'

In Bundesliga 2, a league made of mud, debt and fears, everybody hurt. Most of the time. Mainz, like the majority of clubs, fought a never-ending battle for survival, and aggression – on the pitch and in the stands – was considered a prerequisite. In a typically raucous affair at Waldhof Mannheim's Carl-Benz-Stadion in April 1994, Klopp made the mistake of putting his head through the gaps in the terrace fence to fling insults back at some Mannheim supporters. 'He was smacked in the face,' says Schäfer. 'That was the last time he ever put his head through any stadium fence.'

Klopp's essential problem was that of the division on the whole. He wanted to play better football, but he couldn't.

Schäfer: 'He often said that he had had the right idea – of where the pass or the cross should go – but sadly not the means.' 'He knew how things worked but his body was not able to make it happen,' says Quast. 'He once told me that he felt like a prisoner.'

That type of incarceration ultimately proved liberating, as Klopp was pushed to overcome his shortcomings below the neck-line by thinking a lot harder about the game. Initially, his interest wasn't so much in tactics as in the socio-dynamic aspects of a football team, Hummels observed. 'He was curious about the social relations, inside the dressing room and the club. Jürgen had a strong feel for that. He didn't say: "I couldn't care less, I'm only here to do a job." He always thought of the team as a group of people. He was never an egotistical arsehole. Never, never.'

'The experience he had at Mainz 05 in terms of group dynamics under extreme pressure left a huge a mark on him,' says Peter Krawietz, Klopp's second assistant coach at Liverpool. 'Mainz constantly had their asses to the wall, to put it bluntly. The house was on fire, all the time. They depended on everybody being prepared to put in everything. He learned an incredible amount about the things that make a football team tick in those years, and about the different characters you'll find in the game. I believe he's taken all these years in the dressing room, reflected on them and found that many things can be sorted with a bit of common sense. He has a feel for the situation, for saying the right thing at the right moment in the right manner.'

Looking back at his sports science course at Frankfurt's Goethe University – which he continued with until graduating with the equivalent of a Bachelor's degree in

1995 – Klopp believes his studies were just as beneficial, however. 'They are the basis of everything I later did,' he said in December 2013. He learned about training theory, ergotherapy and psychomotility, the connection between mental traits and bodily movement. 'Without knowing it at the time, I was working on the thing I could do best and wanted to do most: coaching.' Klopp added that studying also taught him 'to work independently', and the importance of effort: 'You either benefit very directly or things blow up in your face, if you don't put enough in. You can't learn these things as easily at other places.'

In an interview with *Der Tagesspiegel* in 2012, he admitted that he was 'not a model student. I had a family and had to earn money playing football.' But, he added, 'dealing with educators, psychologists and sociologists, and knowing about methodology has perhaps helped me find solutions as a coach, without me realising. Studying possibly saved me from early failure [as a coach].'

Despite his tight finances and even tighter schedule, he found being a student enjoyable. His only problems pertained to the course's quaint practical modules. Swimming wasn't his thing, nor was gymnastics, pole-vaulting even less so. But why did a man whose football is so concerned with running do his university thesis on walking?

According to Klopp, he had at first wanted to write about *Rückenschule* (preventative back pain therapy). Professor Klaus Bös, his tutor, didn't agree: there had been dozens of similar papers already. (That might have been part of the attraction for Klopp, in fact.) Bös instead pointed him to walking, a new 'trend sport' from the US that nobody had examined scientifically before in Germany. 'Together with a fellow student, we conducted a proper study and collated statistics, it was cool,' Klopp said.

Klopp's footballing higher education was provided by Mainz coach Wolfgang Frank. His first spell at the Bruchweg (1995–1997) was tantamount to a tactical awakening for Klopp. He suddenly understood that a game could be seen in structural terms, as a series of patterns that a well-drilled team could impose on the other side. But neither his nor Frank's interest was driven by an abstract concern for artistic expression or aesthetics. Tactics, Professor Frank taught, were a means to an end. 'I was never interested in re-inventing football,' Klopp later said, 'all I wanted was to find ways that made us win more often.'

Having served as Frank's 'right-hand man on the pitch' (Schäfer), Klopp had no tolerance for any of the inferior coaches who populated the FSV bench. Quast recalls an incident when the late Dirk Karkuth was in charge, shortly after Frank's second spell at the Bruchweg had finished in April 2000. 'Klopp was substituted three minutes from the end, Mainz were leading 2-0 against Stuttgarter Kickers. Machado, a Brazilian, was supposed to come on, and Karkuth was talking to him on the touchline. Klopp went over, pushed Karkuth out of the way and gave Machado a different pep talk, slapping his back and gesticulating, telling him what he was supposed to do on the pitch. Then Kloppo went off and kicked a bucket in frustration.'

As the repurposed defender got older and slower, his game – 'in your face, strong challenges, good at headers, dangerous in the opposition box', as former FSV midfielder Sandro Schwarz puts it – became a testament to the idea that application could trump ability. More naturally talented teams were shown that it was feasible to consistently play at the very limit or even beyond. 'He made the impossible possible,' Schwarz says. Aged nineteen, he had only just made the move up from the youth team, and frequently sought out Klopp, then thirty, for support and advice. Many players did. 'He was the one guy you'd go to, as a player or as the coach, if you had any questions or problems,' he says. 'He was the absolute leader in the dressing room but also very socially-minded.' When the teenage midfielder tore his cruciate ligament in 1998, Klopp became even more of a personal role model to him. 'He had suffered the same injury [two years earlier] and come back in record time, in only three months. He really helped me through the rehabilitation process, making sure I stayed optimistic.'

Professionals usually need a minimum of six months before playing again after a cruciate ligament tear. Klopp's rush back on to the pitch underlined his extraordinary devotion to the team and his profession, but also reflected his precarious financial situation. German football clubs are legally required to the pay full salaries of injured players for only the first six weeks of their absence, after which national insurance pays out 80 per cent of the monthly wage. For Klopp, 20 per cent less of very little was more than he could afford. 'As a second division player in the mid-nineties, he feared for his existence,' says Krawietz. 'He was on a few thousand DM a month, he had a small child at home and he knew that relegation could mean the end of the club and of him as a footballer.' Klopp's will to win went well beyond the sporting competitiveness he had inherited from his father. He wanted to win so badly because he had to. The life he was living depended on it.

'We were often in extremely dire straits,' says Schäfer. 'A few weeks before the end of the campaign, we usually didn't know whether we would still be professional footballers next season. Can I keep paying the rent for my flat? These were real, serious questions at our level. After ten years at Mainz, two in the third division and eight in the second, I had earned enough to buy half of a flat.'

Klopp felt he owed it to himself to play his heart out, Krawietz says. 'The ability to work towards the game for the whole week, to completely focus on the chance to win and stay alive, as it were, and then to put everything into it during those ninety minutes – that's something he developed for himself at Mainz as a player. Today, he passes that notion on to his team as a manager.'

10. FIRE ON THE RHINE

Mainz 2001–2006

Klopp's 1-0 win over Duisburg in his debut game as coach earned him a second match. 'Everybody wanted to know who we would appoint as "the real coach" after the Duisburg game, because I had sold him to the press as a caretaker manager,' says Christian Heidel. 'So I said: "Jürgen Klopp will stay until the weekend at least."' The weekend came and brought a 3-1 home win over Chemnitz. Mainz were still in the relegation zone (fifteenth) but only on goal difference. Klopp was appointed manager until the end of the season. He reluctantly emptied his team locker and moved into the small office of the coach. 'It was hard for me,' he told Reinhard Rehberg.

'We had momentum,' says Sandro Schwarz. 'We felt that the coach was one of us, that we were one big community, with one guy, our Kloppo, carrying the flag at the front. There was a sense that it was all in our hands, that it was all up to us. We had this indomitable belief, but also a good plan for winning. One thing led to another.'

Klopp would watch the sessions on top of a little hill next to the council-owned pitch that Mainz used for training. 'I didn't have the eye then, to get a clear overview from the pitch,' he said. 'The team played eleven-v-eleven, and when I blew my whistle, everybody had to freeze, like in the "Mannequin Challenge" and wait for me to run down and show them where the distances [between the lines] had become too big.'

'Klopp could not stand losing,' Jürgen Kramny remembers of those early days. 'That was a very important factor, the tactical changes aside. He would often join with the reserve players for a five-a-side the day after a match. Whoever was on his team did not have a nice life. He was driven by ambition. He could be very direct with people.'

Schwarz recalls training sessions of 'maximum intensity', geared towards getting the team into shape for the upcoming final. There was a final every weekend. 'We thought of nothing else but to perform in that next game. We were completely blinkered. We went on a run that took on a life of its own. It was a logical consequence of the way we treated each other and of our performances.'

Mainz picked up eight points from the next four games to leave the relegation zone. After a 4-2 win at Hannover 96, where they'd been 2-0 down at half-time, they were as good as safe with one month to go. 'Driving back from Hannover, we stopped at a service station and Christof Babatz's parents gave us some drinks to take on the bus,' Schwarz says. 'We drove straight to a nightclub called Euro Palace outside Mainz. Kloppo was at the centre of the party. He wanted to be with us, his boys, not sit at home on the sofa. But the next day, 10 a.m., everyone was there and we carried on. Video analysis, looking at mistakes, ways to improve. He was our coach but he wanted to be there when it was time to celebrate. That was great.'

Mainz's improbable escape was confirmed with a 2-2 home draw against LR Ahlen on the penultimate matchday. 'Jürgen, Jürgen, Jürgen,' the fans were shouting as he ran towards them, locking arms with his players. 'I felt uneasy,' he said later, 'I hadn't played.'

There was nothing left to play for away to Waldhof Mannheim but Klopp and Heidel felt a special celebration with the supporters was in order. The club hired around sixty buses for the away fans and then chartered 'the biggest boat allowed on the Rhine' (Heidel) to take them, the team, and the entire staff upstream back to Mainz. 'Flares were still legal then,' says Heidel. 'The whole boat was in flames. An incredible scene. A wall of fire, floating down river in the evening twilight.'

Heidel and Klopp learned an important lesson in those weeks. Little old Mainz could only grow as a club if the supporters were on board. They had to feel truly involved, feel that they were an important part of Mainz's success. 'You have to get people onside at an emotional level,' says Heidel. 'We had to be one big unit. That was the programme and there was no other way. You have to explain what it is you want, and you have to make sure they take part in the success. You can only do that with someone like Klopp leading the way. He could go into the hardcore section at the stadium and tell them: "You're all mad." They accept that, coming from him. He always pushed for getting the supporters involved. He's a *Menschenfänger* [literally somebody who captures people, and wins them round].

That's clear. He works with emotions but also with a plan. We bounced off each other in that respect.'

The gamble had paid off. Klopp's tenure on the bench was made permanent, he signed a two-year deal, after asking for a bit of advice from fellow manager Ralf Rangnick on the phone. Klopp was officially declared *Teamchef*, team boss, since he lacked the pro licence necessary to coach a Bundesliga or Bundesliga 2 team. He was able to satisfy the German FA's strict criteria for coaching a professional side by upgrading his badge a couple of years later. 'We noticed that the team accepted their former player as coach. It wasn't a huge change because he already had a special status as a player, he was the intellectual leader, or perhaps I should say he was the team's brains,' says Strutz. 'He saw the bigger picture. You have to appreciate we weren't the club we are today. People either took pity on us or found it funny that we wanted to get promoted. They smirked and said: "You'll never make it." But I never doubted that Klopp would work out. Not one minute of doubt. Not one second. He was predestined to be a coach.'

Quast isn't so sure. 'Strutz told me the same thing one day. I said to him: "Nonsense. If you really hadn't had any doubts, why didn't you appoint Klopp back in the autumn, before getting Krautzun in?" With hindsight, everybody knew. It's the same with the old coaches. They tell you how amazing Klopp was in training. "He always had the vision," etc. It's their way of skimming off a bit of the glory. Bullshit. The reality is that you needed somebody as nuts as Kloppo to take such a risk: Christian Heidel. It was like poker, when you move all-in with nothing.'

Klopp himself told Oliver Trust of *Frankfurter Allgemeine Zeitung* in December 2001 that he had been 'more prepared [for coaching] than for anything else in life, as strange as that sounds. I have more confidence in my abilities as a coach than I had in myself as a player.' Years later, he admitted that wasn't perhaps 100 per cent accurate at the time. 'I had a thousand questions but no one to give me any help,' he said. 'I couldn't even ask the questions at first because I had to pretend I knew everything already.' Klopp was aware he needed a confidant. Only one man was in the running: Zeljko Buvac, his former Mainz teammate. 'He was my first choice, and he would have been my second and third choice as well,' Klopp said of the tight-lipped Serbian, who is six years older. 'He is football knowledge incarnate.'

The ex-playmaker, at the Bruchweg from 1992 to 1995, had the ability 'to read the game, to know what the opponent was aiming to do, and to do the right thing, intuitively', as Ansgar Brinkmann, put it. 'Klopp wanted only him,' says Heidel. 'They had spent many hours talking tactics as players in the three years they played together, they put their heads together to find how they could best get this poor team through the season.'

The Serbian had left Mainz to play for Borussia Neunkirchen (third/fourth division) in 1995 and start his coaching career there. 'Klopp and him had made a pact,' says Mainz-based TV editor Jan Doehling. 'They said: whoever became a coach and had a big job first would bring in the other one. In theory, Buvac could have been the Mainz coach and Klopp the assistant. But when you think about it, it had to be this way: Klopp is the salesman, Buvac is the guy for detail in the background. He never talks. In all those years in Mainz, he never said a word to anyone outside the club. Not a word. I remember once standing near the changing room with goalkeeper Péter Disztl, the Hungarian international. He had played alongside Buvac at RW Erfurt. We knocked. Buvac opened a window near the showers and said: "Ah, it's you." Then he closed the window again. I was shocked: he actually talked! That was the only thing I ever heard from him.'

'Chucky', as Buvac was known to the players, was more vocal on the training ground. He also joined in sometimes, earning the respect of the squad with his excellent technique. Most importantly, however, he was the new coach's theoretical sparring partner, 'a brother in spirit' (Klopp). Conveniently, he also had the necessary pro licence to coach in Bundesliga 2, unlike his superior.

'Everybody thought they were always in each other's arms but no: they had big arguments,' reveals Heidel about the duo's dynamics. 'It was always about football, though. Buvac is very emotional: "Kiss my ass! Shit!" He'd leave the room and slam the door. And five minutes later, they'd be in each other's arms again.'

Their training sessions were all open to the public, but few came to take a closer look. Doehling and budding football coach Kosta Runjaić were two of the regulars at the Bruchweg and at the barracks of the state riot police, where Mainz trained if their own pitch was waterlogged. They witnessed a set-up that contained different elements woven into one all-action exercise. Everyone was moving, all the time. 'There's nothing worse for players than to stand around waiting while others do an exercise,' Doehling says. 'Most practice sessions bear no relation to the constant movement and shifts in pace during matches.' Buvac's idea was to simulate precisely that. He had the Mainz players running through obstacle courses, getting their pulse racing before shooting on goal. But there was more. Walls and poles were put up to make the ball ricochet unpredictably once the goalkeeper had made a save, a chance to react and score again. The same randomness that players encountered on the pitch became part of the programme. Doehling: 'They did train to make certain moves second nature, automatisms. But Buvac ensured they never knew what would happen next.'

Klopp later described Zeljko as 'the best transfer I have ever made and will ever make'. Heidel says the appointment proved that Klopp 'doesn't just listen to his gut instincts; he thinks things through, and considers the bigger picture.' In 2001, the 34-year-old rookie was honest enough to admit to himself that he needed help. 'It's one of the biggest strengths in a game that teems with egomaniacs and people high on their own self-importance: to know what you can and can't do,' Doehling says. 'And his ability to learn and absorb knowledge quickly. That's a great advantage.'

The team instantly responded to the more refined set-up, as Mainz transformed their 4-4-2 into a more fluid 4-3-3 going forward. A few weeks into the new season, the inexpensive squad of 'players that nobody else wanted' (Klopp) were leading the Bundesliga 2 table, playing a football that was 'qualitatively and tactically superior than the majority in the division', as *Süddeutsche Zeitung* noted. National newspaper reporters despatched to the Bruchweg to examine this ugly duckling story came back with startling quotes. Klopp professed that Mainz played their game 'independent of the opposition, dead-balls aside' and that 'winning and losing should be explainable, not a question of coincidence or a lost tackle somewhere.' Careful not to come across like a swotty know-it-all in his steel-rimmed glasses and suffer the same fate as Rangnick – who had been widely mocked as 'the professor' after extolling the virtues of a back four on state television in 1998 – Klopp seasoned his theoretical utterances with hearty changing-room speak: His 'only problem' he said, was a 'lack of distance' from his former teammates.

Mainz had spent the grand sum of nil on new transfers. Six leavers had brought in the same amount of money in revenue: nothing. The playing budget for the year was DM14m, €7m, and the stadium was still a crumbling heap of steel and wood, two-thirds empty. After barely surviving the drop in May, supporters greeted the series of wins with self-mocking humour. 'We're only a carnival club,' they were singing in the stands. Klopp's mysterious accomplishments and vague physical resemblance to a certain apprentice wizard had tabloid *Bild* nickname him 'the Harry Potter of the second division'. 'People want explanations for why we're up there,' he shrugged. From the second matchday onwards, Mainz were in the promotion places. A glorious 4-1 home win against rivals Arminia Bielefeld in front of 14,700 fans in mid-April 2002 opened the door to the Bundesliga. Mainz needed just three points from the remaining three games to cap the most extraordinary season in the history of the club. They drew 1-1 against Duisburg. They drew 1-1 at home to bogey team Greuther Fürth. Only a defeat at 1. FC Union Berlin on the final day, coupled with wins for both Bochum and Bielefeld, could see them slip to fourth spot. 'We will go to Berlin, do our job and return as a first division team,' Heidel prophesied.

Mainz travelled to the Alten Försterei stadium – and straight into an ambush. Many neutrals had taken a liking to the high-flying minnows and their entertaining football, but in the eastern suburb of the German capital, the air was heavy with politically-charged rancour. 'It was a very aggressive atmosphere, brutal,' says Heidel. 'Even though they had nothing to play for at all, there was raw hatred. They attacked the team bus, they spat at us, they called us arrogant West Germans. Inside the stadium, it felt as if the home team were contesting the World Cup final.' Mainz weren't ready for this pressure cooker.

The atmosphere had been poisoned by some 'creative' writing from a tabloid reporter in Berlin's *Kurier*. ('An idiot,' Strutz bristles.) Some very innocuous lines from Klopp from December about Union's penchant for full-blooded football were heavily spun, making it sound as if Klopp was denigrating the well-supported side from the former GDR as a 'gang of thugs' (*Kloppertruppe*). In addition, Klopp was portrayed as a smart-arse, a self-proclaimed football innovator à la Rangnick and as the loudmouth darling of DSF, the Bundesliga 2 broadcasters.

Union played with a knife between their teeth and took the lead in the fifty-eighth minute. Swiss striker Blaise Nkufo came on, his leg heavily strapped, and scored the equaliser twenty minutes before the end. 'We thought we had made it,' says Heidel. 'But then we conceded in the eighty-second minute, threw everyone forward and conceded a third. The teams below us had won. We were fourth. The whole stadium sang sardonic songs about Klopp's failure. It was his worst defeat ever. He'd always been the *Sonnyboy*, the guy who everybody wanted to interview because of his silly jokes, the guy who made everybody laugh. He'd never tasted such disappointment before.'

Klopp cried bitter tears in the dressing room. 'Our life's dream has been destroyed,' he said, ashen-faced. Heidel, too, was distraught, certain that Mainz would never get a chance to play in the top flight again: 'A few good players were sure to go, I was afraid the whole team might fall apart. I thought, that's it. It felt like the end of the world for us. Little did we know that next year would be much, much worse.'

In Berlin, the Mainz players and coaching stuff drowned their non-promotion sorrows in the team hotel 'until the sun came up', Sandro Schwarz says. 'We said that we somehow had to turn the mood on its head, to transform the sadness into some kind of euphoria for the next season.' Schwarz remembers arriving at the Mainz train station and being surprised that there were a couple of hundred fans there, greeting the team with flags and banners: 'You used to be able to walk through the city with nobody caring. It was only then that we realised that the supporters were really behind us. The day after, that deep sadness was gone, replaced by a real fighting spirit, with Klopp leading from the front.'

But picking up momentum wasn't that easy the second time around. Mainz had to rebuild. Three important players (striker Nkufo, centre-back Manuel Friedrich and left-back Markus Schuler) had all left, and two terraces of the stadium were being reconstructed in anticipation of a first-ever Bundesliga season that had failed to materialise. (The federal state of Rhineland-Palatinate paid for the €5.75m refurbishment, the city council gifted the property to the club and stopped charging them €100,000 for the annual lease.) Injuries to some key personnel made life difficult, too.

Following a win in the opening game away to Union Berlin, of all places, Klopp's team spent the entire season just below the three promotion places. The club were by now thoroughly persuaded that the Swabian (still without his pro licence at that point) was the right man to take them forward. 'He didn't just coach the team, he also understood and accepted the financial framework we were operating in,' says Strutz, implying that the situation had been different with previous coaches.

Klopp's contract was extended by two more years in October 2002, despite a lean spell without a home win that would stretch to two months. 'My interest to extend was as big as that of the club,' he told *Frankfurter Rundschau*. 'It's still a pleasure to work here and to be allowed to develop as a coach. Besides, you don't often have the opportunity in life to be exactly who you are where you are. That's possible here. I don't think I would even have the right clothes [to work] for another club.'

Three games before the end of the season, a dramatic 3-2 win in the derby against big neighbours Eintracht Frankfurt lifted FSV to third spot. 'Nothing in me cries "yippie" or "that's almost it",' Klopp warned. The remaining fixtures were kind. Relegation-threatened Ahlen away, minnows Lübeck at home, relegation-threatened Braunschweig away. 'We want this electrifying football all the time now,' Strutz said.

Sparks certainly did fly at the tiny Wersestadion in Ahlen. Mainz fell 2-0 down before going up 3-2 with ninety minutes gone, but still managed to lose. Two goals from the home side in injury-time saw them drop down to fifth place. Klopp and keeper Dimo Wache nearly came to blows after the final whistle. But just as they thought they were down and out, they were back in. A 5-1 win over Lübeck paved the way for another final, this time at Braunschweig. Mainz had to outscore third-placed Eintracht Frankfurt (at home to Reutlingen) by one goal to quench their Bundesliga desire at last. Klopp took his men to a mini training camp to clear their heads, aware that further failure might turn the erstwhile popular underdog into a bit of a laughing stock. Some had taken to calling them 'a Bayer Leverkusen of Bundesliga 2', a reference to the perennial runners-up from the first division.

On the day, there are no signs of any jitters. Mainz are 2-0 ahead within twenty minutes and leading 4-0 before Braunschweig score a consolation goal in the eightieth minute. Game over in Lower Saxony. As things stand, Mainz are up! Frankfurt are only leading 4-3 against Reutlingen. Klopp moves his hands up and down, as if to suppress the flames of joy. Because the match in Frankfurt is still . . . ongoing. The home side have just scored a fifth goal to make it 5-3. The coach and his players lock arms and form a circle around Axel Schuster, the team manager, who's on the phone to a journalist in Frankfurt. There are less than three minutes of injury-time left to play at the Waldstadion. Two and a half minutes of anxiety and prayers later, the inconceivable happens. Eintracht score to make it 6-3 at the final whistle. Mainz are fourth and in tears for a second year running. 'We thought, is this *Candid Camera*?' says Sandro Schwarz. 'We had enough chances to win 5-0, 6-0. I get goosebumps thinking about it. We were all looking at Axel Schuster's face. Everyone was completely gone after that, not really in this world for a few minutes. It simply beggared belief.'

'*Die Meister der Schmerzen*', the champions of pain, *Frankfurter Rundschau* called them with heartfelt pity. Others were sneering that Mainz should be known as 'The Unpromotables'. 'A horrific experience, what else can you say?' Strutz recalls. He sobbed uncontrollably on the pitch alongside Heidel. Klopp had quickly run inside to escape the media attention and gleeful chants from the home side. Strutz: 'He had a cigarette and didn't say a word. I know because I did the same. You would have thought that it couldn't get any crueller after Berlin.'

Klopp cried when his son Marc, thirteen, asked him whether there'd be school the next day. But on the whole, he kept his composure remarkably well. 'I believe that everything in life happens for a good reason. One day, we'll find out why today happened . . .' he said.

The next day, 8,000 people turned up at the Gutenbergplatz central square in Mainz (named after Johannes Gutenberg, the inventor of the printing press) to welcome the team back in a spirit of defiance. Mainz had been 'smacked in the face twice', says Heidel, 'but Klopp got on the stage and gave these roaring speeches that got everybody going. He emotionalised and inspired people in an incredible way.'

'We will pick ourselves up,' the coach said. 'We are all still young, nobody has to give up just yet. We're determined to do so much more for this city and our fans. I know that people say "Mainz will never do it." But they have a problem. We'll be back. Anyone who writes us off is making a serious mistake.'

The message, Schwarz explains, was believable because the messenger was. 'That day, you saw who Kloppo is as a person. He's a fighter. You felt that he was truly committed to his words himself. I suspect that he felt from the first day onwards all these things were part of life's trials and tribulations, that we could master it all by doing the right thing, by focusing on the here and now, and by disregarding the past. That, in my view, is the essence of Kloppo. He was convincing because he was convinced. He never feigned anything in front of us. He'd ask: "What's the alternative? We can't dissolve the football club." It was obvious that we had to go on, and obvious to him that the next attempt would be successful. I still remember him saying: "We were a point short in 2002. We were a goal short in 2003. You know what comes next, don't you?" And that's how it happened.'

It did. But not quite in the manner anticipated. Klopp's third full season in charge was his worst, points-wise. Ukrainian star forward Andriy Voronin, who had become too prolific for the second division (twenty goals) and moved on to 1. FC Köln, had left a huge, pony-tailed gap up front. The performances were largely indifferent. Heidel warned that too many players were dreaming about life in the Bundesliga instead of concentrating on the hard slog ahead. Klopp defended his team vigorously against outside criticism ('I can't stand it when managers take credit for wins but blame players for defeats') but inconsistency degenerated into a full-blown crisis. Between mid-December and mid-April, FSV won only two league games. They were eighth, six points adrift of third place with five games to go.

'The season was over for us,' says Kramny. 'There was talk about changing the team. After three failures, you couldn't see the same faces in the dressing room any more. Quite a few players were told they could leave. I guess the idea was to try once more with a new squad.' Mainz also had to cut costs, urgently. The club had lost money over the last two campaigns and needed to generate funds to plug higher than anticipated costs for the stadium rebuild.

That spring, Kramny adds, Klopp seemed 'a little bereft of answers for the first time'. The manager conducted a changing-room survey, asking players to anonymously write down their explanations for the malaise. No one came up with anything useful. In a subsequent team meeting, Klopp told his men to stop ruminating on the negatives; they alone were responsible for changing the mood and drawing fresh spirit. 'That's our mission for the last five games,' he decreed.

Luckily for Mainz, Duisburg provided less than feeble opposition in the next game, going down 4-1 at the Bruchweg. In Lübeck, Mainz won 4-1 again. Then 2-0 at home against Unterhaching. But away to Bavarian minnows Regensburg, Klopp's team failed to get on the score-sheet. The 0-0 draw left Mainz in fourth place. They could only go up if they beat Eintracht Trier at home and Alemannia Aachen (third) didn't win at Karlsruher SC on the final day.

Klopp put up a banner in the changing room: '*Jaaaaaaaa!*' it read. 'He wanted to take the huge pressure off the team, by creating a sense of anticipation,' write Rehberg and Karn, 'the prospect of experiencing a moment of joy was supposed to take centre-stage, in place of the need to win.' Mainz did win in front of a sell-out crowd, 2-0. But once again, they were reliant on a result going their way elsewhere. The game in Karlsruhe was still going on after the final whistle at the Bruchweg. Aachen were 1-0 down. A couple of tense minutes later, Mainz had finally done it.

Their tally of fifty-four points marked them out as the worst team to ever win promotion to the Bundesliga. It didn't matter. 'The whole city exploded,' Heidel says. 'It's an emotional town, because of carnival, they love to party and are very proud. What went down on that Sunday, however, no one had ever experienced.' Mainz, a town without any significant footballing background, had fallen in love with the game and their team ninety-nine years after FSV's inception. 'It was chaos. People everywhere.' The team bus took an eternity to travel the short distance from the stadium to Gutenbergplatz through an ocean of smiling, delirious faces. Players and staff went up on the Staatstheater balcony to address the crowd, and of course it was Klopp who took the mic, drenched in champagne and tears. He screamed out one word only: '*Jaaaaaaaa!*'

One celebration was not enough after two heartbreaks, Heidel and the coach spontaneously decided. 'We announced that we would all meet again the next day for another promotion party at the same place. Thirty thousand turned up. On a Monday! The city was packed. The face of it all, you have to say, was Kloppo. Without a doubt. But he never, to this day, was vain enough to take much credit for himself. People who don't know him at all will tell you that he's a straight-up guy, that he's authentic. Because he really is.'

Klopp's speech in the city centre 'brought tears to everyone's eyes and had mothers holding up their babies, yelling that they would name them after him', Doehling says, with only a hint of exaggeration.

'Going up in the third year was the biggest miracle of all,' says Strutz. His father had been president of the club before him. Mainz's first-ever promotion to the top flight was the crowning achievement of more than one person's life's work. 'Usually, teams in our situation break apart after two setbacks of such magnitude. In hindsight, not going up earlier was the best thing that could have happened to us. You know why? Everyone passionate about football was happy for us. Because we were likeable. Because we said: "We won't give up, we'll pick ourselves up again from the floor." No one had really looked at us before. But now we were Mainz 05.' The dwarf-sized club who wouldn't take 'no' for an answer, the serial losers who yelled 'yes' into fate's ugly face. 'That was only possible because of the special relationship between Klopp and his players. To this day, no one feels indifferent about playing for us. Players love playing here and those who played here ten years ago love coming back.'

It's a truism that football teams tend to resemble their coaches after a while but at Mainz the similarities were more blindingly obvious than elsewhere. 'They were limited players, there was no one outstanding in the squad, [centre-back] Manuel Friedrich excepted,' says Quast. 'Many reminded me of Kloppo. There was Toni da Silva, 'the only Brazilian who can't play football', Kloppo once said. He made him a star. There were all these journeymen, quite average players with no chance to do anything special elsewhere. A guy like Marco Rose. He got out of the team bus yelling "Marco Rose is a Bundesliga player. Any objections?" into the camera. He wouldn't have been able to play in the first division in any other city on the planet. Only in Mainz. They all had that mentality that Kloppo himself had. They went for it, they gave their all. They would go for drinks at the Ballplatzcafé together, players and coach. Tell me one coach who does that.'

Promotion for Mainz doubled the club's budget to €20m per season and eased financial concerns about the stadium building works. Long-serving players such as Sandro Schwarz and Jürgen Kramny were offered new contracts after all. But there still wasn't any money for stars.

'Mainz will be in competition with SC Freiburg for being the nicest club in the Bundesliga,' wrote *Süddeutsche Zeitung*, 'but no one should overlook the fact that it'll be very difficult for them. This is a team who work hard but aren't suspected of committing artistry. They slave away while the fans sing carnival songs in the stands, and their game betrays the coach's love of the English style of playing football.'

'The Bundesliga can look forward to having us,' Klopp pronounced. 'We are up for it.'

In June 2004, German football was down and out, disorientated and demoralised. The national team of Rudi Völler had just crashed out of the European championship at the group stage without a win for the second time running, having embarrassed themselves with painfully slow, negative performances that were dubbed 'sleeper train football' and *Rumpelfußball* (from *rumpeln*: to stutter and stumble) by aghast pundits and papers.

The game played by the country's finest had looked so hopelessly behind the times that not one experienced coach wanted to take over the side two years ahead of the World Cup on home soil. Bereft of any mainstream choices, the German FA reluctantly entrusted the task to Jürgen Klinsmann, the California-based reformist who preached the need for more speed and an aggressive, youthful repositioning of the national team's brand. 'Germany has always been a doer nation but we had stopped playing doer football,' he recalled a decade later.

It would take until the end of the competition two years later before the former striker's widely mistrusted ways were formally vindicated. But in the Bundesliga, change came a bit quicker. 2004–05 was the season that Germany's dull, plodding, tactically antiquated league got a move on. Three young Swabian coaches who had learnt in the second division that small teams could get bigger and better courtesy of ingenious strategy and dedicated execution were finding that their formula worked just as well against the traditional giants of the domestic game. 'There's a surge in the Bundesliga,' wrote *Frankfurter Allgemeine.* 'Risky football, defending from the front, pressing and a general sense of acceleration: these are the characteristics of a movement epitomised by these "poor" underdogs.' Sweepers and lazy playmakers had no place in a systemic approach in which the emphasis on the collective pierced the commonly held conviction that individuals made the difference at that level. 'They play concept football, not hero football,' *Berliner Zeitung* noted of the new wave of 'improvement managers' shaking up the status quo.

At Schalke 04, Ralf Rangnick outlawed the back-pass in training and stipulated a maximum of two contacts on the ball. Arminia Bielefeld's Uwe Rapolder, who had led the East-Westphalians to promotion ahead of Mainz, won a surprising amount of games with a well-below-average but perfectly drilled squad that overpowered and outsmarted much more skilful opponents. And Mainz coach Jürgen Klopp, the third and by far loudest part of this triumvirate of south-western football auteurs, oversaw an exhilarating debut campaign that soon disabused cynics of the idea that FSV were set to party all the way to certain relegation. Five wins and three draws in the first ten games proved that the cash-strapped novices could prevail in the big time.

Despite the weighty theoretical underpinnings of their game, Schalke, Bielefeld and Mainz were admired as *Spaßmannschaften*, as fun teams. Their coaches didn't just play a good, modern game. They talked one, too. Klopp, in particular, sparkled in the spotlight, wooing the public with elaborate descriptions of his team's strategies and eulogies to their fighting spirit, stressing that the best scheme was nothing without the legs and the passion to bring it to bear. Two big interviews with *Der Spiegel* and *taz* provided enough interesting quotes to last a decade. They didn't read like regular question-and-answer sessions, more like a manifesto: for a different kind of football, and a different kind of coaching, based on the principles of humanity and respect.

'We want to dominate the game,' the second-youngest coach in the league after Matthias Sammer said about his game plan. 'Especially when we don't have the ball. We want the opponent to play the ball into precisely the areas we want him to play it into. The opponent having the ball is our build-up for scoring a goal. We want to win back the ball so quickly that we'll only need one pass to get in front of goal. We don't run more than others, but we run without taking breaks. Why should we [take breaks]? We train all week to be sharp for ninety minutes. And we have a well-defined system. We don't sting everything in sight like a swarm of hornets. We lure the opponent and then sting him.'

'The experience,' he added, 'is more important than the result. We play *Erlebnisfußball* [football that provides an experience], exactly the kind of football that I want to watch. We want to run incessantly. That's our code of arms. We are the vanguard of the regular guys in the pub. They want us to run and fight. Our entry ticket is well-defined, week after week: passion, willingness to run, will. If one guy leaves the stadium thinking, "they should have run and fought more today", we got it wrong completely. I love this game because it's about power, because it stirs up the dust. You can only get in touch with the game's emotionality via pace and action. A win alone is never emotional. A good game makes the hairs at the back of your neck stand up until Monday or Tuesday. Football is theatre. If we don't put on a superb performance, only two guys will be sitting there at the end.'

Mainz's elevated levels of coherence on the pitch were underwritten by a special bond off it, Klopp explained. Two years earlier, he had taken his team to a remote Black Forest hut where they had to cook and clean for themselves. Ahead of their first Bundesliga season, an extremely unpleasant survival trip to Sweden had yielded four days of almost non-stop rain, plenty of mosquito bites, a near-mutiny by the squad ('they wanted to charter a helicopter to get us out of there') but also a new-found closeness as a result of the shared experience. Klopp asked the players to write a letter to themselves in the glow of the campfire, detailing their impressions and feelings about the journey to the heart of the Scandinavian wilderness. The letters were put in envelopes and collected by Klopp, who told his men they'd be kept, to be revisited in case the team experienced a crisis in the months ahead. 'Each of them could then read what he had written down at that time, sitting around the fire with his teammates, and remember those special and invigorating emotions.'

The Mainz players were also shown a documentary on the New Zealand All Blacks rugby team. Klopp asked his men how they felt about calling themselves the All Reds. Would they feel embarrassed? Or could they put on the 05 shirt and vow to themselves that they would push to the very limits as long they wore it? Mainz never performed the haka in the changing room. But Maori chants were played on the team bus stereo driving into stadiums.

Since the club couldn't afford to buy players that didn't fit the footballing and psychological profile, Heidel and Klopp conducted extensive job interviews with prospective recruits. If possible, the player was invited to Mainz with his wife or girlfriend. Klopp would speak to him alone at first, for three, four, five hours, talking football while Heidel was showing off Mainz's most beautiful spots to the wife or girlfriend. Afterwards, Heidel would talk to the player. 'I wanted to find out about his background and his family, I wanted to get an impression of him as a person,' he says. 'And I told him many things about Jürgen Klopp. It would have been silly to do that with him in the room. I said to the player that he would eventually love this coach. That kind of stuff.

'There were two key questions. "Do you like to train?" If somebody said: "Well, not really, but I'm at my best at the weekend" – goodbye. No chance. And: "Do you like running?" If somebody said: "I prefer doing it with my technique," or "I don't need that", we didn't take them. I always said to them: "If you think you'll score three goals at the weekend without training hard please tell me now. Because you'll never play here. Regardless of your name." Players responded to such honesty. There were many we didn't take because we felt they couldn't deliver what was needed. Also if someone said: "It's only Mainz . . ." We sent him away. Kloppo always said: "I want to get the feeling that you can only imagine playing for one club right now: Mainz. If you don't have that feeling, if you think you have to talk to others first, leave it. If you haven't caught fire after I told you about the club, you shouldn't come here. And be honest, because it won't work." The players were impressed by that. And then we sent him home, without a concrete offer. We said: "Think about it. Can you imagine playing here?" We told him that we would also deliberate. "We will tell you if we want you. If it doesn't work out because of money, so be it." But it almost always worked. The players we hooked we got. We knocked them out. Once they signed, Kloppo and I high-fived each other. It was clockwork.'

Egyptian striker Mohamed Zidan was a good case in point. His agent dismissed a move to 05 from Werder Bremen, saying 'Mainz? What does he want in Mainz?' Heidel remembers. 'But after we had talked to him, he was as keen as can be. He only wanted to join us, no one else.' Apart from a functioning system that made the most of everybody's qualities and thus increased the players' marketability ('whoever performs in Mainz will, at some stage, get the chance to earn what others are earning,' Klopp predicted), the club also offered an appealing work–life balance. Heidel: 'There are worse cities to live in. You can live a normal life as a footballer there. In Cologne, you can't go on the street. In Mainz, that's still possible. You will hardly find a player who didn't enjoy playing for us. We never had to penalise people for indiscretions. It wasn't necessary.'

That is not to say that the usual rules didn't apply. Late arrivals for training were sanctioned with a couple of hundred euros fee. There was also a tariff for the coach himself being tardy: 500 euros. One day, when Mainz were still in the second division and Klopp was still living in Frankfurt's lower middle-class Gallusviertel area, he arrived at Michael Thurk's apartment in the same neighbourhood to pick up the striker for their daily commute down the notoriously congested A66 Autobahn. Repeated rings of the doorbell brought no answer. Klopp rang all the bells until someone let him in, then knocked on Thurk's door. After a while the door opened: Thurk, in pants. 'Oh, Coach, sorry . . .'

'I'll give you exactly two minutes, otherwise I'll drive off without you.'

A good ninety seconds later, Thurk was down at the car, wearing a jumble of thrown-together clothes. The drive to Mainz was 'pretty stressful', says Quast, who shared the ride. 'Traffic jams, everything blocked. Kloppo was sweating because he wasn't on much money then. Five hundred euros was a lot. Thurk also started sweating – Klopp told him he'd have to pay if they were late. They somehow made it with two seconds to spare.'

Klopp made a point of treating his players the way he wished former coaches had treated him as a player. Midfielder Fabian Gerber was given a day off training to celebrate his mother's birthday – a newsworthy, fiercely debated event in the machismo-infused Bundesliga. 'I wasn't allowed to be with my son for his first day of school ten years ago and still ask myself why I was stupid enough to heed that order from the coach,' Klopp explained his leniency. 'I want people around me to do well. That's what life is about. Okay, we play football, there's rough language and sometimes more. But I don't have to step on people's toes. I don't have to threaten punishment to get them to perform. I have to show players targets in a way that they automatically want to achieve them. That's what I believe in.'

05 strikers Benjamin Auer and Thurk sometimes argued for a more relaxed playing style, without success. Klopp was uncompromising when it came to his footballing agenda. 'But only one player,' Heidel insists, 'didn't get along at all in Mainz: Hanno Balitsch. He always said that Klopp and the team behaved like a cult, that they were laughing their heads off all day. He couldn't stand that, and he also thought it strange that players were addressing the coach with "*Du*" [not the more formal "*Sie*"]. Hanno and me still laugh about it now when we bump into each other. But I challenge you to find others, even those who didn't play regularly, who'll say one bad word about Mainz. They won't. I always told prospective players to call and ask former players about their opinion. They had no reason to lie.'

Mainz won plenty of plaudits for a courageous showing in the 4-2 defeat against Felix Magath's Bayern at the Olympic stadium at the end of November. But darkness was closing in. Seven more defeats and one goalless draw against Rapolder's Bielefeld left them in fifteenth place, four points ahead of the relegation zone. There were no more insightful interviews in highbrow publications with the manager, but questions about his job security. The Mainz board, however, made it clear that Klopp would stay on as manager even in the case of relegation. The questions receded again. 'Getting rid of him was never discussed,' says Strutz, 'we were convinced of him as a coach and a human being.'

Klopp told the fans at the Bruchweg to stop swaying to the carnival music and celebrate every won tackle instead.

He had sleepless nights and later admitted to feeling lonely amidst the wave of bad results ('I couldn't ask anyone because coaches don't tend to outlive eight defeats in a row') but stayed upbeat in the dressing room and projected calmness. 'The players never started doubting themselves, that was his real achievement as a coach,' write Rehberg and Karn. A tactical tweak – Mainz started playing 4-3-2-1 – also helped them to find their feet again. Wins against Freiburg (5-0), Schalke (2-1), Hannover (2-0) and Bochum (6-2) eased fears of the drop. After matchday 32, a 4-2 home defeat by champions Bayern, they were mathematically safe. Both teams celebrated together with the fans, swilling big jugs of beer on the pitch. Mainz finished their first-ever Bundesliga season in eleventh place.

Klopp's ability to sell himself, his football and his club to others, even at times of struggle, distinguished him from Wolfgang Frank, says Doehling. 'Frank didn't have that talent. He lost his nerve after every defeat, bemoaning Mainz not doing better and the stadium being empty. Klopp learned from that. He knew how to talk to people. Do you say to them: "You're all idiots because you don't understand how great our football is"? Or do you say: "This is a full-throttle event. Everyone who doesn't come to experience that will really miss out. You'd better come." He's got a talent for being positive. And, you will have heard that before, he captures people. There aren't many people in Germany who can do that. Can you get people behind you, behind your idea? Politics is no different to coaching. He's a born politician. But you mustn't drive people into the fire. You can only do that once, then they're gone. You have to lead them in and out of the battle again – alive. You have to deliver them. Then they will follow you.'

Staying up in 2004–05 was a 'football fairy-tale', says Quast. People in Mainz had almost become used to miracles; the extraordinary had become routine. He recalls Bayern fans standing outside the ground with open mouths, staring at Klopp partying with supporters in the club's stadium pub, the Haasekessel, after the final whistle. '"Hold on, isn't that your coach?" the visiting supporters wondered. They went up to him to take some photos. He was always there, drinking with the twenty-five fans who had seen him score four goals at Erfurt. He didn't want to change. That was him. And that was Mainz.'

A couple of weeks after securing top-flight survival, Mainz's fortunes took a turn for the even more fantastical. The Bundesliga's smallest club found itself experiencing a dream within a dream, like the marks in Christopher Nolan's *Inception*. Thanks to the congenial demeanour of players, officials and fans – as well as a hefty dose of luck – FSV became one of two European teams allowed into the UEFA Cup by way of the Fair Play ranking. (Their role as the league's nicest, most fun-loving club didn't win universal approval, however. Ultras from Hannover 96 held up a banner saying 'Your likability makes us vomit' months later.)

Jürgen Klopp played things cool. 'UEFA Cup feeling? Is that like heart burn?' he replied to questions about Mainz's completely unexpected excursion into European football. Worries about the heightened demands on the inexperienced, close-knit squad were similarly brushed aside: 'We shouldn't talk ourselves into having a problem. The only difference is that we'll see less of our wives.'

But that wasn't the only difference. Adventurous trips to Armenia (4-0 on aggregate v FK Mika Ashtarak), Iceland

(4-0 on aggregate v Keflavik) and Spain (0-2 defeat on aggregate v Seville) brought huge excitement but also fatigue and exhaustion in the early stages of the 2005–06 season. Mainz lost the first five Bundesliga games. Ah, second-season syndrome, many said, the party was over. Gravity was bringing the high-flyers back down to their natural level at last. 'It's questionable how long Mainz's fun society will continue to exist under increased pressure,' wrote *Neue Zürcher Zeitung* ominously.

Klopp sought inspiration in a comic strip he had read as a teenager. 'Clever and Smart', drawn by Spanish illustrator Francisco Ibanez ('Mort and Phil' in English), are secret agents who constantly suffer terrible mishaps and grave mutilations without any lasting damage, appearing as good as new in the very next panel. 'I loved these comics,' Klopp said. 'The time needed for regeneration by the characters was brilliant. It didn't matter whether you were flattened by a steamroller or fell off a cliff 800 metres high – things simply carried on!'

In 'Clever and Smart', the laws of physics and biology didn't apply. But the Bundesliga was a much less forgiving environment. Mainz's form recovered after their UEFA Cup exit at the end of September. The results didn't. Ten games into the season, FSV were in the relegation zone with seven points on the board. A 3-1 defeat away to Hertha BSC was typical of an inexplicable disconnect between splendid attacking football and depressing scorelines. Klopp instructed everybody to look past the numbers. 'We will analyse this match independently of the result,' he told reporters in Germany's capital. Local broadsheet *taz* was a little surprised to note that the players continued to keep the faith, determined 'to stay the good-mood-gang of the league, to keep acting courageously, to keep playing offensively, fast and with a plan, and above all, to keep presenting themselves in such a way that even the most critical observers can't help but notice that these men enjoy playing football.'

Klopp himself still enjoyed football, that much was obvious to those closest to him. He regularly turned out as a player for the team of Kemweb, a small media agency whose offices were close to his house in the suburb of Gonsenheim. Kemweb played against other firms – banks, supermarkets, building firms – in a dedicated amateur league, and they were often short of men. Peter Krawietz, who worked for them, had one day asked Klopp if he felt like making up the numbers. He did. Every three or four weeks, whenever Mainz's Bundesliga scheduled allowed it, he'd play somewhere in the countryside between vineyards and fields of turnips 'against men with huge beer bellies and incredibly bad players who were all world champions of the "third half"', as Martin Quast recalls. 'Kloppo was at his happiest there, among those guys. He stood on the pitch and keeled over laughing when some bloke tried to shoot on goal and hit the corner flag instead. Afterwards, everybody huddled around Kloppo in a tent or in a pub, and he didn't stop laughing all night. That barking laugh of his. All you saw were his big teeth. Completely random people working at a bank or at Blendax, the toothpaste factory, went home saying: "Herr Klopp, we knew you as a coach, but we had no idea you're such a cool guy. Sensational. You could still play in the seventh division, right?" That was the biggest praise to his ears. Because he never pretended to be someone he wasn't.'

As the days drew shorter, Mainz 05's strong attacking department – playmaker da Silva, strikers Michael Thurk, Benny Auer, Petr Ruman and Mohamed Zidan – started to turn a heap of goal-scoring opportunities into tangible success at last. By Christmas, Mainz had amassed 16 points. The positive momentum could not be overlooked. Klopp was offered a two-year contract extension until the 2008 winter break, and he accepted. Christian Heidel didn't deny reports the coach's salary had been raised to €1.2m, which would have put him not far off the Bundesliga elite at the time.

'Mainz 05 are a fantastic club,' Klopp told *Frankfurter Rundschau* in a double-interview alongside Heidel in January 2006. 'They have literally exploded in terms of their development over the last five years, without changing their character. Working there is still a great, fun challenge. Looking for another challenge right now was never up for debate.'

Klopp, the fuse for Mainz's explosion, denied being changed by the spotlight but did concede that his high profile was beginning to have a negative impact. 'You get used to getting recognised, your private life suffers,' he said. 'If somebody had beamed me into the year 2005 five years ago, I would have been shocked. I would have been able to run through Mainz naked then, nobody would have known my name.'

Streaking through the genteel streets of Gonsenheim was perhaps no longer an option but Klopp didn't exactly hide either. His name was on the doorbell of his house. (It was still there in November 2016.) You would find him on the sun deck of Café Raab a short walk away or renting DVDs from Video Toni in the evenings. One day, Toni, the owner, said to Klopp he'd get free videos for life if his shop was shown on television. Hearing that, Martin Quast included Toni in a feature on Klopp for Sport1. Toni kept his word. 'Now Kloppo will never pay again,' he said.

Heidel did warn Klopp that he would go from being 'the most famous person in Mainz' to somebody known 'by eighty million Germans, including every grandad and grandma', after working for ZDF at the World Cup in five months' time. If the subtext of the *Rundschau* conversation – that Klopp was slowly outgrowing Mainz 05 – was lost on anyone, the coach made sure to spell it out. 'My willingness to be a coach at Mainz won't last for ever,' he said. 'I can't imagine still being here in ten years. I'm too curious for that. I'd kick myself up the back-side [to make a move then].'

Klopp's winsomeness might have created unwanted attention for him, but it translated into cold hard cash for the club, Heidel says: 'No one was jealous. On the contrary: we took advantage of his popularity. The Kloppo effect helped us win sponsors and sell tickets.' The club were beginning to think big, far beyond the next game and the immediate need to stave off relegation for a second time. They conducted a feasibility study into building a new stadium. And after fifteen years in the job, Heidel finally went full-time as the club's general manager. 'We have a chance here to create an infrastructure that we wouldn't have dreamt about a couple of years ago,' Klopp said. 'I want to be part of that challenge. When I leave, I want the club to have benefited from me. That was always the plan. I want to leave a mark.'

'Negotiations with Kloppo lasted two minutes,' Heidel says. 'I gave him a piece of paper with a number. He was

allowed to put the year next to it. Shake of hands, end of
story. We never negotiated. He always agreed to my proposal.
You know, he always complains about earning so little as a
player, but he was, for sure, the best-paid manager in the
second division. By a distance. And he wasn't a pauper in
the first division either. Because I knew how important he
was. He earned as much as three, four players put together.
He would say: "Come on, that's too much." "No. You're
worth it." Sometimes people called to lure him away and he
would laugh his head off. Because no one realised how
much we were paying him. Seven figures. There were many
Bundesliga coaches who didn't make that. Klopp filled up the
whole stadium. He was an advertising icon for Mainz 05.
You can't measure that effect in pecuniary terms. It went far
beyond his work in training.'

The team's obvious top-heaviness, meanwhile, necessitated
a tactical rethink. Mainz's best players were all in attack, so a
new 4-4-2 system with a diamond in midfield – and Thurk
behind two strikers – was put in place to bring their qualities
to bear. Away to Dortmund in February, the new formation
seemed to leave the midfield far too exposed, however. The
coaching staff were mulling over abandoning the experiment
at half-time, with Mainz 1-0 down and not in the game at all.
But they stuck with it. Somehow, things fell into place, Thurk
scored and the visitors were in the end unlucky not to take all
three points. 'That was a very tough moment,' Klopp later
said, 'one of many valuable lessons for us.' Seven points from
the next three games lifted them clear of the relegation
places.

Recognition for Klopp's good work also arrived in
another shape: centre-back Manuel Friedrich was called up

by Jürgen Klinsmann – the first-ever Mainz player in the *Nationalmannschaft.* 'Manu is a class defender and super lad. I'm happy for Jürgen Klinsmann that he'll be able to get to know him,' Klopp quipped, beaming with pride.

Mainz only lost one match in seven, 3-0 away to Nürnberg, in their modified shape. Nevertheless, results elsewhere conspired against them ahead of the home game against league leaders FC Bayern Munich on matchday 31. The team were confined to a bleak, cheerless place. But that had nothing to do with their unexpected slip into the relegation places. On the invitation of Rhineland-Palatinate minister of justice Herbert Mertin, Klopp had taken the squad for a visit to the Rohrbach federal prison. One inmate told the coach that he had once sat next to him on a fan bus journey to a Mainz second division game when Klopp had been suspended and travelled with the supporters. The Mainz manager listened attentively to the inmate's life story. 'Man, you have to get your life in order when you get out,' he advised him, *Frankfurter Rundschau* reported. Klopp told the paper it was important for his players 'to experience a completely different world that's anything but fun and luxury. That kind of thing helps you grow as a human being and as a player, even if it doesn't quite help you win against Bayern.'

The best part of the unusual trip, however, was the chance 'to get the boys in here a few extra hours outside their cells', he added. Having been told that there was no live football on television inside the jail, Klopp asked Mertin to install a pay TV decoder to enable the inmates to watch Mainz's match v Bayern. The politician only smiled at the brazen suggestion but felt that the team visit might have served as a 'kick-start' for the rehabilitation of some of the convicts.

Back on the pitch, Mainz drew 2-2 with Bayern. 'It would be disaster if Mainz were to go down,' Bayern general manager Uli Hoeness said after the evenly contested ninety minutes. A nervy 3-0 win away to VfL Wolfsburg put the club into a very promising position. And on the penultimate matchday it was carnival time at the Bruchweg once more. Mainz beat Schalke 1-0. They were safe. A tearful, beer-drained Klopp mounted the stadium fence to sing punch-drunk songs with the fans. 'He's the ultra among the Bundesliga coaches,' *Süddeutsche Zeitung* wrote, and 'Mainz 05 has become the expression of his personality', a club where both players and the crowd were 'whipped into a frenzy' by the man on the sideline and 'tens of thousands were living in step with the emotions prescribed by their coach.'

After a 0-0 at Duisburg on the final day of the season, the poorest side in the league (their wage bill of €13m was less than half of the average for the other seventeen sides, €28m) were once again ranked the eleventh-best team in the country. Some players wondered whether they had actually underachieved in view of their playing capabilities, but Friedrich maintained that the club knew exactly what they had done. 'Being able to play in the Bundesliga again next year is the greatest thing for us,' he said. 'We still experience each game as a present, like a kid with wide eyes.'

Like a discreetly out of tune violin among a philharmonic orchestra, however, two small, annoying quibbles jarred with the celebrations ever so slightly. Mainz fans had angrily jeered former FSV midfielder Mimoun Azaouagh during the Schalke match; a sign, perhaps, that the self-styled party club was becoming a bit less special, more like a normal one. 'That's not who we are,' Klopp castigated the supporters. Secondly, regular observers noted that Heidel protested a little too vigorously when someone put it to him that the losses of playmaker da Silva (to Stuttgart) and key striker Mohamed Zidan (back to Werder) would be tough to compensate. 'We've been hearing that for fifteen years now,' he said dismissively.

But that summer, the floodgates opened. In addition to da Silva and Zidan, striker Benny Auer and defender Mathias Abel also left. Most damaging, in more ways than one, was the departure of a fifth regular, Michael Thurk. The forward's twelve goals in 2005–06 had gone a long way to keeping Mainz safe, as had his six goals in the second half of the previous season. Thurk was the type of striker Germans call a *Schlitzohr*, literally: a cut-up ear. The expression goes back a few hundred years, to when apprentice craftsmen wore golden earrings and had them ripped out as a punishment for misdemeanours. Thurk was a street hustler on the pitch, a lovable hoodlum and serial irritant for defenders. He'd grown up in the Gallus quarter of Frankfurt, an industrial, working-class district wedged in by two major railway lines. Locals referred to the area as '*Kamerun*', due to its high level of immigrants.

Thurk's brace on the final day of the 2003–04 season against Eintracht Trier had lifted Mainz to the Bundesliga, but he had cast a solitary, distraught figure amidst the ecstatic festivities. Thurk had agreed to move to Energie Cottbus for the coming season, in anticipation of the East German club's promotion to the top division. But in Energie's place, Mainz had gone up. 'I feel like shit. Do I really have to go there?' Thurk muttered throughout the party in the city centre, crying inconsolably.

Heidel had promised the forward that he'd be welcome to return if his transfer to Cottbus didn't work out. When it didn't, Thurk paid part of his transfer fee to facilitate his return in January 2005. 'In Mainz's history, we have made two incredibly [good] personnel decisions,' Strutz said later, 'One is Klopp. The other one was to take back Thurk from Cottbus. What this guy is on the pitch is incredible.'

In July 2006, Thurk learned of interest from Eintracht Frankfurt. The move to his hometown was hugely attractive to him, emotionally and financially. Mainz wanted him to stay. Thurk provoked a falling-out with Heidel and Klopp to force through his sale. He professed himself disappointed that the Mainz general manager had not informed him of Eintracht's enquiries, then attacked Klopp for not backing him enough in relation to a possible call-up by the national team. 'I have to think about that,' the Mainz coach had – truthfully – answered when someone had asked him about Thurk's prospects with Klinsmann. 'That's not simply a negative statement about a player,' Thurk complained, 'I felt as if he was making fun of me.' But the thirty-year-old went further, much further. Klopp, Thurk said, was some kind of 'super guru' whose man-management prowess was vastly overrated: 'This constant cheerfulness, always a funny quip. The stuff he says in the team meetings, his way of motivating. I switch off, because I've heard it a thousand times before. It's worn thin. Many of the things he says, I can't hear any more.'

There was no going back after that. Mainz sold him to their local rivals. The switch didn't work out for Thurk, however. He only scored four goals in thirty-six games before moving on to FC Augsburg. 'The stuff Thurk said was unforgivable, it was scorched-earth stuff,' says Quast. 'Kloppo was God in Mainz, you can't do that. It got very personal. After their many car journeys together to and from Frankfurt, they had become very close, like *Topf und Arsch* [pot and bum]. It was calculated by Micha. He knew the club had to sell him. But how do you deal with a guy like that? For a while, their relationship was very tense. I was sure Kloppo would break off all contact. But then, 2015–16, Augsburg are playing at Liverpool. And who's there, sitting in the VIP box next to Ulla [Klopp's wife]? Michael Thurk! Kloppo had invited him as a guest of honour. Thurk had played for Augsburg, so it was his game, too, in a way. There was no grudge, no ill-feeling at all. That's cool. I respect people who can let bygones be bygones like that.'

The start to the 2006–07 season was spectacular. Rafael Benítez's Liverpool were demolished 5-0 in a friendly at the Bruchweg. Mainz beat VfL Bochum 2-1 in the first Bundesliga game of the season. But that was it, as far as wins were concerned. The newly built team couldn't make the demanding system work. Eight draws and eight defeats left them propping up the table at the halfway mark.

Thurk's attack supplied an easy explanation for Mainz's terrible results: Klopp could no longer inspire the dressing room. Maybe he was too busy analysing the national team's games for ZDF to pay attention to mundane Bundesliga matters, the tabloids wondered.

Strutz says that wasn't the problem. 'Before one game, against Schalke 04, Klopp made an unbelievable speech in the press conference. He just talked and talked, and at the end, I was sure that we would go and win. I asked one of the cameramen to give me the tape.' 'We will keep our naive belief,' Klopp had said, 'we won't go to Schalke feeling small with our backs bowed or broken. Whoever stays the course, never gives up, never stops working will be rewarded at the end. That's my fundamental belief. We will keep on fighting until someone tells us: "You can stop now, the season's over." ' Mainz lost the game, 4-0.

The match before the winter break, at home to FC Bayern, brought the same scoreline. A Mexican wave swept through the sold-out Bruchweg, one part defiance, two parts gallows humour. Strutz didn't like it. 'I would have preferred if the crowd had really jeered the players instead.' The club bosses agreed that the team, especially some of the new recruits, lacked ability and application. There would be some changes during the holidays, but not on the bench. Heidel declared Klopp unsackable. 'We would jump for joy if he extended his contract beyond 2008 with us,' he told the press.

Klopp denied that his team had been afraid of the Bavarians' visit – 'we didn't shit ourselves, I had a look before' – and stayed stoically upbeat. The break would offer a chance to make the requisite changes. In any case, he told reporters, finishing the year bottom of the Bundesliga wasn't his worst-ever Christmas: 'When I was five years old, I wanted a Bonanza bike. I got one but our neighbour Franz, who played Santa Claus, sat down on it as a joke. The wheel rim was bent like an "eight". I couldn't ride it and was very upset.'

'It didn't feel as if the house was on fire,' says Neven Subotić, sitting in the quaint Tasty Pasty Company, an exposed brick café run by a very chatty British expat in Cologne. 'That season, it wasn't pure chaos or anarchy. It was business as usual. We trained hard and played with a clear plan at the weekend, knowing that winning a point would be great. That was our focus. There was no sense of grave frustration, it didn't feel as if nothing was working for us. I think everybody knew that we didn't have the quality of the bigger sides, that we basically belonged down there. As a young player, I was very preoccupied with myself anyway.'

Heidel spent money to stem the tide. Mohamed 'Little Pharaoh' Zidan, a happy-go-lucky striker who – like Thurk – only ever fulfilled his potential under Klopp, was brought back from Werder Bremen for €2.8m in January, a record signing for Mainz. Danish midfielder Leon Andreasen (also from Werder) came in on a six-month loan to shore up the centre, Colombian winger Elkin Soto was plucked from utter obscurity (he was out of contract after a spell at CD Once Caldas). The supporters, too, got a move on. They started a campaign called 'Mission Possible 15' to save Mainz 05 from relegation. (Fifteenth place was enough for survival.) The Mainz ultras promised themselves to make the Bruchwegstadion, where FSV had become a bit of a pushover, a noisy cauldron once more.

Klopp, described as 'a young, unshaven man forever jumping up and down on an imaginary bouncy castle' in the *Guardian*, made the most of the restart. Zidan, Andreasen and, to a lesser extent, the soon to be injured Soto, were key factors in winning five of their first six games in the *Rückrunde*. Mainz were tenth. There was talk about reaching the UEFA Cup for a second time. 'My teammates fight as if the opponents are threatening to take away their children,' Andreasen said admiringly. Strutz hailed the team 'the Bravehearts of the Bundesliga'. Any similarities with Scottish insurgents proved superficial, however. Underneath Mainz's kilts, there wasn't that much going on.

Refereeing mistakes, injuries, goal-scoring opportunities wasted, silly goals conceded. The familiar litany of relegated sides since time eternal. All of it true, all of it was to blame, to an extent, for Mainz losing seven of the following nine games. More importantly, the disastrous first half of the season had made the margin for error too small for a side of 05's limited capabilities. A home win on the penultimate day of the season, 3-0 v Gladbach, came too late. Mainz would have had to beat FC Bayern 7-0 away to have had a shot of staying up. There was no realistic prospect of achieving such a result on a PlayStation, let alone in the Allianz Arena. The Bundesliga adventure was over. FSV were going down after 102 games at the top.

For Subotić, it was relegation in his first season as a professional football player but, surprisingly, not that painful. 'The mood in the dressing room was good until the very end,' he says. 'We stayed a team, we stayed together. That was a very important experience for me. It helped me to grow as a player. It didn't get significantly worse or louder towards the end. Maybe a little, but not by much.'

The Bruchweg certainly didn't lose its voice. Standing ovations accompanied a lap of honour after the final whistle in the Gladbach game. 'We want to see the team' chants forced the squad to come out of the dressing room for a second round. They sang 'You'll Never Walk Alone' again. 'My handkerchiefs are wet,' German FA president Dr Theo Zwanziger admitted. 'Football can't achieve more than it has here, with us,' Strutz said about the emotional farewell.

Klopp took the microphone. Once again, a cartoon figure provided the impulse for his speech. Paraphrasing the end credits of the German version of the animated *Pink Panther* show, he promised that 'this is not the end of all days, we'll be back, without doubt – like the pink philosopher said.' Klopp 'almost sounded happy about the relegation, for bringing out the true football soul of Mainz', *Frankfurter Allgemeine* felt. The drop down wasn't treated as a catastrophe but accepted as a rather inevitable setback. 'All that has happened is what everybody had always expected,' the broadsheet wrote. Klopp: 'It's amazing to see how people deal with relegation. That's what life is about. If you've given it your all and have failed, you can deal with the situation. People and the club have reacted in a classy manner. Here, players will never be idiots for losing a game.' In Munich, FSV players and officials wore red top hats before kick-off and held up a banner in front of their travelling supporters. 'We take our hats off to you,' it read.

Klopp confessed to a spell of introspection ('I questioned myself. If I had found I was 90 per cent responsible for relegation, I would have had to draw the necessary conclusions. That's not the case.') but pledged his allegiance. 'I don't have the right to stop now. I want to make sure I can live in Mainz after I retire or get fired somewhere, without there being any open questions.' He accepted that some players wanted to leave for other Bundesliga clubs, he added, but the situation was different for him. 'I'm nearly forty, I can do my job for a few more years. I'm not running out of time. Players have less time, they have to do these things. For me, it's about living up to my responsibility. I'm happy to do that.'

Top left: Norbert and Jürgen Klopp on a trip to Bad Kreuznach in 1975.

Top right: Have 'Abitur', will travel: on a post-graduation trip through Southern Europe.

Bottom: 'Klopple' (fourth from right) lining up for TSV Glatten.

Top: Four generations of Klopps: father Norbert, son Marc, Jürgen and Opa Karl.

Bottom: Playing for his second club, TuS Ergenzingen (centre-right).

Top: A move to Bundesliga side Eintracht Frankfurt failed to work out. Klopp (bottom left) hardly played for the 'Eagles'.

Bottom left: Klopp and TuS Ergenzingen came second in a hat-trick competition and received an award from Germany legend Uwe Seeler.

Bottom right: Mainz 05 coach Wolfgang Frank was a football revolutionary and Jürgen Klopp's most important mentor.

Alongside sporting director Christian Heidel, Klopp took 'Carnival club' FSV Mainz 05 to the Bundesliga for the first time in their history in dramatic fashion.

Klopp crying at his farewell from Mainz.

A 5-2 triumph over FC Bayern in the DFB Pokal final marked Klopp's high point with the Black and Yellows. A year later, Dortmund narrowly missed out on a Champions League win against their German rivals at Wembley.

With former Eintracht teammate Sven Müller at Anfield, and talking tactics with his trusted coaching staff Zeljko Buvac (centre) and Peter Krawietz at Melwood.

Return to the Yellow Wall: Klopp came up against Dortmund in the Europa League in 2016 and beat Thomas Tuchel's men in spectacular fashion.

Top: A last-minute goal by Adam Lallana saw Liverpool beat Norwich City 5-4 in January 2016. Klopp broke his glasses celebrating with his players.

Bottom: Klopp-Apocalypse now: the LFC manager going wild at the Anfield touchline.

11. ONE, TWO AND ALMOST THREE

Dortmund 2010–2013

Nuri Şahin, Mats Hummels, Marcel Schmelzer, Neven Subotić and Sven Bender looked at each other and started giggling in disbelief, like schoolboys who had just pulled off the most elaborate prank on their teacher. The moment lasted only 'two seconds', says Hummels, 'but it felt like two hours'. The 80,000 punch-drunk, screaming supporters on the terraces were shaking the Signal Iduna Park so hard that time itself became unstuck.

Stadium announcer Norbert Dickel had set off the earthquake, crying out that Köln were 2-0 up at Leverkusen, Dortmund's last remaining rival for the top spot. BVB were leading 2-0 against 1. FC Nürnberg, only twenty minutes away from winning the Bundesliga title, with two games to spare. 'We knew then that he had done it but couldn't quite comprehend it,' says Hummels of that unforgettable day in April 2011. Subotić: 'We were babies, most of us weren't even twenty-three yet. We had no idea what was happening to us. We knew we were there. But we didn't quite know

how we got there and what being there actually meant.'
Bender: 'I had goosebumps like never before in my life. It
was a brutally emotional moment, a realisation: we, a bunch
of kids, had done it. Looking back I'm almost sad I couldn't
enjoy it more. But it was just too unreal and over too quickly
to take in in its entirety.' Klopp was equally unable to fully
appreciate the occasion. 'I thought it would feel better, more
euphoric,' he said, almost apologetically. 'Perhaps the
pressure on us was a little stronger than we were prepared
to admit.'

For everyone else, the minutes, hours and days afterwards
were a blur. Kevin Großkreutz, running around with a
partially shaved head like a madman (the batteries of the
electric razor had run out). Keeper Roman Weidenfeller,
telling an Al-Jazeera reporter in a hilarious mix of German
and English 'we have a grandios saison gespielt'. 'Fans
hugging, crying. Five hundred thousand people in the streets
of Dortmund. Beer. Champagne' (Subotić). 'Two weeks of
emergency rule' (BVB president Reinhard Rauball). 'It was
total ecstasy, impossible to put into words,' Hummels says.
'You had a town mad about football, a club mad about
football, and a coach in Kloppo who always put the
supporters at the heart of things in a very extreme manner.
The combination of all of that created an energy that people
still talk about today and will never stop talking about.'

Sebastian Kehl, one of a handful of players over thirty,
had experienced winning the title with Dortmund before, in
2002, as had Weidenfeller. Borussia's financial near-death
experience in the intervening years made the 2010–11 league
win more special still, he explains. 'To see the joy in people's
eyes after they had been worried for so long about the future

of their club and had wished for the glory days to return . . .
we felt so incredibly happy for them. We were able to give
something in return to them after all those difficult years. I
think people there have never forgotten and will never forget
it either.'

Nothing had prepared anyone of a Black and Yellow
disposition for this triumph. 'No disrespect to the guys from
the 1950s but in my view this is the biggest success in the
history of the club,' said Michael Zorc. The sporting director
had won the Champions League with Borussia as a player
in 1997 but felt that this side, the youngest-ever Bundesliga
champions, had achieved more. 'No one expected us to
have a chance, let alone dominate the league to such an
extent,' he said. 'When we won previous titles, we were at
least among the favourites.' Another Europa League spot
had been seen as a realistic target for a team without
expensive stars – striker Robert Lewandowski commanding
the only significant outlay – and a coach who had never
come near a trophy as player or manager before.

Klopp's guidance was 'the essential factor' in making
Borussia great again, Hans-Joachim Watzke says, but the club
also benefited from Zorc firing magic bullets in the transfer
market ahead of the campaign. 'We got very lucky with
quite a few of the signings Zorc made, in close cooperation
with Jürgen and me,' Dortmund's CEO admits. In that
respect, the summer of 2010 was probably the luckiest of
all. The arrival of Lewandowski, a muscular but very mobile
centre-forward, reduced Klopp's reliance on the less
technically gifted Lucas Barrios, and increased his tactical
options. The unknown Pole, a future world-class number 9,
was often deployed as second striker or number 10 behind

his Argentinian teammate in his debut Bundesliga season. In attacking midfield, Shinji Kagawa (twenty-one), bought from Japanese second division side Cerezo Osaka for the bargain-basement sum of €350,000, added agility and guile next to another de-facto new addition, eighteen-year-old Mario Götze. The son of an IT professor and product of Borussia's youth system effortlessly fizzed past opponents to inject even more speed into Borussia's offensive game. Matthias Sammer, the German FA sporting director, hailed 'Super Mario' (*Bild*) as 'one of the greatest talents we ever had'.

The trio's interlocking moves gave Dortmund another dimension in the final third, 'they opened up our game', says Subotić. The biggest improvement stemmed from the squad's tactical progress, however. After two full seasons, Klopp's *Jagdfußball* (hunting football) was becoming second nature, a collective ritual, accepted and practised without hesitation.

'We kept the core of the team, most of us, very young,' says Subotić. 'We didn't get in players who were already at the height of their powers and perhaps on their way down again. Our guys hadn't fulfilled their potential yet; they wanted to do anything to get there. That was hugely important, as was the fact that we had people who had completely bought into the system. They believed in it, they lived it.' They had signed up to it, too. Ahead of the campaign, Klopp asked his players to put their name to 'a promise', containing seven rules. BVB players agreed to: 'unconditional dedication', 'passionate devotion', 'a determination [to win], independent of the scoreline', a readiness 'to support everybody', a readiness 'to accept help', a readiness 'to put [their] quality wholly at the service of the team', a readiness 'to take on individual responsibility'.

'It might sound stupid but when things go like clockwork, you're happy to run,' says Bender. 'You don't even feel it any more. We were so united in our purpose, so clear, eager to help each other. We were blood brothers.' 'We stopped asking questions,' adds Hummels. 'We knew exactly what the coach wanted us to do, and it was actually fun to play that way, almost addictive. His classic phrase was: "Run like there is no tomorrow." It came easily to us.'

The team could see itself grow, says Subotić: 'Many were on the way up. That was fun. We had this confidence, we felt that we would play everybody off the park. When we didn't, we simply said, "Okay, lesson learned, we'll smash them next time." The first two years were like that. And in the third year, we did smash everybody.'

Any remnants of inhibition were discarded when Dortmund racked up seven consecutive wins after a 2-0 opening day defeat in the Signal Iduna Park to Bayer 04 Leverkusen. The irresistible run included a 3-1 win in the derby at Schalke, an edgy 2-0 home triumph over FC Bayern in October – Klopp's first league success against the Bavarians – and a fortuitous 2-1 over 1. FC Köln that showed that even the team's deficiencies could work in their favour. Klopp had worked in pre-season on toning down the wildness, to make Dortmund's game a bit more rational, especially in possession. But 'full throttle [was] what they do best', Watzke remarked after the win against the Billy Goats, 'they're not good at winding down a game'. Instead of settling for a respectable 1-1 draw at the RheinEnergieStadion, Dortmund pushed forward with abandon in the final minutes, propelled by a will to win that was much greater than the fear of losing. 'None of us had won any significant titles, of course we were hungry,' Hummels said. Nuri Şahin popped up with a last-second strike that secured three points – and top place in the table for the very first time under Klopp. Borussia hadn't occupied first place since winning the *Meisterschaft* in 2002.

At Mainz and in the early months at Dortmund, Klopp's watchword had been *geil*. Both an adjective or an adverb, it carries a faint whiff of 1980s pop culture and literally translates as 'horny', but it can also refer to something very inspiring or impressive. '*Geil* is the word that best describes my excitement,' Klopp told *taz* in 2004. 'The language I use is important, I need to get through to my players. But I don't use *geil* to come across as young or cool. I simply don't have a better word to describe something I happen to find exorbitantly beautiful.'

Geil was complemented by *Gier*, greed, in Klopp's phraseology in 2010–11. The team needed to be greedy in chasing the ball, in covering the pitch and in the pursuit of results, he stipulated. Traditionally sinful traits – lust, gluttony, avarice – were thus recast as footballing virtues. There was to be no distinction between work and play, pain and pleasure: self-sacrificial toiling could be a sensual, arousing experience. Klopp, feverishly saluting won tackles and clearances on the sidelines, was the physical manifestation of his teachings. 'He said things like "I'm looking forward to this game with every fibre in my body" and it was so believable that one second later, you felt the same,' Bender says. 'We learned to be completely in the moment, to think only from game to game.' The idea that big targets had to be clearly articulated in order to be achieved was dismissed as counter-productive. 'Whoever says that has no idea,' the coach explained. He set his men immediate, achievable targets. They had to win the next game. 'A slalom skier would never throw his hands up in the air in celebration after clearing the first gate, would he?' he asked.

Klopp set 'an example to the boys' by behaving in accordance with his own convictions, says Fritz Lünschermann, the BVB team manager. 'His style, his mentality . . . He's quite a unit, too. He's not a 1.75m man, he's 1.93m. A demolition bomb, pure dynamite. You only have to light the fuse. He used to say: "Get on the wild ride." Most of the time, that's what happened. The other important advantage was the age of the team. It had become quite young, quite quickly. Neven, Mats, all these guys. They were all still kids and followed him like Jesus' disciples. They had a very strong bond.'

The extraordinary togetherness of the players wasn't limited to football matters. 'We used to get together, ten of us, and play online, for hours on end,' says Subotić. 'We knew that wouldn't last for ever – you get older, you have other interests – but at the time, it was a hugely important tool for us that brought us together.' Looking back, Hummels says, 'it was a unique situation: a highly talented group, with world-class players, happy to hang out with each other like a gang. That special combination made everything possible.' Dickel: 'There's an old saying in football: "You have to be eleven friends." It's not totally wrong. If there are eight friends in the team, that's already quite good.'

A united team, created in Klopp's image, delivering a string of victories: there was no longer a need to deal with tactical dissidents because there weren't any. Even if somebody did harbour private doubts, the intensity in training had ramped up so much that natural selection precluded any deviation from the course. Only the fittest, most devoted followers could survive life in the fast lane.

'In the first year, it was rather normal football, with a pinch of Klopp tactics,' says Subotić. 'In the second year, it got spicier. In the third year: boom! We reached a whole new level, because all twenty-five players now truly got it. Training felt like war. The starting eleven playing v subs. By the middle of the week, you sort of knew the line-ups. You can't imagine how difficult these games were. You were used to having a bit of space and air to breathe but that was all gone. Everyone attacked the ball, everyone defended. Everyone pressed. These games were as hard as the real ones, perhaps even harder.'

The training week had a fixed pattern. Monday was a rest day. Tuesday: gym sessions, sprints, four-a-side games, tournament-style, the winner stays. (Subotić: 'Fun to start your week that way but very demanding. You sprint all the time, challenge for the ball all the time. It's a workout, but you don't realise it.') Wednesday: eleven-a-side. Two halves of ten minutes. Preceded by a warm-up with passing. Thursday: shooting on goal. For everybody, including defenders. 'After two extremely tough days, you needed to have a bit of fun. We sometimes adjusted the sessions to concentrate on a particular weakness of the opponent, to cross the ball in a certain way, for example. But you could shoot on goal unobstructed. I think every pub player would have said: "I'll be happy to join in that session!"'

Fridays were devoted to dead-balls. Free-kicks, but mostly corners. The same two teams were always up against each other, and the ball was live – there would be counter-attacks, and counter-counter-attacks on a very small pitch, 30 metres long, with boards along the touchline to keep the ball in play. Subotić: 'Short and sweet but tough as hell. Two hundred miles an hour for a few minutes. The score was kept throughout the season. The motivation was very high, nobody wanted to lose. No prisoners. It was also your last chance to show the coach: "I'm here, I'm ready." A last short, sharp jolt.' Saturday was game time. Sundays were spent regenerating and doing warm-downs. On top of these physical exertions, there were short and concise video analysis sessions. After a quick introduction by Klopp, Krawietz took over and showed the team clips of the next opponents, their dead-ball pieces, their basic defence and attacking shapes, where they had problems or gaps.

The whole routine was 'so brutal that there was no time to think at all', Subotić recalls. Which is just as well, because Klopp mandated that his men should live only for the moment and never contemplate matters beyond the next game. Metre by metre, tackle by tackle, and goal by goal, Dortmund were running away with the league, racking up win after win, while champions Bayern were ignominiously stuck in mid-table, slowly self-destructing under the high-handed leadership of Louis van Gaal. Bayer Leverkusen were doing much better, but they were Leverkusen, weren't they? A club with a well-deserved reputation for being bottlers. Three months into the campaign, it dawned on Klopp and his men that they could go all the way.

To keep the pressure off the team, any mention of winning the league was strictly banned, from the very top down. 'We are not talking about the *Meisterschaft*, I couldn't care less about the table,' Klopp kept insisting. 'I have 0.0 per cent interest in the table. Anyone talking about winning the league now has no idea about football,' said Zorc. Watzke, too, preached silence. 'It's totally unrealistic to talk about the championship. We are not ready to burden our seven, eight players who aren't even twenty-three years old yet with that kind of baggage. Setbacks are guaranteed to happen.'

A few weeks later indeed, Klopp found himself answering uncomfortable questions in a TV interview. 'Why did the team play so poorly against Hannover?' WDR's Arnd Zeigler enquired. 'We have problems, so many problems,' Klopp said, rubbing his eyes underneath his glasses. 'The boys don't adhere to instructions, I can't get through to them. I'm not sure I'm the right coach any more. We have to analyse the situation critically during the week. Maybe the players want to get rid of me. I'm a bit clueless at the moment, to be honest.' The BVB coach also lamented that there were no alternatives to the 29-year-old Roman Weidenfeller in goal. 'Today he was okay but in the morning, after getting up, he looks horrible. We have no choice other than to drink enough until he looks better in our eyes.' It was all a very good joke, of course, a feature for Zeigler's satirical football show. Dortmund had in fact won 4-0 at Hannover. And yet, the skit served a serious purpose, too, like many of Klopp's funny lines. His comedic qualities helped to release tension inside the dressing room and also guaranteed that his players listened attentively. 'His punchlines are perfect,' says Watzke. 'Jürgen is never monotonous or predictable. That keeps everybody's concentration.'

By January, BVB had opened up a twelve-point gap. Mario Götze performed so well in the 3-1 win at Leverkusen that

Klopp was forced to substitute him, to save him from even more media hype and potential retribution from humiliated opponents. He had played himself into a dream-like state where every flick and turn was coming off. 'Playing this well was so much fun, more than winning itself,' Subotić smiles. 'Our system gave us a huge advantage over everybody else. It was like fishing with the best bait in the world. Or with a shotgun.' True to Klopp's maxim of 'staying greedy', the team's physical output never dropped. They were to space what World Cup winner Takeru Kobayashi was to hot dogs: they ate it up until the opposition was blue in the face and going down with cramps. Subotić: 'We ran our opponents into the ground, and they were totally shell-shocked.' Their pressing game had by then become so refined that they were able to systematically direct the other team's attacking moves into the most congested areas or dead-ends. 'When there's little pressure on the opposition defence and midfield, you can't stay too close to an attacker as a defender,' Subotić explains. 'They can simply play a long ball over the top, and the attacker can run past me, and it's a goal. But by pressurising their build-up play, you force them to play the ball early, under duress. Knowing that, I can anticipate where the ball is going to go, get really close to the attacker and get ready to tackle before the pass has even been made.' '*Gegenpressing* is the world's best playmaker,' Klopp later said about his team's propensity to win the ball when opponents were in total disarray, in areas on the pitch where only one or two clever moves were needed to get through on goal. In Şahin, they had the perfect man for those killer balls. 'Sometimes it felt as if he was 90 per cent of the team,' says Subotić. 'It was like: get the ball to Nuri, he'll do something.

If you saw him without a shirt you thought, "what, this tiny guy?" But you couldn't get the ball off him. He was the brain and the leader.'

It was Şahin who effectively swung the game at Bayern on matchday 24 with a wonderfully executed free-kick, Dortmund's second on the night. Borussia hadn't won in Bavaria's capital for nineteen years, 'most of my boys were still being breast-fed then', Klopp joked. Before the game, general manager Uli Hoeness had predicted 'a win with two goals or more', noting that 'man for man', the champions had the better side. As far as the teams went, there was no comparison, however. 'Bayern were driftwood in a sea of Yellow and Black,' wrote *Süddeutsche Zeitung* in view of the hosts' helplessness against Dortmund's targeted aggression. Wherever star winger Arjen Robben went, two BVB players were already there, stepping on his toes. So emphatic, definitive and hugely symbolic was the visitors' 3-1 triumph that Bayern officials were queuing up to congratulate them on winning the title.

Klopp lost a pair of glasses and a few drops of blood hugging his players a bit too forcefully after the final whistle. But that was a small price to pay for a result that knocked Bayern out of the title race and made the *Meisterschaft* Dortmund's to lose. They were twelve points clear with ten games to go. 'We've now come to a point where we can say: we can and want to be champions,' Watzke declared, irrespective of Klopp's protestations. 'I couldn't give a shit about the championship today, I'm too happy with the way we played,' the coach insisted.

Almost seven years later, Watzke recalls sitting in the team bus outside the Allianz Arena after the game. 'I was sat next to Michael Zorc. I asked him: "Was that it?" He said: "Not yet, but it's coming." I'll never forget that moment. We had been dead as a dodo a few years before. And here we were, on the verge of a league title. It was unfathomable.'

Following a small wobble, with a defeat in Hoffenheim and a draw against Mainz, Bayern employed mind games one more time. 'If I was wearing black-and-yellow pants, I wouldn't sleep soundly,' Hoeness said ahead of Dortmund's home game against Hannover. But Germany's most decorated club found that they weren't even best in class in talking a good game any more. 'I wonder what Hoeness' pants looked like before he went to bed,' Klopp responded. Borussia won the game 4-1. Seven points ahead of Leverkusen with five games to go, they were almost champions.

Watzke was perhaps the last remaining pessimist. 'I'm a born sceptic. That made for a good partnership with Klopp, because scepticism is completely alien to him. He once said to me: "I don't think about defeats." It's true, he's never spent a minute wondering what might happen if a game is lost. I'm the complete opposite. And I just could not believe that we could win the league with this team. One week before we won it, I doubted everything again. We had lost 1-0 at Gladbach.' But Dortmund could not be denied. They were unstoppable.

'With every game, Klopp's team talks got clearer, louder and more precise,' says Bender. 'He explained that we were in charge now; it was all down to us. We hardly needed any motivation but his speeches were the icing on the cake. We went out and ran even more.'

The team were so infused with the need to exert maximum effort each time that they hated themselves for meekly capitulating 2-0 at Werder Bremen a week after the title celebrations. Possibly still suffering from the after-effects of the party, Dortmund were a shadow of themselves. 'We all sat in the bus in silence, ashamed,' says Bender. 'But thirty minutes in, we looked at each other and thought: "Have we lost our minds? Are we totally insane?" We were German champions! Who cares about losing that game. Let's sing!' They sang all the way back to Dortmund.

Bayern's unimaginative transfer dealings and discontinuity at a coaching level had let in outsiders before, VfB Stuttgart (2007) and VfL Wolfsburg (2009) seizing the crown had come as shocks as well. This was different, however, much bigger. Borussia's *Meisterschaft* under Klopp opened up people's eyes to the potency of a collectivist approach. Ingenious tactics, faithfully implemented, could lift a team of youngsters, cheap left-field foreigners and a handful of veterans to the point where they didn't just upset the odds but set a new benchmark. The disruptive innovation underpinning their success was especially relevant to the Bundesliga, a league that had been steadily losing ground internationally due to financial restraints and a culture of passive coaching. Klopp's Dortmund showed a way to increase productivity with purely natural, renewable resources: a blue-collar work ethic, humility, cleverness.

Outside Germany, experts took note, too. Three months before the title win, the technical staff of Italy's national team, coached by Cesare Prandelli, came to look at Borussia's training. The team's movement reminded them of Sacchi's Milan, they told a beaming Klopp afterwards. Watzke: 'The football we played was our unique selling point at the time. One shouldn't forget that Bayern weren't as good then, they didn't have today's quality and didn't spend that much money yet. It was a bit easier for us, but we were on this unbelievable run. You could feel that this team was only at the beginning of its development.'

Success brought its own trappings. Half the team received lucrative offers to switch clubs. But of the regulars, only Şahin moved on. José Mourinho's Real Madrid exercised a €12m release clause to take the midfielder to the Bernabéu.

Şahin's successor was twenty-year-old İlkay Gündoğan, from 1. FC Nürnberg. Sitting in a Spanish restaurant in Manchester's city centre six years later, the Gelsenkirchen-born son of Turkish immigrants remembers meeting Zorc and Klopp in a Düsseldorf airport hotel in spring 2011. 'I was playing for Nürnberg and the season was still going on, it was very hush-hush,' he says. 'I have to say I was a little intimidated by him at first. He was so tall. We talked for half an hour by ourselves and it was obvious to me that I wanted to go to Dortmund afterwards. He's got this gift: he can totally captivate you, dazzle you, make you feel euphoric. I've never met any other coach like him. He asked me: "What would be your targets if you came to us?" I said: "To play as often and well as possible." "You see, that's already the first mistake," he replied. "It's not about playing often but making the most of your time on the pitch. I can't promise that you'll play often. That's not possible. But I can promise that you will learn an incredible amount, and that we will be extremely successful if you all bring your potential to bear." I remember that clearly. That was the first time in football that somebody didn't promise me the stars but was open and honest with me. I found that fascinating.'

Gündoğan found the step-up from Nürnberg very difficult, starting with the pre-season fitness regime. Players had to go on the notorious 'Chucky runs' set up by assistant coach Zeljko Buvac. Eleven runs back and forth, with and without the ball, on a parkour that stretched the entire length of the pitch. After the eleventh run, players had to hit the crossbar from the halfway line. Those who missed had to go on a twelfth run. 'The hardest thing I had ever done. It was sick,' Gündoğan sighs, reliving the horror in his mind. 'But it was important: surviving that session gave us plenty to talk about, it brought the team closer. You felt camaraderie with your fellow sufferers. Mats [Hummels] always complained. But he ran, too.'

Gündoğan's problems extended into the first half of the season. He was introverted and immature, he says, spending a little too much time with family and friends, playing with the handbrake on, worried about making mistakes. 'Klopp saw that,' he says. 'And he scared me a bit, to be honest. I sometimes didn't immediately understand what it was he wanted me to do. It took time until the penny dropped for me.'

For the legs and for the head, Dortmund's specific way of playing was tough to adjust to, let alone the higher quality of his teammates. Gündoğan: 'We practised a lot of *Gegenpressing*. Klopp said the first one, two seconds after losing the ball were decisive. We shouldn't be upset about losing the ball but actually be happy about being able to win it back. The idea was to attack the ball straight away, to surprise the opponent. They felt secure, they weren't ready for that.'

The new arrival's strife in the first half of the season coincided with Dortmund's failure to make their mark on the Champions League. History repeated itself on the international stage. Having got knocked out in the Europa League group stage in the previous year, when Paris

Saint-Germain, Sevilla and Karpaty Lviv had proved too strong and Dortmund too gung-ho, Klopp's men finished last in a group with Arsenal, Marseille and Olympiacos. 'We lacked experience,' says Watzke. 'Neither the team nor the coach had been in the Champions League before. We turned up in Athens, Marseille and London and played the way we played in the Bundesliga, but the level is beyond compare. In the Champions League, every little mistake gets punished. We pressed really high up the pitch, that didn't work. Every game was the same. We were the better team, we created good chances, we didn't score; we lost 2-0 or 3-0. The year after that, we changed our style of playing. We were up against Real Madrid and Manchester City in the group stage then, and we went through.'

It was a learning process for the team, Gündoğan says. 'We were all quite young and naive, these European teams were a little too street-smart for us. But we heeded the lessons, just as I did for my game.' Introspection came by way of an involuntary spell in the stands. 'Klopp took me aside one day and said: "This won't be easy for you, but you won't be involved at the weekend." There was no explanation. He had never criticised me or told me "you're playing shit", or stuff like that. But he's a clever guy. You knew he had his reasons for not including me in the squad. It was like a riddle that I had to solve. What was I supposed to do? What am I doing here? I had a thousand questions in my head but after a while I cracked it. I deciphered the code.'

Gündoğan came on nine minutes into the game against Hannover in February 2012, after Sven Bender had picked up one of his many injuries. He was a revelation. 'It kind of clicked. The shackles were off. I became part of the first team and everything kind of just happened, it all flowed naturally. My football, the relationship with my teammates and with Jürgen.'

One awkward incident in training sealed their bond. Gündoğan had been due to play in the first team against the reserves in the important Wednesday session, when the weekend's match was simulated. Getting up in the morning, he felt a tightness in his hamstring. Players with injury concerns were supposed to come in ninety minutes to two hours early, to get assessed by the physio and enable the coaching staff to find a replacement from the amateur team or under-19s if need be. Gündoğan thought he could train but decided to seek out the physio thirty minutes before the session started. 'He looked at it and said: "I have to tell the coach, there's a danger you might get injured." I said: "Okay, but please tell him that I can play." A few minutes later, the door opened and Jürgen walks in. This giant of a man, looking at me angrily. "What the hell are you playing at?" he shouted. "It's okay, Coach, I can play, I just wanted to make sure . . ." He reminded me about coming in an hour and a half early. He was quite upset with me. "Do whatever you want!" he said and left. I thought: "Shit. What do I do now?"' Gündoğan was the first man out on the pitch. Klopp called him over. 'He walks a few steps with me, away from the boys, and goes: "My friend, you can understand me, right?" "Yes, I do. I just wanted to—" "No. You don't understand. The next time you have any problems, even if it's just a little twinge, or your bum is itchy, or whatever, you call the doctor, or the physio. You can even call me first thing in the morning and break my balls. Just tell us." "Okay, Coach." "You'll join in

the warm-up, but then you go off before the game starts."
"But I want to train." "Be quiet. You'll go off." Then he
laughed and hugged me. I asked once more if I shouldn't
stay for training, but he sent me back in after another hug.
He became more than a coach for me after that. We had a
special connection, and a very successful one.'

Dortmund's European woes had no negative impact on
their form in the league. On the contrary: from October
2011 onwards, they went on a domestic rampage of twenty-
eight games without defeat. Once more, a win over Bayern,
Dortmund's fourth successive defeat of the Bavarians,
decided the title race. The home side's perfect midfield
positioning created a 'kill zone' near the halfway line where
most Bayern attacking moves went to die in the first half.
Bayern did a little better after the break as the Black and
Yellows tired but Arjen Robben missed a penalty and
Lewandowski's goal secured all three points in the heaving
Signal Iduna Park. Dortmund moved six points clear at the
top with four games to go. 'We can hardly play any better,'
Klopp exclaimed. The 44-year-old was reluctant to
acknowledge the true importance of the win as far as the
title race was concerned. 'A lot can happen before the end
of the season,' he cautioned. 'But we'll have three days to
celebrate and enjoy tonight's extraordinary event.'

A few players took that declaration perhaps too seriously.
Gündoğan: 'That Wednesday after the Bayern game, five
of us went out partying. We didn't drink but stayed in a club
until two or three.' The problem was: they had a game
against Schalke on Saturday. The derby. Schalke went 1-0
up but Dortmund won 2-1. The players went partying
again. The next morning, Klopp addressed the team at the

training ground: 'Somebody told me a few of you went out during the week . . . I don't know who, I don't want to know. But I can tell you: these players should be happy we won yesterday. Otherwise we would have seen the biggest punishment in the history of club football.' 'The players looked at each other and thought: "Fuck, thank God we turned that game around!" We went out quite often as a team then, eight or ten people at a time, there were a lot of singles in the squad. Sometimes, you could see the after-effects in training on Sunday morning. But I don't think we ever overdid it. It made us more of a unit, I believe.'

Klopp's ambition to win every game did not diminish after Dortmund were confirmed as champions again. His team duly went on to set a new points record for the Bundesliga: eighty-one. 'Generally speaking, all our games that year were amazing,' Gündoğan smiles. 'We dominated the opposition, Klopp-style. They didn't know what hit them. We basically mugged them, they couldn't deal with it. That gave us an extra-good feeling. We didn't steal the points, we knew: they have no chance against us. One game, against Köln, we were 1-0 down at half-time, no one knew why. We won 6-1. We were so good that it didn't matter if the opposition took the lead.'

'In those years, we played a new kind of football in Germany,' Kehl adds. 'We simply swamped or overwhelmed other teams. They were completely helpless.'

Borussia's appetite was not yet satisfied. Four weeks after winning the league, they had the chance to achieve the club's first-ever double. Jupp Heynckes' Bayern stood in their way in the final in Berlin. It would, as Watzke puts it, turn into 'a game of fundamental importance for both clubs'.

Throughout his first successful cup run as a coach, Klopp had shown the team edited highlights from previous wins, underlaid with dramatic music. The night before the final, a motivational video comprising historic achievements, such as the moon landing, Boris Becker's win at Wimbledon in 1985, and Muhammad Ali's 'Rumble in the Jungle', ramped up the emotional temperature. 'We told the boys: our own film is not over yet,' Klopp said in an interview with *RedaktionsNetzwerk Deutschland*. 'You have to wait for the right moment with these things, then they're great.'

Twenty-three years had passed since Dortmund's last win in the cup. Less than three minutes into the match, Dortmund were 1-0 up through Shinji Kagawa. Robben and Hummels both converted penalties, then Lewandowski scored BVB's third on the stroke of half-time. The 3-1 lead enabled the Black and Yellows to play on the counter-attack after the break, setting up traps that the Bavarians stumbled into like a pack of doddering bears. 'Dortmund played more defensively, more sneakily, more calculatedly,' *Süddeutsche Zeitung* wrote, full of admiration. 'They aren't just German champions but also cup winners in the forcing of opposition errors.'

The mighty Bayern were dismantled, humiliated, as Klopp's men romped to victory in the Olympic stadium. Lewandowski ended up with a hat-trick in the 5-2 win. 'This was not coincidence,' Bayern CEO Karl-Heinz Rummenigge conceded in front of sponsors and VIP guests at the midnight banquet. 'This was an embarrassment. Every goal was like a slap in the face for us.' On the pitch, Watzke and Zorc had quietly shed tears of joy, on 'the most extraordinary moment in [Borussia's] history', as Klopp acknowledged. He had 'danced in the dressing room with a beer in his hand, like one of us', Gündoğan smiles. The coach told reporters that Norbert Dickel, goal-scorer in the 1989 final, had given him his right shoe as a good luck token the night before. 'It had been in his basement for more than twenty years and smelt a bit,' he laughed. But supernatural powers or good luck didn't come into it, neutral experts noted. Dortmund beating Bayern for the fifth time running was a feat both unparalleled and well deserved. Their superior system, application and transfer policy had negated the giants' array of star individualists and huge financial advantage. It's 'a power shift', *Die Welt* attested. 'Dortmund have replaced Bayern at the top of the German football food chain.'

'The system that Jürgen, Zeljko and Pete played dominated German football for two years,' says Dickel. 'Nobody had the faintest idea how to deal with our aggressive pressing, and our doubling-up, or tripling-up, on players. Even Bayern didn't know what was going on. It was a wonderful time, more spectacular than the wins in the mid-nineties. We were carried along on this wave, we went into every game knowing we would destroy the other team. We were drunk on euphoria, we had all gone BVB-crazy. It was a trip.'

That night in Berlin, Klopp was Mr Big, a shell-suit pusher, delivering a (legal) high of almost unbearable potency to millions of Borussia loyalists. The name of his drug was: love. 'I relish the total intensification, when bangs go off everywhere,' he told *Die Zeit* a few months later, 'that phase of "all or nothing", when it feels as if people don't dare to breathe.'

Martin Quast had watched the cup final in an old Jürgen Kohler shirt in the stadium. Afterwards, he saw Klopp and his team singing songs in the little tent that broadcasters

ZDF had put up behind the Marathon Gate. At the end of the live programme, as Klopp was carrying the golden cup and silver championship trophy – affectionately known as the Salad Bowl – Quast shouted '*Gude*', the traditional Mainz greeting, at his friend and told him that his shoelaces had come untied. 'He was laughing his head off. Then he gives me the bowl and the cup and goes: "Hold this for a second." And then he ties his laces. A quick high-five, and then he says: "It's a shame, but I have to go," picking up the cup and the bowl again. Cool, isn't it? It could have been a bottle of wine and a ring of sausages, he didn't think about it for one moment. Cup, championship trophy – so what? That's him. What normal person would do such a thing?'

Alex Ferguson was another observer who had enjoyed the show in Berlin. The Manchester United coach had travelled to Germany to cast an eye over Kagawa and Lewandowski. 'He sat four places to the left of me,' Watzke says. 'I told him he could have one – Kagawa – but not the other. He looked at me a little dumbfounded.' The Japanese midfielder would leave for the Premier League at the end of the season. Barrios, now surplus to requirements, was sold to Guangzhou Evergrande. All the other regulars stayed, plenty of attractive bids notwithstanding.

Watzke was under no illusions about the size of the challenge that awaited him and Zorc, however. The Bavarian empire was poised to strike back. 'We were intoxicated. It was an epochal evening for us but also the high point, the best day in the job for me – I felt it. I remember lying awake in bed at 4 a.m., staring at the Brandenburg Gate. You just knew it would get difficult from now on, that there would be a reaction, that Bayern would be out for revenge and start targeting our players. They had played forty finals before, I think, but never conceded five goals. They felt humiliated. That moment, they radically changed policy. They went all in, investing money like never before in the squad. And it paid off for them.' Dortmund's trick of being much bigger than the sum of their parts – a feat of football alchemy conjured up by grand wizard Klopp – had, to some extent at least, relied on the biggest team failing to make the most of their potential.

Bayern broke their own transfer record to buy holding midfielder Javi Martínez from Athletic Bilbao (€40m), as well as Mario Mandžukić (€11m, VfL Wolfsburg), winger Xherdan Shaqiri (€11.8m, FC Basel) and defender Danté (€4.7m, Borussia Mönchengladbach). The increase in individual quality, especially at the back, had a very welcome tactical knock-on effect, Bayern's former sporting director Matthias Sammer explains: 'More stability in defence made it possible for midfield and attack to press higher. Bayern's game became more flexible, more dynamic.'

Klopp wasn't the only one who found the Bavarian new direction eerily familiar. 'They have done to us what the Chinese do in industry,' he complained. 'They see what others are doing, copy it, and then go down the same route with more money than other players.'

'Bayern have taken on elements of Dortmund's game and become more like Dortmund than Dortmund themselves,' Ralf Rangnick observed. Imitation might be the sincerest form of flattery but that was scant consolation to Klopp, whose careful, four-year building work was put in the shade by a shiny, super-expensive skyscraper next door, partially using his own blueprint.

Bayern's novel sense of humility without the ball, their much improved intensity and tactical awakening made for a devastating combination. Heynckes' men won the Bundesliga with a new points record (ninety-one), notching up ten more than Dortmund in the previous season, before adding the DFB Pokal to their trophy cabinet.

After two seasons of 'dragging Bayern down to our level' (Klopp), Borussia's excellence had inadvertently raised the Reds' game. The effect on the rest of the league was similar. Taking inspiration from the double-winners, more and more teams started to include pressing and *Gegenpressing* in their tactical repertoire, fighting fire with fire. 'Suddenly, everybody did it. That's when we realised how brutally difficult it is to play against a team like that,' Subotić says.

Opponents also adopted a second counter-measure. Since Dortmund's game was built on rapid moments of transition after winning the ball, teams happily ceded both the ball and space, forcing BVB to play a slower, possession game. Klopp's racing car of a side now frequently got stuck in traffic. 'Our way of playing had encouraged all smaller teams,' says Gündoğan. 'They thought: we can beat teams who are actually better than us by adopting these tactics and getting it right.'

Dortmund picked up fifteen points fewer than in the previous season, but second place was not seen as failure. They needed to grow as a club; Champions League qualification was more important than defending their trophies.

The slight domestic setback was more than compensated by a thrilling international adventure. Klopp's men, dubbed 'the hottest team in Europe' by *FourFourTwo* magazine, outsmarted a number of sides ill-prepared for the ferocity of their finely honed drive-by-shooting approach. An early indication of Borussia's greater maturity in matches against the Continent's elite came in the second game of the group stage, away to Manchester City.

The visitors, spurred on by their fanatical travelling support, played the world's most expensively assembled team off the pitch at the Etihad; 'they were in charge for most of the game, flowing forward in yellow-and-black waves like New York taxicabs rushing to collect wealthy fares on Wall Street,' gushed the *Daily Telegraph*. Dortmund took the lead through Marco Reus and had enough chances to score three more. A last-minute penalty, converted by Man City substitute striker Mario Balotelli, made a mockery of their dominance – 'they were different class tonight, starting with their fans,' City keeper Joe Hart admitted – but the manner of the 1-1 draw left Klopp 'satisfied, verging on proud'. The BVB coach was more unnerved by the questions about the penalty decisions than the two dropped points. 'Such a fantastic game, and the first question is about the penalty?' he grumbled. His poor results in previous years had clearly irked him, but now 'an important step to represent Borussia Dortmund differently in the Champions League' had been made. 'It was one of the best games I've ever seen, and I've seen a few,' Klopp told *FourFourTwo* a few weeks later, 'we were almost terrified out there at how perfectly our plan came together.' 'Maybe one day, this night will be remembered as the team's European birth,' wondered *Die Welt*. Klopp's football had been proven feasible outside German borders, too, at last.

'To be honest, Manchester City were shit that year, not very strong,' Watzke shrugs. 'Their team was slow, overweight, I don't know.' But Dortmund also took four points from two games v Real Madrid and qualified for the last 16 as group leaders. They truly had arrived. 'We're a little surprised that everybody else is surprised about that,' Zorc said, a little indignantly.

Subotić puts the improvement in 2012–13 down to greater collective intuition. 'You can practise being ready to counter-press and win back the ball, the mindset. But you can't train the exact movement because you don't know where you'll lose the ball on the pitch. Everybody had both the power and responsibility to act as the trigger; then everybody had to join in. Getting the right feel for it took a couple of years. Then it became a natural reaction, a reflex.'

Dortmund had little trouble dispatching a leggy Shakhtar Donetsk in the next round – 'it's always good to get Russians or Ukrainians then, they're still on a winter break,' Watzke says – but Málaga in the quarter-finals was a very different story. Borussia were 2-1 down on aggregate at home in the second leg after ninety minutes. What happened next would go down as the 'miracle of Dortmund' (Klopp): the Black and Yellows scored twice in injury-time, the second from an offside position, to edge the Spaniards 3-2. The Signal Iduna Park erupted, spewing out happiness like molten lava. 'I ran on to the pitch, hugged Marco [Reus] and never wanted to let go again,' Gündoğan remembers. 'It was the craziest moment of my football history for sure,' Subotić says. 'That was something straight out of a Hollywood movie. We knew we could get one goal, and then just push and see if we can get lucky. Luck was on our side that day.' 'It's crazy, just crazy what happened in this stadium,' Klopp shook his head, bewildered by the turn of events, before he hugged Marcel Schmelzer in the mixed zone. 'Rarely has a football team been seen as so united and enthralled with themselves,' *Süddeutsche Zeitung* wrote. Dortmund were in the semi-finals of the Champions League. 'It's phenomenal – people here are as happy as if they had a second hole in their backside,' Klopp diagnosed.

The madness of Málaga, an unforgettable moment of otherworldliness, was 'one of those stories that will still be told in twenty years' time', Klopp told author Christoph Biermann a few months later in his book *Wenn wir vom Fußball träumen*. 'My motivation [as a coach] is to collect that kind of stuff, for people to tell and retell it. That's what this club is about. Its most important pillar is made up from the stories it has written since its foundation. That's also the reason why I love experiencing this time here so much: it gives us the chance to write such stories.' Football, he added, was a shared collection of stories, a shared history, an identity. 'You win and you lose, but you're with people you like. You're at home, you belong. That's what we all want. Ten million people want to belong here.'

The next chapter pitted the Black and Yellows against José Mourinho's Real Madrid. Two nights before the first leg, on the stroke of midnight, Gündoğan was on his mobile phone, looking at a headline that didn't seem to make sense. 'I had this routine, I would read *Bild* online before going to bed,' he says. 'Next day's articles went live after 12 a.m., and there it was, in big, fat letters: Götze is moving to Bayern!' I texted Marco Reus; him and Mario had the same agents and were best friends. "Can this be true?" "Yes, I've known since yesterday." I had trouble believing it.'

Götze, twenty, was the wonderkid of German football, 'the talent of the century' (Sammer). He had been with BVB since he was eight years old, a symbol both of their renaissance under Klopp and the promise of an even greater future. Dortmund had resigned themselves to losing the odd player each year, but not a true Dortmunder. Not Mario. Everybody was in shock. 'Some of the players couldn't sleep,' Klopp told the *Guardian*. 'It was like a heart attack. I couldn't speak. I couldn't go out with my wife that night.'

Bayern had exercised a €37m release clause, *Bild* reported, to make him the first big-name signing of the Pep Guardiola reign, which was to start later that summer. But who had leaked the story and why at such a sensitive time, forty-eight hours before the tie against the Spanish ensemble of superstars?

Suspicions quickly fell on the Bayern hierarchy. Their signing of Götze was a classic Bayern powerplay. Why should they mind if news of the transfer further unsettled their domestic rivals ahead of a hugely important match? 'Bayern tried to destroy us,' Watzke later claimed. Whether the Bavarians were really the culprits is uncertain, however. Dortmund had known about Götze's decision twelve days before, and it's quite possible a third party – say an agent representing a player negotiating to join Bayern next season, or a thwarted club who had also shown an interest in Götze – spilled the beans without malice aforethought. Bayern had their own semi-final, against Barcelona, to contend with and could have done without the controversy. The forward's release clause, in any case, had to be activated by 30 April.

Either way, Klopp was left 'emotionally the worse for wear' by the prodigy's defection south, Watzke says. 'He found it hard to accept that Mario wanted to leave, that he wanted to join up with Guardiola. That turned out to be the mistake of the century, and Klopp had foreseen it. He knew, he was 100 per cent convinced, that the lad was making an error. It hurt him. The kid that he had brought through was leaving. He told him it was a mistake in a meeting, just the two of them. We met with him and his agent, too. Klopp repeated: "You're making a mistake." But the decision was made. That played a lot on Klopp's mind. But in the sense that he was worried about Mario, not about the team.'

Gündoğan remembers a few ultras turning up at the training ground looking to make their displeasure known. Klopp played it cool. 'He said that he regretted Mario's decision, but that it was a normal thing in football, and okay, and that the show had to go on. Mario was still our player until the end of the season, and he was convinced that he'd do his best. And that was it.'

'I explained to Mario that people will definitely not forget him moving to Bayern Munich,' Klopp said after the final whistle. 'But they will be busy with other things tonight, because the club is the most important thing. Fortunately, that's what happened. The atmosphere put everything I've ever experienced in the shade.'

Having sown passion for almost four years, Klopp reaped pandemonium that night. Madrid were buried under a deluge of screams and attacks, barely escaping with their footballing lives after an epic 4-1 drubbing. Neither Götze nor his teammates had been adversely affected by the *Bild* story, as Dortmund completed a hugely impressive Bundesliga double over La Liga: Bayern had beaten Barcelona 4-0 in their first leg. A showdown in the final in

north London beckoned. More bad blood, too. Robert
Lewandowski, scorer of all four goals against the Spaniards,
had agreed terms with Bayern to accompany Götze on his
move to the Allianz Arena, a piece in *Der Spiegel* had alleged
just before kick-off. The Polish striker and his camp did
nothing to quell the speculation. 'We intend to change clubs
this summer,' agent Maik Barthel was quoted as saying.
Lewandowski's contract at Dortmund expired in the
summer of 2014.

Klopp defused the situation with self-deprecating humour,
reminding reporters at the Signal Iduna Park that he, too,
had scored four goals in a game once: 'At Erfurt'. But deep
down, he was much more troubled than he let on, Watzke
reveals. 'Robert Lewandowski was an issue that bugged
him, in the extreme. We couldn't quite agree, either: should
we have sold him in 2013 or let him leave in 2014 for free?
Jürgen was more of a mind to sell him. But Robert is a
professional, like very few others. He's not the emotional
type, he'll never kiss the badge, but to have him in your
team is a gift. He's like a machine. Nevertheless, Klopp was
quite annoyed with the way things went down. All of us
were angrier and more upset that we lost these players than
we let on. Once you admit that, people immediately accuse
you of moaning.'

There was no time for that in May 2013. History
beckoned. Dortmund v Bayern, a Bundesliga derby on the
hallowed turf of Wembley. 'German football has arrived in
the present after learning from the past,' cheered *Süddeutsche
Zeitung*, outlining how both teams' tactical sophistication,
inspired by the great historical sides (Ajax, Milan, Barcelona)
had taken them to a first-ever all-German final in the

Champions League. Klopp's injection of energy in particular, *Frankfurter Rundschau* claimed, informed 'a new, German school of football. He has reinvented the old, physical game of German teams, feared and despised in equal measure, paired with strategic finesse and technical maturity.'

There was another plotline. The final, Klopp explained to a world-wide audience via his *Guardian* interview, pitted 'the most interesting football project in the world, the new story, the special story' against a Bayern side behaving 'like a James Bond villain'. Dortmund were rank outsiders in financial terms, football romantics fighting against aristocratic moneybags who didn't just want to beat them but dismantle them altogether. Klopp, a huge sports film buff – 'I grew up on movies likes *Major League*' – firmly believed the underdog could carry the day. 'We are not the best team in the world but we can beat the best team in the world,' he predicted.

Dortmund so nearly did at Wembley. A typically full-throttle Borussia hunted and harangued Bayern, took control and created decent goal-scoring opportunities. 'I remember we should have been 2-0 or 3-0 up after thirty minutes,' says Gündoğan. Once Bayern had weathered the first storm, the game slowly drifted away from Dortmund. 'I think it was impossible for us to keep the same pace after the first forty-five minutes, it had been incredibly high,' Bender says. A Mario Mandžukić goal saw Jupp Heynckes' team take a 1-0 lead on the hour mark.

Eight minutes later, Gündoğan equalised from the spot. Dortmund were in it again but felt aggrieved, too. Bayern defender Danté, already on a yellow card, was not sent off for fouling Marco Reus in the box. Gündoğan: 'Referee

[Nicola] Rizzoli said: "What do you want? You got a penalty, didn't you?"' Bayern, unperturbed, had more energy and class towards the end of the tense nail-biter. Arjen Robben scored the winner in the eighty-ninth minute.

Klopp and his players were applauded off the pitch by the Dortmund fans. They were gracious losers. 'We have to respect Bayern's win,' the coach said calmly. 'We shouldn't forget that many teams wanted to get to the final, and that Bayern shot half of Europe to pieces on the way here.' Bayern were 'that little bit better than us that year', Watzke concedes. But Rizzoli's lenience still rankles. 'It was a catastrophically bad decision. Out of a hundred referees, ninety-nine would have probably sent him off. I would have liked to see how the game had gone then . . .'

Immediately after the match, Klopp had vented his anger in the tunnel, shouting at Pierluigi Collina, UEFA's head of referees. 'One or two decisions certainly could have gone the other way,' was all he said in the press conference, adding that the pride he felt for his team would soon take centre-stage again. In the dressing room, he consoled his tearful players by pointing at the bigger picture. 'You know that on a different day, with a different referee, you beat them. But Klopp didn't overdramatise it,' says Subotić. 'He said: "Remember where we were at the beginning of the season, how far we have come. Did anyone think we would make it to the Champions League final? It's all good, boys. Enjoy the evening." He's the man who sets the mood. For the club, for the team, for everybody. Especially at such testing times, when everybody's looking for a bit of direction.' Klopp's philosophical take paved the way for 'a great post-match party' at the Natural History Museum,

Josef Schneck says. 'After a while, nobody was thinking about the defeat any more. We've always been pretty good at partying.'

Looking back, Kehl wonders if Dortmund winning at Wembley might have been 'too much of a fairy-tale'. 'Nobody would have liked to see that movie, it would have been unrealistic crap,' Klopp told Biermann. A little later, in an interview for UEFA.com, he wasn't so sure any more, however. 'It would have been crazy if we had won the Champions League last season,' he said. 'I think we would have lost our minds, it would have been an incredible story – I would have loved to watch that story if it was a movie. A story like, I don't know, the Cleveland Indians in *Major League*, the Dortmund Indians. But it really would have been very crazy. So that is why everything is OK, and still very special. And there is still a lot of time for us to win even more.'

12. CHAOS AND THEORY

Liverpool 2016–2017

The Reds' 2016 pre-season tour to the US offered a long-overdue chance to work on fundamentals. At least one of the daily double-sessions was devoted to detailed tactical drills. Members of the LFC press corps were so impressed by the complexity of some of the choreographed exercises on show on the Stanford University pitch that they questioned whether training should in fact be open to the public at all. The journalists were used to Premier League coaches hiding their trade secrets behind ten-foot walls, fearful of spies sent by rivals.

Jürgen Klopp had no such qualms. When the German heard of the reporters' concerns, he put on his best silent-movie-comic 'I don't understand what you're talking about' face. 'That? That's kindergarten stuff,' he said to an LFC staffer, waving away an imaginary fly. 'I don't think for a second that Arsène Wenger will be surprised by any of that.' The Frenchman's team, Arsenal, were Liverpool's opponents on the opening day of the coming season, when LFC won 4-3.

A critical appraisal of Klopp's first eight months on Merseyside had earmarked three areas ripe for an upgrade. The first one – the obvious need for a much more thorough and systematic implementation of the coaching staff's main idea of play – was at last addressed under the Californian sun. An absence of European engagements during the season would offer more time for match preparation.

The squad, a mish-mash of genuine talent, loyal stalwarts and speculative investments that hadn't quite come off, was added to by the arrival of Bundesliga centre-backs Joël Matip and Ragnar Klavan, goalkeeper Loris Karius from Klopp's alma mater Mainz 05, all-action midfielder Georginio Wijnaldum (Newcastle United) and Southampton's Sadio Mané, a Senegalese striker who had been offered to LFC two seasons earlier for a third of his £37m price tag but who had not been ranked highly enough in the club's technical department's player evaluation model.

Thirdly, Klopp and his staff deemed that the Premier League's physical exertions warranted improved conditioning. Andreas Kornmayer, a stubbly, bespectacled mini-Klopp ('It's funny how they look alike,' Adam Lallana laughs) was brought in as head of fitness and Mona Nemmer was appointed head of nutrition. Lallana, unprompted, says the work of the two former Bayern Munich employees had a discernible positive effect on the 2016–17 season: 'Putting Mona in there has been unbelievable. She has come and reached new levels with the food we're eating. And Andreas, the fitness coach, comes in and we had a good pre-season under him. He got us fit for how the manager wants us to play, which is demanding.'

A trip to Wembley in early August offered a glimpse of the exciting prospects ahead. European giants Barcelona, leggy and behind their English opponents in terms of preparation, were beaten 4-0 by the Reds in the International Champions Cup, a semi-competitive fixture, with Mané the star attraction. Twenty-four hours later, however, Klopp's much-changed side crashed to a 4-0 friendly defeat at Mainz, of all places. Spectators at the Opel Arena, many thousands of whom had come to the ground early to welcome their former hero with standing ovations, sent Klopp home with another round of applause after the final whistle. The LFC coach professed himself grateful that his team had accompanied him on his slightly uneasy lap of honour. 'It would have been hugely embarrassing for me to run about by myself there,' he laughed. 'That way, it was cool. My boys showed that they have good manners, even if they can't play football. They showed their appreciation of the extraordinary atmosphere.'

The two contrasting 4-0 scorelines, as well as another pair of wildly differing games – a breathless 4-3 win at Arsenal and a sorry 2-0 defeat at newly promoted Burnley – set the tone for the entire campaign, a riveting, exhausting ride that ended in relief rather than euphoria, just like any other overly long roller coaster. Liverpool were prone to stunning performances against some of the best sides that year and at the same time liable to suffer embarrassing defeats at the hands of the decidedly lesser lights. That unnerving pattern ultimately precluded a better finish than fourth spot, but in the run-up to Christmas, hope burned brightly on Merseyside that more than an inglorious quarter of a century without a league title might come to an end.

Following on from the Burnley reversal, the Reds won against champions Leicester (4-1), future champions Chelsea at Stamford Bridge (2-1) and ten other sides in an unbeaten fifteen-match run that briefly took the club to the top of the table and 'made Liverpool supporters enjoy, well, being Liverpool supporters again', as the *Liverpool Echo* wrote. 'The fans like watching their team. They can't wait to come to Anfield, the sense of the new heightened by a redeveloped Main Stand that's allowing the ground to rediscover a consistent volume not heard in four decades.' Gone was the resigned, apathetic silence that had hung over the ground for much of the time since the failed championship challenge in 2014. 'We were bulldozing teams,' Lallana says. As promised, heavy metal football had arrived.

'Klopp is the best coach in the world for the spectators, he creates teams that attack the back four,' said Manchester City manager Pep Guardiola. Neither the Catalan nor his prominent colleagues José Mourinho (Manchester United), Arsène Wenger (Arsenal), Antonio Conte (Chelsea) and Mauricio Pochettino (Tottenham Hotspur) were able to inflict a single defeat on Liverpool that season.

Mané's inclusion gave the attack an extra level of pace and flexibility. The former Red Bull Salzburg winger and his two Brazilian teammates Philippe Coutinho and Roberto Firmino constantly switched positions in pre-programmed ways to find a path towards goal, even against 'sides so deep that their last line of defence is right next to the terrace', as Klopp's chief scout Peter Krawietz puts it.

In a celebrated appearance on Sky Sports' *Monday Night Football* in September, the Liverpool coach reiterated his mantra of *Gegenpressing* being 'the best playmaker'. But at Melwood, the emphasis had quietly shifted from working against the ball to working with it. Liverpool, the coaches realised, needed better active solutions for those games where they were the dominant side.

'After getting used to one another in the first season, there was a much bigger focus on possession football for the second year,' Krawietz reveals. 'The idea was to control the pace of the game with the ball, and to use the time between games to adopt a footballing idea that could – ideally – be reproduced in a flexible manner under pressure.' To that end, the coaching staff spent many training hours getting the team to adhere to certain patterns of movement. While the routine never included precise, pre-determined runs, it consisted of 'agreed procedures' (Krawietz) for creating spaces in the specific areas where opposition teams were suspected to be most vulnerable. One such procedure, for example, entailed two players dragging their opponents away from the centre with dummy runs, thus clearing a channel for the third one to run through on goal unopposed. A simple enough move, but very effective if executed in perfect synchronicity.

Krawietz: 'The system by itself is not really important in football. The point of coaching is to try to make football, a game based on many random events, less random, to force your luck in a sense. My favourite quote is by Lukas Podolski: "Football is like chess, but without dice." I'd change that slightly, to make it: "Football is like chess, but with dice." What I mean by that: every coach spends an incredible amount of time pondering about all the different factors, about the opponent, the weather, and so on, knowing full well that total control of the ball is unattainable. All you can really do then is to find a general order, a system of orientation for your own players that brings out the best of your specific squad. Successful combination football depends on two people having the same idea at the same time. One has the ball, the other starts making a move. A coach's job is to practise these sequences to instil an idea, repetition and situations, to increase the chance that they will work under real live conditions, when there's pressure and an opponent interfering. The alternative is to rely on total individual quality, on being simply superior. But that's not our approach. We can't afford these players; we have never been able to afford these players at any of the clubs we have worked for. That's why the idea always takes precedence for us.'

In those golden autumn months, the succinctness of Klopp's playing concept threatened to trump all rivals, most of whom had trouble making the most of their players' potential. Whereas Liverpool's last title challenge, under Brendan Rodgers in 2013–14, had owed much of its drive to one superstar striker (Luis Suárez), this was a true team, moving and playing as if connected by invisible nerve cords.

In the slipstream of the strong showings, players who had long been written off suddenly shone. James Milner, one of the most important leaders in the dressing room, was reinvented as a left-back. 'It was cool to see that players who had already played hundreds of Premier League games were ready to try out a different style, to adapt to it,' Krawietz says.

Centre-back Dejan Lovren was another player who confounded his critics. 'When we came to Liverpool, everybody told us about his problems, about the things he couldn't do but we were determined to look at him and everybody else with fresh eyes,' says Krawietz. 'We felt from the very first day that we had a player here, and his development has been great. I think a new coach, trying out new things and different players, taking responsibility for any failure, was seen as a chance by many to improve their situation. And many have seized it.' Adam Lallana and Roberto Firmino, who found it easy to adjust to the new tactics due to their past at pressing bastions Southampton and TSG Hoffenheim respectively, emerged as real pillars of the side, as did veteran midfielder Lucas Leiva. His experience, footballing intelligence, communicative skills and ability to learn made the Brazilian a key part of the new set-up.

Klopp had insisted on his first day at Anfield that Liverpool weren't nearly as bad as vast sections of the media and their own supporters feared. Maybe the squad itself had started feeling that way, too. 'He would sometimes get frustrated, telling us that we don't believe how good we are,' Lallana says. The coach and his staff also feel that the public in England are generally too quick to make up their mind about players and too slow to revise their views in light of evidence to the contrary. Krawietz: 'Once they have convinced themselves, for example, that a goalkeeper is shit, he remains shit for eternity. They will wait as long as it takes until he does make a mistake and then say: "See, we told you so." It's a self-fulfilling prophecy, in a negative sense. It's quite prevalent here.'

A late blunder from Loris Karius in the 4-3 defeat at Bournemouth in early December put an end to Liverpool's unbeaten run and led to the young German getting dropped for Simon Mignolet for the remainder of the term. The timing of the awful result – the Reds had been 3-1 up with fifteen minutes to go – couldn't have been much worse, either: the team were scheduled to fly to Spain for a Christmas party. Klopp was unperturbed, however. 'When we landed in Barcelona, music came on in the plane and he got on the microphone,' Lallana recalls with a huge smile. 'He was like: "Listen, lads. If we can party when we win, we can party when we fucking lose." So everyone got off the plane thinking: "You are right, it is the time to party. Let's party. Let's have a drink." Which just shows: there is more to life than football. Yeah, we did our best; we lost. And yeah, it feels shit to lose, but there is more to that. The older you get, I think the more it hurts, but the quicker you get over it.' Klopp, who lives directly opposite Lallana's former home in Formby, a genteel coastal town, is 'just a cool guy', he adds. 'You see him having a fag, a smoke . . .' Before the England midfielder moved to Cheshire, his young son Arthur would often wave at the tall, blond neighbour across the road, shouting 'Klopp, Klopp!', imitating the coach's touchline fist pump. And Klopp would unfailingly smile back with a wave, to the obvious delight of Lallana Jr.

Smiles and fist pumps got harder to come by after the turn of the year, however. A horrific run of only two wins in twelve games in January and February saw the team crash out of both domestic cup competitions. Fans awoke from their title dreams to fears of losing out on the Champions League altogether.

The selection of weakened teams for the League Cup and FA Cup was 'the only way to approach such a spell of games, to get through it and the one that follows after', Krawietz insists. Getting used to a fixture calendar with no time off at Christmas has been one of the main challenges for the Germans. 'It makes a huge difference. You can't appreciate how big if you haven't experienced it yourself. It's really not funny.'

As embarrassing and disappointing as the exits at the hands of Southampton and Championship side Wolverhampton Wanderers were, they also offered up the opportunity to go away for a warm-weather training camp in La Manga in mid-February. After experiencing their first campaign without a winter break, the German coaching staff had come to fully appreciate the almost absurd physical and mental burden of non-stop football. LFC owners FSG agreed with Klopp that the team should have one week together in the sun to recharge their batteries each year, at the earliest opportunity.

The trip to Spain failed to have the desired effect, in the short term at least. Liverpool suffered a 3-1 defeat away to Leicester on their return to domestic duties, putting in one of the worst performances of the season. Lallana: 'The Leicester game, we lost 3-1 on a Monday night. That was a bad, bad moment. A bad result. I didn't see it coming. That game, you felt that you had let him down. You know, you tried your best, but your best was just nowhere near good enough that night. Yes, [the Europa League final v] Seville was disappointing, but . . . they were fantastic, they have won it three years on the bounce. I will never get over that, but I can understand why they beat us, if that makes sense. Leicester was just really poor.'

Klopp, well-versed in navigating crises, pleaded for perspective in those difficult weeks. 'We have to believe in the long-term project. Nobody wants to hear it but losing is a part of football,' he said. 'I don't care about all this talk about reaching a low point. I love driving to training in the morning and working with the boys, even if it's difficult. You can't give up because you're losing. You have to try again in the next game.' He and the team had fallen victim to their own success in the autumn, to an extent. Liverpool's winning streak, at full strength, had created the expectation of more of the same to come, but in the absence of the injured Coutinho, and Mané, who played for his country at the Africa Cup of Nations, the lack of depth up front was laid bare in brutal fashion.

The team's cause wasn't helped by a foul air of fatalism that engulfed Merseyside like a rank Victorian pea-souper. Liverpool, as a club, had to rid itself of the attitude that these types of losses were somehow 'part of the DNA', Klopp told lfc.tv after the season. He sees changing that defeatist mindset into a much more confident outlook as one of the main objectives for the coming years. He wants a bad result to be shrugged off as a blip, rather than being seen as a harbinger of inevitable doom. 'This club and maybe this city have to learn to take moments like that for what they are. Don't make them bigger. In life, you cannot ignore the negative things that have happened. If you can change them, change them: if you can't change them, ignore them. That's how it is. It's all about the reaction. In football, and in life. If you get up in the morning and the first hour is bad, does that mean you go back to bed? No, it means let's try another one.'

After reaching a kind of nadir at the King Power stadium, Liverpool's form recovered sufficiently to secure fourth spot, with an angst-laden opening half against Middlesbrough at Anfield on the last day of the season eventually turning into a deluge of goals.

Liverpool director Mike Gordon describes the 3-0 win as 'one of the happiest moments' of his tenure. 'Finishing in the top four, with this group that had worked so hard for it, with my partners John [W. Henry] and Tom [Werner] in attendance, being able to celebrate with Jürgen and his staff . . . you feel this happiness, to the core. It was really great.'

But in hindsight, are there any regrets about a big opportunity missed? With the notable exceptions of Chelsea and Tottenham, all the big teams underperformed in one way or another. Could Liverpool have sneaked the league with one or two useful signings in the January transfer window?

'I would regret it if we hadn't tried to bring in additional players,' says Gordon, having pondered the question very carefully. 'But we clearly did try. The availability of players in the January window is continuing to diminish, it's now an anomaly if you're able to do something. I don't know what it would have meant for the rest of the season if we had found the right solution. Would we have strengthened? Nobody knows. But showing discipline [in the transfer market] and staying true to your principles is really important, and that's one of the reasons we didn't add to the squad. We tried. And the same goes for all windows. We look for any advantage and opportunity to improve.'

Krawietz says the coaching staff don't look back in anger, either. 'Are we upset [about not doing better]? No. Football is a learning system, a game of constant development. We wanted to give the many young players we had a chance, an outlook. Financially, I don't know if it would have been possible [to make additions in January]. Spending big money is not exciting. We have wonderful guys in prospect. Trent Alexander-Arnold, Ben Woodburn, Ovie Ejaria. We want them to have the opportunity to train with us, and evaluate their true potential. We knew we didn't have any

international games. We played a great first half of the
season, with many great games. In January, we fell into a
hole, a little bit. We got a little unlucky with refereeing
decisions, and unfortunately we had some injuries. You
have to factor them in but we are, of course, trying to avoid
them as best we can. We have made outstanding progress
in terms of the players' athletic development, and we're
exhausting all possibilities of injury prevention. Luck and
bad luck will always be a factor, though. Would we have
liked to win the title? Obviously. That's what we're fighting
for. But we don't go around second-guessing past decisions
and bemoaning missed opportunities. We take it on board
and stash it in our rucksack of experience. And then we
make all of that part of future deliberations.'

For 2017–18, when Liverpool will once again play twice a
week, juggling the demands of the Premier League and
European football, players, coaching staff and the club
hierarchy all agree that an expanded, enhanced squad is
mandatory. 'We understand the importance of depth,' says
Gordon. 'It's not just about the best XI. It's a very long season
in an especially demanding sport, and many of the best
players also play for their countries in addition to club football.
We need reinforcements. That lesson has become particularly
acute and relevant over the last season and a half.'

Lallana's assessment is equally candid. 'I think we need
three, four more top, top players. No disrespect to our younger
lads. But if you look at our bench in the last three months,
there are a lot of young players on there. When you look at
Chelsea's bench, they bring on [Cesc] Fàbregas, Willian. At
times, just having them on the bench is enough to keep the
players in the starting XI on their toes, subconsciously that is.

Another three, four top, top players keeps everyone on their toes, raises the quality that bit more. And it is only going to help us. Europe next year, you are going to need more bodies. We've had a lot of injuries this year as well. There is no shying away from the fact that we need four or five more top players and the manager understands all that. [Jürgen] is not stupid. He rotated his players at Dortmund quite a lot, for big games. If he has got the squad and he has got the trust in the players, he will rotate. I have no doubt about that.'

Krawietz agrees. 'Rotation and a broad squad is the only way forward, that's the conclusion. We need to be in a position to be competitive in all competitions and rotate at a high level of quality.'

One interesting theory put forward by English newspapers was that Liverpool could have done with a more orthodox striker to function as a lighthouse during those dark days of January and February, an expert in forcing the issue when the football's not freeflowing. Somebody you can boot the ball up to when your legs and mind can't make their way up the pitch themselves any more.

Krawietz is unconvinced. 'I won't deny that's an option that could work. I don't want to sound naive, either. But staying true to your own ideas is important. You have to adapt them, of course, but you're still trying to succeed with it. You can't say: "Listen, lads, up until now we played one way, but now it's January, and bad weather, and windy, you should forget all of that. Let's play shit football and see how we get on!" No. It can't work like that. There are many ways of winning a game. Sometimes you have to defend all the time, leave one guy up front and win 1-0 with a counterattack. That can happen. But we won't make that a strategy going into a game or start bending our own rules. We have our own principles of playing, and we don't give them up. We stick to the plan.'

But why does the plan work so much better against the best Premier League sides than it does against those situated in the mid-table or the bottom? Liverpool would have won a mini-league consisting of the top six (five wins, five draws) but they lost to Burnley, Bournemouth, Hull City, Swansea and Crystal Palace, and drew against Sunderland and Bournemouth. Is there an argument that Klopp's football could do with taking its foot off the gas for everyday commutes to less glamorous destinations and learn to get there with a lower rpm?

Lallana, interestingly, thinks the opposite is true. He blames LFC's troubles in nominally easier games on the subconscious belief that 80 or 90 per cent of effort will suffice. 'It's a mentality thing. When your mentality is right, your tactical play is going to be better. The manager knows that, and it's not something that you can change overnight. But he is emphasising that we need to get that right. As soon as we get it right for those games, I feel we can go on and achieve something really special.'

'If Adam says that, we're one step closer to illumination,' Krawietz notes contentedly when the midfielder's thoughts are put to him. 'I think it's only human to think [about smaller games] that way. Even for journalists, I guess. You go to Aston Villa v Burnley, you think, "okay, let's check it out". But for Chelsea v Spurs, your pencil is sharpened. Nevertheless, it must be forbidden to think that way as a player. We fight against that. We reiterate that the same number of points is at stake, regardless of the opposition.

What we want is a consistently high energy. Having the ball and dominating the rhythm of the game comes with a certain level of intensity. That's just how it is. Ninety minutes of football are a) unhealthy and b) exhausting. That won't change.'

Former Liverpool defender and Sky football expert Jamie Carragher points the finger in a different direction. 'I don't think it is an attitude problem with Liverpool. You would never criticise a Jürgen Klopp team for its attitude. Every team can have an off day now and again, of course, but I think it is tactical. Liverpool's game suits playing against teams who build from the back, who push up their full-backs and leave spaces to attack in counter-attacks. If the possession stats are 50–50, that means Liverpool have less of a chance of getting caught on the counter-attack. That's what seems to happen in the smaller games. The best two ways of scoring for the smaller teams are set-pieces and counter-attacks. And that's where Liverpool are really weak. You have to address that, you have to change. Liverpool need to buy a couple of taller players. Even in attacking positions, I think. You can also keep your full-backs back a bit more in some games, to make yourself less vulnerable on counter-attacks. Maybe sometimes it makes sense to let smaller teams have the ball. Because they're not set up for it.'

Klopp's staff are very aware that set-pieces have been an Achilles' heel. Krawietz, in particular, is full of admiration for the high calibre of dead-ball routines he has encountered in England. 'It's a tradition,' he says. 'You can look all the way down to the fourth division here, and you'll find real choreographies, really good ideas. Every team has at least one guy who delivers really dangerous balls and five, six giant guys who'll attack the ball fearlessly, with pace and unbelievable power. The Premier League is full of these players. They might not be stars but their individual quality is incredible. In addition, the goalkeeper is not protected as much as in Germany. You touch his shirt in the Bundesliga – it's a foul. Here, that's part of the warm-up. And then all hell breaks loose in the box. We understand that. We understand the importance of defending dead-balls. On top of that, we spend a lot of time thinking about ways to avoid facing set-pieces in the first place.'

The smaller sides' ability to import an element of chaos into the game with simple but hugely effective measures might also explain why Klopp's Liverpool have found it easier, paradoxically, to play against the better teams. Their game follows more recognisable patterns, a code that the coaching staff are able to decipher and disrupt. Their programmes are hackable, because they are programmes. The much more random operating mode of the teams below the Champions League places, on the other hand, necessitate a much more spontaneous and muscular response that Liverpool have not always mustered.

'As I said earlier: we are learning. All the time. It's a process,' Krawietz emphasises. 'You might feel as if you're in control but then the referee blows for a free-kick in the eighty-ninth minute and the stadium is on fire and the pitch becomes a sauna. You can't ignore that. It's a huge challenge for us but we are ready to deal with it, ready to prepare for it, ready to adjust to it. We know full well that we'll fall flat on our faces if we don't.'

13. SMALL-SCREEN TRIUMPHS

In the years after Germany's win at the 1990 World Cup, commercial TV started taking an ever greater interest in the nation's favourite sport. SAT1 revolutionised the way Bundesliga highlights were broadcast on Saturday evening by devoting as much airtime to the spectacle surrounding the pitch – players' girlfriends in the VIP seats, angry club presidents, managers' sweaty armpits – as to the matches themselves.

The docu-soap format of their *ran* show fed off the whole gamut of human emotions, providing storylines and entertainment that didn't depend on the football being particularly riveting. *ran*'s emphasis on showbiz elements involuntarily impacted on the protagonists, and even more so on the way football was being talked and thought about in Germany. Winners won because they wanted it more, losers lost because . . . that's what losers do, isn't it? Players and coaches who didn't bark grandiose, adrenalin-drenched statements into the SAT1 microphones after the final whistle were seen as weak and hapless. They obviously lacked the confidence and mettle needed to thrive in an alpha-male world.

The game's transformation from the rather uncouth pastime of the proletariat and other undesirables into a mass-market-compatible commodity pumped millions of Deutsche Marks into a sport that had never been profitable before. The deliberate dumbing down of its presentation came at a heavy price, however: *ran*'s version of the Bundesliga had a hollow centre. This was football de-footballised, not concerned with the how, only with the wow. The wanton lack of any attempt at serious public analysis contributed to clubs and the national team getting left hopelessly behind over the following decade. It lacked the vocabulary and technical framework for introspection.

'I ask myself if anyone really wants to get valid information about the game in Germany,' Klopp told *Der Spiegel* in November 2004. 'Does anyone want to hear, "They shouldn't have run more, they should have run in a smarter way"? I doubt that. Maybe on [some niche channel], in a programme for exotics.' The time was indeed ripe for a change by then. Within eighteen months, the Mainz coach would emerge as the main beneficiary of football's analytical void and as a catalyst for a transformation, winning awards for his punditry and the acclaim of Franz Beckenbauer. But, unbeknown to most, his overnight success on the box had been a very long time in the making.

SAT1, the first privately owned TV station in Germany, had started broadcasting in 1985. Their regional office for the state of Rhineland-Palatinate was based in the capital, Mainz, and SAT1 CEO Jürgen Doetz was on the FSV board. When the club was once again struggling to pay their bills ahead of the 1990–91 season, the TV boss stepped in to help out. He made SAT1 Mainz's shirt sponsor.

Not long later, one of the club's players started an internship at the regional sports desk: Klopp. 'He was already the loudest guy in the team, a world champion in talking,' says Martin Quast. 'Doetz said to him: "Kloppo, if this thing with football doesn't work out for you, I'll make you director of communications at SAT1. No problem."' Doetz was quite serious. SAT1 was still a small start-up channel at the time. Only a minority of people with cable connections were able to watch the programmes. Rhineland-Palatinate's tiny regional sports department was housed in a couple of metal containers attached to an office building. It was staffed by a band of freelancers on fixed-term contracts, and a changing array of students and school-leavers eager to learn the trade. Klopp, who was always worried that his low-paying career could come to an end if Mainz were relegated to the semi-pro third division, jumped at the chance to test himself in the new medium after training and between his sports science lectures at Frankfurt University.

One day, the presenter of the 'Wir im Südwesten' Thursday evening sports section announced to viewers a feature on the Röschinger sisters from Bad Vilbel, the two most successful snowboarders from the Hesse region – 'by Jürgen Klopp'. He had interviewed them, done the voice over, and edited the piece. Quast remembers it as being quite good, packed with interesting details and asides. 'He was talented, and he had fun. He later said: "If football hadn't worked out, I probably would have ended up being a sports reporter."'

On 15 May 1992, Klopp's knack of talking himself into (and out of) tight spots delivered a genuine coup. One of the closest title races in the history of the Bundesliga had left league leaders Eintracht Frankfurt tied on points with VfB Stuttgart and Borussia Dortmund ahead of the final day of the 1991–92 season. Frankfurt's much-admired 'Fußball 2000' team of Andy Möller, Uwe Bein and Anthony Yeboah had a superior goal difference to their rivals. A win at relegated Hansa Rostock would deliver their first league title since 1959.

Eintracht coach Dragoslav 'Stepi' Stepanović had ordered a media blackout on the day Frankfurt flew off to the north-east of the country. Everybody tried to speak to the immensely quotable Serbian ahead of the season's dramatic conclusion, but Stepanović refused to do any interviews. SAT1 sent intern Klopp as their secret weapon, the guy who always got things done somehow. He had played under Stepanović at Rot-Weiß Frankfurt a few years earlier but his key contact proved to be Mainz 05 teammate Hendrik Weiß, whose mother worked as the press officer for Frankfurt airport. She allowed Klopp through security and all the way to the doors of the plane, where he intercepted Stepanović and obtained the only pre-match interview in the whole of Germany. 'That was his outstanding journalistic achievement,' says Quast. For Eintracht, the outcome was far less happy, however. They went on to lose 2-1 at Rostock in controversial circumstances the next day, opening the door for an unexpected triumph by VfB Stuttgart.

Everyday life inside the SAT1 container compound was not quite as stirring. As the youngest member of the editorial team, Klopp's main task consisted of procuring a regular supply of cola-bottle sweets from the nearby wholesale store. 'He was happy to do that, but he said that we should make it a game. Everything was a competition with Kloppo,' says Quast, one of the sports editors on the desk. 'We sat there and threw cola-bottles into each other's mouths from three, four metres, best of ten. The loser had to buy everyone else a beer. These scenes come to my mind when I see him now, being the coach of Liverpool.'

After his formal internship of three months was up, Klopp kept returning to the containers to do the odd feature, or simply hang out with ex-colleagues who had become close friends. One of them was Martin Schwalb, a young handball player. He later won the handball Champions League in 2013 as coach of HSV Hamburg.

Klopp's witticisms in the 'flash interviews' right after the final whistle as a player and coach at Mainz made him a favourite with the reporters from DSF, the commercial channel broadcasting Bundesliga 2 in Germany. In September 2001, Klopp and Ralf Rangnick – who were first and second in the second division with Mainz and Hannover 96 respectively – were invited to the station's *Viererkette* talkshow to discuss the crisis in German football with 1974 World Cup winner Paul Breitner, one of the most prominent pundits. Following on from the excruciatingly bad Euro 2000 tournament, the national team was in acute danger of missing out on the 2002 World Cup after a 0-0 draw in the first leg of their play-off against Ukraine.

Breitner at first was reluctant to share the stage with Klopp and Rangnick, says *Viererkette*'s producer Jörg Krause. They were second division coaches. What did they know about the national team's problems? The former Bayern Munich and Real Madrid midfielder in the end agreed to sit down with these relative nobodies. Prompted by presenter Rudi Brückner, Breitner suggested a flurry of partially contradictory reasons for Germany's fall from grace, including too much pressure from the German FA, an absence of long-term planning by the authorities, and a weak mentality in the *Nationalmannschaft* squad. Rangnick, bruised by his infamous appearance on *ZDF Sportstudio* three years earlier, when he had pontificated on the virtues of zonal marking and earned the scorn of Bundesliga colleagues and of the tabloid media in return, was careful not to contradict the authoritatively suited-and-booted Breitner too openly. Klopp, thirty-four, clean-shaven in a student's uniform of a brown polo shirt, khaki trousers and trainers, could hardly fit his rangy frame into the leather armchairs. He was also deferential to begin with, even a little nervous. His voice, lightly charged with a Swabian lilt, betrayed a sense of unease in the opening exchanges.

Rangnick (in a grey shirt over a black T-shirt, like an off-duty graphic designer) and Klopp grew in confidence as the programme progressed. Between them, they quietly pinpointed the two most important reasons for German football's problems: weaknesses in youth development and the failure to understand football as a collective game. 'Young players get ten hours a week training, and the club caretaker decides if they're allowed on the pitch during school holidays,' said Rangnick. 'We have to get them to train thirty, forty hours per week.' He went on to explain that young professional players, too, expected to keep on learning their trade, instructed by coaches 'who put on proper training sessions, treat them respectfully, point out mistakes and aim to develop them further'.

Breitner protested that Bundesliga pros were, by definition, so good that they didn't need to be taught the ins and outs of the game – least of all by self-appointed modernisers and upstarts who had never played at the highest level themselves. 'I don't want to put anybody down here,' he said, feigning diplomacy, 'but the individual quality [of the best players] is so high that many coaches won't be able to keep up. You learn from looking at your peers at this level, like I learned from looking at Franz [Beckenbauer] and Gerd [Müller] in training [at Bayern]. You don't need a coach to explain to you why you only hit the outside of the post from twenty metres rather than the inside, or point out a small technical mistake.'

Klopp was moved to object forcefully, but an advertising break spared Breitner the ignominy of getting contradicted live on TV by a bespectacled, profusely side-burned coach from Mainz 05. When the cameras returned, Klopp smiled beatifically and joked that the shooting technique in Bundesliga 2 wasn't 'that bad'. 'In any case,' he added, 'what's much more interesting is improving the team as a whole, preparing each player so that the combination of them all functions well.' Klopp readily admitted that he hadn't been the best of players, more of a second division warhorse. But why should that disqualify him as a coach? 'Yes: I teach them more than I ever knew,' he cheerily agreed with Brückner.

Getting Mainz to the Bundesliga and to a mid-table position without significant investment in the squad and almost no first division experience within the team proved Klopp's point a few years later. Ever the teacher, he seemed to enjoy talking about his ideas and methods in public almost as much as coaching the players. 'Most things I learned in life I learned because somebody gave me the right advice in the right moment, without me asking,' he would tell the *Sunday Times* years later. 'I was a lucky guy. I met some nice people in the beginning: teachers, coaches. And of course my parents and all that stuff. I think that's what life should be: that you make your own experiences and whether they're good or bad you share them – so somebody else can avoid the same mistakes. That's how I think football should work too.'

Unlike one or two of his young, iconoclastic contemporaries, he buffered his mission statements with self-lacerating humour, carefully downplaying his own importance and stressing that of his fellow travellers on the journey towards a faster, more joined-up game. Klopp's enthusiastic dissemination of the new doctrine never crossed the line into self-aggrandisement or open disrespect to the establishment.

Dieter Gruschwitz, the former sports editor of state broadcaster ZDF, enjoyed talking football with Klopp over a beer in a pub not far from the FSV coach's house in the suburb of Gonsenheim. 'We would see each other all the time and started to become friendly,' Gruschwitz says. 'Klopp had this very winning, captivating way of talking to people. So I started thinking . . .'

ZDF owned the rights to the upcoming 2005 Confederations Cup, held in Germany as a test run for the 2006 World Cup. Their (friendly) rivals from ARD had the award-winning duo of presenter Gerhard Delling and expert Günter Netzer, the former Germany international playmaker, whose acerbic wit and sometimes toe-curling honesty had brought a measure of relief during the mostly inept performances of the national team at the turn of the century and beyond. Netzer, a youthful rebel turned aristocratic elder statesman – if he had lived in Britain, he'd long have been Lord Netzer or at least Sir Günter – served as a visual reminder of much better, glorious times and looked forever personally insulted by crude attempts at football that violated his heightened aesthetic sensibilities.

ZDF's big name for the two major tournaments on German soil was Franz Beckenbauer. But as head of the organising committee, he would only be available for a few broadcasts. Gruschwitz: 'Beckenbauer aside, we didn't have anyone at Netzer's level. And we couldn't pretend to either. The only way out was to do things very differently. With a referee as an expert – Urs Meier. With Jürgen Klopp, as an analyst, on a new tool: a touchscreen that combined video images and the ability to draw on top of the frames. And to do everything in front of a live audience in Berlin.'

Klopp didn't have to deliberate too long about the offer: 'Gruschwitz came into my living room and asked whether I could see myself working as an analyst. All I thought was "I can watch World Cup games!" Then I asked whether my two sons could get free tickets. He said yes. That made the decision easy.'

The ZDF executive had one grave concern, however: 'I knew he could analyse a game, there was no question of that. But would the TV viewers believe a second division coach talking about international football at the highest level? Was the gap between Mainz and Brazil not too wide?'

Beckenbauer seemed to think so. 'Der Kaiser' looked a little suspicious and bemused by Klopp's studio deliberations at first. 'But after the second and third time, he said: "Wow, it's really great, the way he explains the game,"' says Gruschwitz. 'A couple of matches into the Confed Cup, Beckenbauer was totally in awe of Jürgen.' 'Beckenbauer's approval was like getting knighted for Klopp. If the Kaiser thought he knew his stuff – he really knew his stuff,' says Jan Doehling, who worked as an editor on the shows.

There had been no trial run. 'Jürgen just got up and did it. He's a natural,' says Gruschwitz. 'Straightaway no one was worried any more whether he would connect with the audience. He could tell you about football without being moralistic, or hurtful, or being too scientific. Even a grandma understood what he was on about. At a World Cup, you don't just get the football supporters, entire families sit in front of the television, including many people who don't really care that much about football in day-to-day life. He was perfect at getting the game's intricacies across to those people, too, in an informative and entertaining way. That's who he is. It's a gift of his, his great talent.'

Klopp's smart-casual attire befitted his choice of words. Interesting little observations – a left-back was too deep, a midfielder had switched off – were packaged into unfussy, un-TV-like language that didn't sound put on or patronising, but simply like a clued-up guy talking to his friends in the pub. Twenty-five million people were watching, but you wouldn't have known it from Klopp's demeanour. Gruschwitz: 'He had a lightness, an assuredness and an authenticity that immediately won over everyone – including Pelé, who was an occasional guest on the World Cup shows. He took a shine to him as well.'

What came across best, Gruschwitz adds, was the young coach's passion for the game. The combination of his antics on the touchline at Mainz and the enthusiasm with which he could talk about Costa Rica's formation showed the viewer that 'here was someone who really lived for the sport'.

Klopp's relaxed yet substantive style of punditry 'changed the way we looked at football in the [ZDF] office', the former TV boss reveals. Doehling agrees: 'He taught us how to analyse. The first and most important thing I learned from him was that there was not one absolute truth. You don't look at a clip and only see one particular thing. It's open to interpretation. He also said he had to see a game two or three times, that you couldn't really see things clearly the first time around. You might see that there's something wrong. But you won't see *what* is wrong immediately. That helped me overcome my own fears. You can feel your way in. You can become skilled. You can adopt a routine, you can develop. It's a process, a craft. Not a question of "you either can do it or you can't". That's what I tell my colleagues today: video analysis is not wizardry. You won't be able to do it straightaway. But you can learn it.'

ZDF's compelling offering, the perfect complement to Germany's unexpectedly exciting run to the semi-final, the fantastic weather and the nation-wide party atmosphere essentially taught viewers the same lesson. Decades of the kind of armchair psychology that involved vague musings about one team's nervousness and another one's mental strength, which had been the preserve of top footballers, was swept aside in favour of factual expositions of the little, tangible, readily identifiable things that could make all the difference. 'Klopp continues something that didn't exist before his debut at the Confederations Cup: he simply talks about what's happening on the pitch,' wrote Christoph Biermann, one of the first German football journalists to cover tactics extensively, in *Süddeutsche Zeitung*. Klopp's focus on the machinations of a match closely reflected his footballing education under Wolfgang Frank. 'Everybody used to play man marking,' he said. 'The question: "Would this goal have gone in if that guy hadn't lost his one-v-one?" was relevant then. Today, there is zonal marking, but many questions still relate to the concept from back then. We should talk less about players, more about the game.'

Viewers felt emancipated. They were given the tools to think about football in a far less abstract manner. By championing insight over status and experience, ZDF's coverage democratised the public discourse about the game. If a second division coach could persuade Beckenbauer to take note, maybe everybody could.

But it went much further than that. Klopp's success on the World Cup touchscreen changed age-old perceptions about the basic requirements of coaching, Doehling believes. 'If you had played first division football, you were meant to be a first division coach. If you had played second division, you were a second division coach. That's how it used to be. What Klopp did was to demonstrate – in front of millions of people – that knowledge could be gathered, that coaching was a trade that could be learned. You serve your apprenticeship, you graduate, you get to the next level, you take another exam. You develop, step by step, until you become a coach; by virtue of what you can do on the sidelines, not what you have done on the pitch. A whole generation of young managers who had never made it to the highest levels as players was inspired by that.'

Klopp's results with Mainz and his triumphant stint as the *'Fernseh-Bundestrainer'* (Gruschwitz), TV's national manager, opened the door for even more anonymous coaches to succeed in the Bundesliga. Men like Thomas Tuchel and Julian Nagelsmann realised that their limited practical skills were not necessarily a bar to progress. Clubs, too, felt emboldened to look past prior playing experience.

On the whole, the World Cup shook German football out of its staidness and strengthened the hand of reformers. Within weeks, many of Jürgen Klinsmann's most controversial methods – more proactive goalkeepers who enabled a higher defensive line, core-stability exercises with American fitness coaches, a strong emphasis on personality development and help from sports psychologists – became accepted practice in the top flight.

For Klopp, working with ZDF offered an opportunity to closely study the games of international teams who were rarely seen on German screens. The time on stage also delivered a couple of other valuable lessons to him. Firstly, he recognised the potential of the new visual aid and was quick to utilise the touchscreen technology for his own work at Mainz. 'That was his second question in 2005: "Can I use that on my laptop in the changing room?"' says Doehling. 'The first question was: "Where is the loo?" Klopp's clever like that. He thinks about things. He's not one of these coaches concerned with lining his pockets as much as possible in a short space of time. He cared about making things work, about getting the maximum out of it. Maximum fun, maximum use. He wanted to learn. No one really knew the possibilities of that system at the time, no one was working with anything like that in the Bundesliga. We made it possible for him, and it was great for us that he used it during the season, because that made him better when it came to doing it on TV at the World Cup. It was Peter Krawietz's job to put together the clips for use at half-time or in pre-match team-talks at Mainz.'

A second realisation concerned the power of the crowd to push a team to its limits and beyond. Like many experts, Klopp had been sceptical about the *Nationalmannschaft*'s chances at both competitions, Doehling says. 'Everyone knew that Klinsmann wasn't the world's best tactician, and we all underestimated the influence of [his assistant] Löw. Germany's success came as a surprise. I suspect that Klopp picked up on the difference motivation made. Motivation had carried the team past the odd tactical weakness and the odd deficiency in tradecraft. Klopp had always played with the support of the crowd, but at the World Cup he saw how the crowd could really play the game. That's what happened against Poland. [Substitute] David Odonkor, surfing on a wave of euphoria, put in the cross of his life [to decide the game]. Pure spirit. You could see the same thing when Klopp whipped up the crowd for Liverpool's game against Borussia Dortmund. The Anfield crowd carried the inferior team that night. They even scored the decisive goal for them.'

Gruschwitz sounds as if he's about to well up reminiscing about those summers working with Klopp. 'He was an incredible team player,' he says. 'He didn't just turn up shortly before we went on air but got involved hours before, giving his thoughts. There were long discussions about what should be shown; he left nothing to chance. On days off, we went out to eat together. He wanted to be a genuine part of the team. He truly was one of us. There's no other way to put it.'

That is not to say that there wasn't the occasional ill-tempered outburst. The day before the World Cup, an angry Klopp kicked a hole in one of the paper walls at the studio reception and shouted at people as the system had failed. 'But that was okay, no problem,' says Doehling. 'He did that once because he wanted things to work well. Outstandingly well. He always said: "Let us put something together that works outstandingly well tomorrow." He was interested in the job, not in looking good on television. So he lost it once, and everybody ran a bit quicker as a result, and the damn thing worked, and everybody had a good time. And Klopp mentioned these people's name on air, the ones who worked behind the scenes, to make them feel part of it. "Mike, roll the tape," he'd say. The bosses told him that wasn't the done thing on TV. But Klopp didn't care.'

His popularity approached the levels of the national team and their coaches in those days. People stopped to take pictures with him and asked for autographs outside the stadium in Berlin. German FA president Dr Theo Zwanziger joked at a get-together of Bavarian coaches that his aunt had told him to appoint Klopp – the guest of honour at the event – as the next *Bundestrainer*.

At Mainz's first off-season friendly after the tournament, the stadium announcer in the minuscule Bad Göging ground introduced Klopp as 'that famous guy from television' and asked him whether he'd continue working in football. The

Mainz coach warily acknowledged that people needed 'a mug' to represent and symbolise the club but railed against being the sole focus of attention. Eyewitnesses at the game reported that many fans wanted Klopp's autograph. But nobody asked any of the Mainz players for theirs.

The ZDF coverage of the World Cup won the German TV award for best sports programme in November 2006. Klopp's contract with the channel was extended to Euro 2008. Two years later, he won the German TV award again, for his punditry at the 2010 World Cup for RTL. More coveted trophies would follow not long after.

14. 60,000 TEARS

Mainz 2007–08

In May 2007, a few weeks after Jürgen Klopp's first relegation as player or manager, he was running a youth hostel in rural Thuringia, right in the former 'death strip' of the inner-German border. Temporarily. Klopp had taken the Mainz 05 squad to a similar, no-mod-cons hut for a team-building exercise four years earlier, in the run-up to the promotion-winning 2003–04 season. The back-to-the-woods trip with the 2007–08 players was supposed to have the same positive effect and outcome.

Thirty men were sleeping on bunkbeds in one room. The days started at six in the morning, with Klopp blaring out German *Schlager* classic 'Guten Morgen, Sonnenschein' on a boom box. 'I'll never forget that,' says Neven Subotić, even though he can't remember quite whether that aural pleasure consisted of the original acoustic version by Greek singer Nana Mouskouri or Ireen Sheer's cover from 1989. 'We were totally shot every morning. But we had to get up, make our own breakfast; prepare lunch and dinner. Peel the carrots, that sort of thing. [Midfielder] Milorad Peković was injured. He couldn't join in the exercises – games in the woods where we had to cooperate to achieve a common goal – so he was the "mother" of the group: he stirred the gigantic soup pot for a few hours until everybody came back in for lunch.'

A stone's throw from the modest lodgings, a section of the wired fence, a guard tower and a museum reminded the visitors of Germany's division. 'The players, as much as they're susceptible to such associations, could understand the choice of the team base as symbolic: Mainz 05 are keen to cross the same border that they recently had crossed in the opposite direction due to relegation,' wrote *Die Welt*. In physical terms, Klopp joked, they had already 'crossed the line' during the training camp.

The forty-year-old saw the step back down as an opportunity to hone his tradecraft. 'In the second division, the playing style – the work of the coaching staff – has a much bigger influence on success and failure than in the Bundesliga, where individual quality by the opposition can ruin the best plan,' he said. A good run, *Die Welt* suspected, 'might enable Klopp to cross a personal line [to a new club] afterwards'.

The city of Mainz kept the faith. All 15,000 season tickets were sold, and locally based credit company Coface agreed to buy the naming rights to the modern, first-class football stadium (cost €60m, capacity 35,000) that the council were planning to build on a brownfield site, a five-minute drive outside town, not far from Klopp's domicile in Gonsenheim.

Three of last season's best performers – Manuel Friedrich, Leon Andreasen, Mohamed Zidan – did not go down with

Mainz. There was an almost entirely new midfield in Miroslav Karhan, the Slovakian international and former VfL Wolfsburg stalwart, Tim Hoogland (Schalke) and Daniel Gunkel (Energie Cottbus), and a teenage centre-back who by playing with the coolness of a much older head quickly made himself indispensable: Subotić. Having had a taster of first-team action in the Bundesliga denouement against Bayern, the Serbian rapidly improved to play thirty-three out of thirty-four games in the second division, making very few mistakes. He credits Klopp's careful but not always gentle handling of him for his good performances.

'Klopp has a very broad spectrum,' he says. 'He could be very harsh. I thought: "Hey, this guy is screaming at me. Chill, dude." But I probably needed it then. He'd be better placed to judge that. That side of him was old school. A hard school. But there were also these moments where he came up to me and asked: "Everything okay? If there's anything you need, let us know. We want to help. We're there for you. We want you to play well." He was like a colleague in that sense, not like a superior. I felt I could approach him. That took away a lot of my insecurities. I was a teenager, on my own on a different continent, in a flat, getting paid to play football. Ridiculous, really. It was a very strange situation. The last thing you need is a coach telling you: "You have to perform now, otherwise you'll be gone next year." I was given time to grow.'

The decibel levels might have gone up from time to time at the training ground, but Klopp's censure would always be directed at the player, not the person, Subotić explains. 'Getting shouted at was always like hearing an alarm bell for me. I knew I had made a mistake then; that I could have done better. It was always respectful, never the kind of insults you'd sometimes hear from Bundesliga 2 coaches. That stuff made you piss yourself with laughter.'

Watching many training sessions from the sidelines, Doehling didn't notice anything out of the ordinary in the way Klopp addressed his players. 'But if you saw how they reacted to him during the game, you immediately realised that he had found a way to communicate with them in the dressing room. You cannot treat everybody the same way. That's social intelligence: you have to gauge how you have to talk to somebody. I'm sure he sometimes hit the wrong note but, mostly, he got it spot on. These stories that you hear of some other top coaches – they don't talk to players for weeks or kill them in front of the group – you never heard of Kloppo. He didn't play those games.'

'With Klopp, it was all very humane,' Subotić confirms. 'I knew these things were said for a reason, for motivation, as a means to an end to get to the top. Klopp had it both: the rough and the smooth.'

There were two different sides to his Mainz team, too, that year. 05 started the season well, with a 4-1 win against Koblenz. Three defeats against the league's better teams – bogey side Greuther Fürth (3-0), Kickers Offenbach (2-0), coached by Klopp's mentor Wolfgang Frank, and TSG Hoffenheim (1-0), an expensive ensemble under the expert direction of Ralf Rangnick – in the following seven matches offered a glimpse of possible shortcomings, however. They went into the winter break in second place on thirty-one points, a whisker ahead of Köln, Freiburg (both on thirty), Fürth (twenty-nine) and 1860 (twenty-eight).

On 9 January 2008, Klopp's mobile phone rang. Unknown number. Heidel, sitting next to him at the winter training camp hotel in Costa Ballena, Spain, immediately knew it was important: 'Klopp sat up straight, nodding "yes, yes" like a good boy.' Bayern's general manager Uli Hoeness was on the line. The most powerful man in German football was calling Mainz 05, was calling Klopp. The record title-holders were in the market for a new manager to succeed veteran Ottmar Hitzfeld for the next season. Hoeness: 'We're looking at a big, international option, and at a smaller, German one. You are the German option. Can you see yourself coming here in the case we decide to go for the German option?' 'We can talk about it,' Klopp replied demurely.

'I told him he had to go for it,' Heidel says. 'I said: you're absolutely crazy if you don't do it.' Their relationship was so close, he adds, that Klopp always confided in him about approaches from other clubs. Bayern's advances were hugely alluring. Klopp was aware he was only second choice for the Allianz Arena role, a back-up contender if the Bavarians' complex, highly secret negotiations with the unknown international heavyweight were to fail. But that didn't do much to lessen his disappointment when Hoeness phoned again with bad news two days later. 'We have decided to go with the other Jürgen,' the Bayern patriarch declared. 'What other Jürgen?' Klopp replied, dumbfounded for a moment. He had thought Germany's biggest club had worked on reeling in a foreign super-coach. But 'the big, international option', it now transpired, was California-based Jürgen Klinsmann, the former German national team manager. Heidel: 'Hoeness added that Bayern's choice was 'quite similar to you, Mr Klopp'. He didn't really admit it but I could see that it was a blow for him. He was a little hurt.' Mainz reporter Reinhard Rehberg later recalled Klopp taking training in a bad mood that day. 'But he quickly got over it,' Heidel says. 'Klopp's very good at overcoming setbacks.'

As much as the Mainz coach was irked by losing out to his namesake and fellow Swabian, this was a defeat that turned into a win before too long. Hoeness' public confirmation that Klopp, the second division coach who had presided over relegation seven months earlier, had been a very serious alternative for the most glamorous job in German club football 'amounted to his beatification', *Frankfurter Rundschau* wrote. 'He wrongly used to get reduced to being a motivational guru, with talent for PR honed as a TV expert. His selection as a contender to succeed Hitzfeld, by itself, has directed attention towards other qualities [of his].' 'Bayern thinking about me was an honour,' Klopp said.

In Heidel's view, 'Bayern didn't have the balls' to opt for a coach without a top football background, ignoring the fact that Klopp was a much more experienced manager than Klinsmann at the time. 'I was talked into trying out the Klinsmann adventure,' a rueful Hoeness later admitted, 'we signed up the wrong Jürgen. We all know that was a big mistake.' Klinsmann's reformist agenda, while 'convincing on paper' (Hoeness), failed to win over the team and the club due to a severe lack of tactical detail. The former VfB Stuttgart striker was fired ten months into his first season, with Bayern in danger of missing out on the Champions League.

In the second half of the season, Mainz's results continued to be decent, without ever building up any real momentum. Klopp's men were easily the best footballing side behind Borussia Mönchengladbach and Hoffenheim, patient on the ball and technically much more sophisticated than the vast majority of opponents. That superiority, unfortunately, translated into a bit of complacency. Games that should have been won were drawn. Games that should have been drawn were lost.

But Mainz never lost touch with the promotion places. And Klopp's marketability was not damaged by his team's underwhelming run either. On the contrary: encouraged by Bayern's earlier enquiry, a number of Bundesliga clubs thought that FSV's uncertain prospects might make it easier for them to prise Klopp away from his natural habitat at the Bruchweg. 1. FC Köln, coached by the idiosyncratic Christoph Daum – who had missed out on getting appointed as Germany's national team coach after failing a drugs test in October 2000 – got in touch. Heidel: 'Things were always open and transparent between us. Kloppo said to me: "I'm going to meet with [Köln sporting director Michael] Meier. I don't really want to go there but I want to hear what they'll say. I want you to know that." I said, "No problem. Go, and listen to him. You're only going to find out how good life is for you at Mainz. But please make sure no one finds out."' Just like Heidel predicted, the secret rendezvous at one of Meier's relatives' homes in Frankfurt came to nothing. Klopp had left the meeting deeply unimpressed. (Köln, a promotion rival, later brazenly complained that Mainz were trying to seed discord by falsely claiming that Meier had contacted Klopp, which led to Heidel making the failed approach public.)

That February, a senior delegation from Hamburger SV – sporting director Dietmar 'Didi' Beiersdorfer, CEO Bernd Hoffmann and marketing and communications director Katja Kraus – also visited the Klopps at their house in Gonsenheim. Over pizza, cake and coffee, the northerners probed the Mainz coach's willingness and suitability to take over at one of the historic greats of the league for the next season. Hoffmann and Kraus were certain that they had found their man, a young, energetic manager who would make the fairly expensively put-together side a championship contender once more. Beiersdorfer was less sure. Could a club of HSV's stature appoint a coach nicknamed 'Kloppo', the former defender wondered in Klopp's presence. 'You have a sporting director called Didi, don't you?' the Mainz coach shot back with a smile.

Scouts were instructed to discreetly watch Klopp (and other candidates for the post, such as Bruno Labbadia, and Dutchmen Fred Rutten and Martin Jol) at work. The results were collected in a dossier and presented at a board meeting. Klopp's coaching and brand of football were much commended but HSV's spies also noted that he had been unshaven, late for training, dressed in shabby jeans and talked rudely to the local sports reporters.

'A typical Hamburg story,' says Heidel, shaking his head. 'Holes in his trousers, they said. This rumour that he was late for training? Jürgen Klopp was never late for training, not once in all those years. And they said he was brash with journalists. Yes, he was. He had known these guys for fifteen years, was on first-name terms with all of them. They had already slaughtered him as a player. They were like friends. When he said to them "you've fucking lost your mind" in a press conference, with no camera running, they knew exactly how to take that. But those guys from Hamburg were like: "Oh my God, he can't go to Hamburg. Impossible."'

Klopp was not pleased when the scout's findings were relayed to him. 'Those who work in football should have known how I work, and the way I look. You don't have to put a scout on the touchline for that. That's amateurish,' he said to *Bild am Sonntag* in 2011. 'It hurt me to hear I wasn't punctual. There's probably no one more punctual than me. Unshaven – only that much was true. I called Mr Beiersdorfer and said: "If you're still interested in me – I decline. Please never call me again."'

Hamburg's failure to land Klopp, the most promising German coach of his generation, has become part of German football folklore, the Bundesliga's version of Decca Records boss Dick Rowe turning down the Beatles. Whether Klopp's casual demeanour really did tip the scales against him is somewhat doubtful, however. A former HSV official who was directly involved in the search privately insists that Jol – who had led Tottenham Hotspur to fifth place in 2006–07 and was out of contract – had simply been considered the better choice by a majority on the board, irrespective of Klopp's sartorial shortcomings. Either way, after initial success under Jol, who made it to the UEFA Cup and the DFB Pokal semi-finals in 2008–09, HSV soon came to regret their decision. 'We might not have reached the Champions League final with Klopp in charge but I'm sure the club would have been in a better position now,' a mournful Hoffmann told *Sport-Bild* in 2014. Beiersdorfer, too, admitted to having 'a few sleepless nights' over missing out on Klopp. By the time he left Dortmund in 2015, Hamburger SV had appointed twelve different coaches (including Labbadia for two spells), traded stints in Europe for regular relegation battles and turned into a byword for serial incompetence.

Back in April 2008, media chatter about Klopp's unresolved future – he was out of contract in June – was reaching a crescendo. Mainz ultras were so worried the coach might leave that they disobeyed a pre-season agreement not to call him over to their section for the customary 'Humba' singing session after the final whistle. Klopp had wanted the players to be the sole focus of the crowd's praise. But after the 3-0 win in the derby against SV Wehen Wiesbaden on matchday 27, the chant 'Jürgen to the fence' went out, again and again, until finally the coach relented. The show of adulation from the terraces was an obvious attempt to sway Klopp's decision. 'I understand their cause, that's why I agreed [to sing with them],' he said, adding that he was well aware of the strength of feeling in the stadium.

A couple of days later, Klopp told reporters that he had made up his mind. He would sign a new contract with the club – if they were promoted back to the Bundesliga for the next season. 'We've had plenty of emotional discussions and agreed that failure to go up would be a good time to part ways,' he said. The newspapers recorded Klopp's declaration as 'a clear "Jein"' to his club – it was both a '*Ja*' and a '*Nein*'. The immediate outlook for Mainz, however, remained sunny, with a high chance of stubbles. With three games to go, FSV were second in the table, two points ahead of Hoffenheim.

Klopp demanded that the crowd at the Bruchweg made themselves heard in the home game against Alemannia Aachen. Mainz's chief 'propagandist' (*Süddeutsche Zeitung*) got his wish. The atmosphere was crackling under the floodlights, the stadium 'louder than it had been for a long time', Rehberg and Karn wrote. But it was one of those games. 05 created plenty of opportunities and took none. An Aachen counter-attack fifteen minutes from time found the

net. Mainz fell down to fourth spot. Three days hence, after
the injury-ravaged team had slumped to a 2-0 defeat at 1. FC
Köln, they were in the same place. There was still hope, still
a possibility. Third-place Hoffenheim had to lose or draw
against Greuther Fürth, Mainz had to beat St Pauli. Klopp's
last game as FSV coach finished with a 5-1 win over the self-
styled punk football club from Hamburg. Hoffenheim had
beaten Fürth 5-0. They went up to the Bundesliga, Mainz
stayed down. Eighteen years of Jürgen Klopp at the
Bruchweg – just under eleven as a player, just over seven as a
manager – ended in silent desperation, football's worst feeling:
total powerlessness. Nothing he or his team could have done
that day would have been enough to lift Mainz to the
Bundesliga and prolong the liaison between club and coach.

Twenty thousand fans in the stadium stood up to serenade
the sobbing manager with 'You'll Never Walk Alone'. Klopp
only managed two thirds of the lap of honour before
breaking down in tears. He escaped to the dressing room,
sprinting across the pitch, away from the sadness. 'For
Mainz, it's the beginning of a new world that we never
wished for,' Heidel said. 'If it was up to me, we could have
continued working together for another ten years.'

Thirty thousand people turned up on Gutenbergplatz
the following Friday evening to give Klopp a second,
happier, send-off. Earlier that day, he had been unveiled as
the new Dortmund coach. Back in his football hometown,
Klopp's voice crumbled under the weight of tears.
'Everything I am, everything I can do, you have made
possible for me – everything,' he stuttered on stage.

'People were crying,' says Subotić. 'Grown-ups, women,
children. Toddlers who didn't understand what was going

on were crying, too, because everybody was crying. The farewell do showed once more how many emotions he stirred up, how he brought people together. I had seen him celebrating, I had seen him lost in thoughts before. But this was a different side to him. It wasn't sorrow, it was affirmative. His life's work was being recognised. He was the star of the team, the main protagonist of an extraordinary story. That night, you could see how much he meant to the whole city. It was very touching, unforgettable.'

'In terms of saying goodbye, Kloppo's number one in the world ranking,' Heidel says proudly. 'I don't know of any coach getting that kind of send-off, with a stage in the city centre, and 30,000 people, all there for one single person. Usually, coaches are fired at the end. Or they leave, somehow, with a bouquet of flowers in their hands. At Mainz, it was very dramatic, with a huge banner: "Thank you, Kloppo". It was the most emotional farewell imaginable. And I don't say that just because I organised it.'

Klopp assured the 05 faithful that he would never forget them and happily celebrate Mainz's promotion in the city square – from a different vantage point – next season. He thanked Christian Heidel and Harald Strutz for 'giving me the chance to choose my dream vocation', then castigated an unnamed local paper for printing critical statements 'by some morons' about his successor, Norwegian Jørn Andersen, and threatened that 'they won't get any interviews any more'. It might have sounded churlish and off-colour to the uninitiated, but the forty-year-old merely reiterated a point he had stressed over and over to reporters in the past. A club of Mainz's stature and means, he lectured on stage, could only succeed 'if everybody is pushing in the same direction, if everybody takes the giant heart of this city into their own hands when going into the stadium or watching Mainz at home to really cheer us on, to step on the gas and to support us with all their might. If we haven't learned that lesson after these eighteen years here, I don't know any more.'

Subotić remembers the evening well for a second, more personal reason. In the midst of the sentimental festivities, Klopp cornered him, to lay the groundwork for the defender's move to Dortmund with him. 'He had ten million things to think about that night, so I thought the last thing he needs is me to congratulate him [on his beautiful farewell] and ask: "How's it going, how do you feel?" But he came up to me and said: "If you want to go somewhere else one day, call me before." There were 30,000 people there, his family, friends, all the players he had ever coached and everybody's grandmother on top of that but he took a few minutes to talk to me. That felt amazing. I will never forget that moment, especially under these circumstances. He had already had a drink. That's fair to say. He deserved to. It wasn't a memorial ceremony but a celebration. And it changed my life for ever.'

15. IN TIMES OF FADING LIGHT

Dortmund 2013–2015

Borussia Dortmund had pushed the best team in Europe extremely close in the 2013 Champions League final at Wembley. And yet, the twenty-five-point gap behind Bayern Munich at the end of the Bundesliga campaign posed an uncomfortable question. Why had Dortmund lost so much ground domestically? Two 1-1 draws in the league games against the treble winners suggested an inability to beat the lesser lights had been the main issue. Klopp and his coaching staff believed the answer was not change, but more of the same: better and faster. 'We want to build a new pressing machine,' he announced, before heading into the summer holidays.

Mario Götze joined up with Pep Guardiola, Robert Lewandowski didn't just yet. Bayern's unwillingness to make a suitable offer to sign the Polish forward before his contract at the Signal Iduna Park was due to expire in 2014 chilled relations between the clubs to well below freezing. Matthias Sammer, the former Borussia icon turned Bayern sporting director, attracted special opprobrium. 'If I were him, I'd thank God that someone had the idea of hiring me every time I walked into the Bayern training ground,' Klopp said. 'I don't know if Bayern would have got one fewer point without Sammer.'

'Jürgen has got this ability to nail the head on the head,' Dortmund's CEO Hans-Joachim Watzke says. 'When he said that thing about Sammer, 200 people told me: "Finally, somebody dared to say it." Without fear of any recriminations. He doesn't care, he's fearless in these moments. He doesn't care what others might say. Sometimes he goes too far, but that makes him even more likeable in my view.'

The unresolved Lewandowski situation did 'zap some of our energy that year', Watzke confesses, however, even if the player himself was scarcely affected by the unedifying tug of war. He would notch up twenty goals in the season, winning his first *Torjägerkanone*, the trophy for the leading goal-scorer.

An emphatic, brilliantly engineered counter-attack victory (4-2) over newly arrived Bayern coach Pep Guardiola in the German Super Cup held out hope for another exciting season. And Klopp's pressing machine 2.0, with shiny add-ons Pierre-Emerick Aubameyang and Henrikh Mkhitaryan, was soon pumping out wins in the Bundesliga, too. Dortmund were only one point off the Bavarians at the top of the table eleven games in.

Then the mood darkened. A loss to Wolfsburg brought attention to a lengthy injury list. Was the Klopp team's high-intensity, super-athletic playing style to blame, one journalist enquired in the pre-match press conference for Bayern's visit to Westphalia. 'A wretched question,' the coach sneered on the podium, with barely controlled rage, 'we are a team that gives their everything, you've all praised us for that countless times.' Klopp pointed to a more convoluted fixture list – half a dozen of his players had become German internationals – as well as to increased pressure as reasons for the physical complaints. 'Bayern have injuries, too, but they can compensate them better,' he added. The harsh tone of his reply left little doubt that he was personally offended by the suggestion. It was also dangerous, threatening the team's morale, he stressed: 'The moment your coverage manages to take away the players' appetite for movement, we'll automatically face tough times.'

And the tough times were coming. Bayern's 3-0 win at the Signal Iduna Park, a game that swung on the opener by substitute Mario Götze, of all people, ushered in a spell of poor results. Dortmund finished a 'shit final third of the year' (Klopp) in a disappointing fourth spot, twelve points behind leaders Bayern, who had a game in hand.

Dortmund missed too many chances and had problems creating openings against teams who were happy to sit deep. It became clearer than ever before that as tactical trailblazers, they had made a rod for their own back: even newly promoted teams who were individually not on the same page had learned to adopt smart counter-measures. 'You play the same ball you've played the year before, but the opponents are there. You play the ball again. And they're there again,' Subotić recounts. 'It's always harder if you're forced to play through opponents rather than to concentrate on the transition,' says Hummels. 'We found it tough going.'

An increasingly curt and irritated Klopp refused to believe that the problem was 'a lack of plan B', as countless media observers claimed. The issue, he insisted, lay with application, not strategy. And the injuries? Simply bad luck. Or maybe not? Some wondered whether the rot had set in due to the departure of athletics coach Oliver Bartlett in 2012. But that explanation is not corroborated by any of the players or BVB officials who contributed to this book.

Unsurprisingly, 'things got a little disquiet in training', says Hermann Hummels. 'It wasn't always nice. But it's normal. Being with a coach for such a long time is like being in a relationship. There is tension. It's unavoidable.'

There were arguments about tactics, too. Some of the more experienced players were possibly a little less receptive to the 'run, run' mantra than they had been before. Subotić: 'When you get the feeling as a player that you've already achieved something, that you have a bit of experience, you suddenly don't want to say yes to everything any more. I guess that's human nature. If it was necessary, Klopp upped the volume. He shook us up a bit, to wake us up. Not by saying: "You have to play something different, boys, it'll be tough." No, he went up to a player and slapped him across the face. You think: "Oh, he might slap him back." That was a rougher move. But you knew he didn't do it to let off steam but to up the intensity. We understood. And the aggression was always contained. Never uncontained, that wouldn't have worked.'

'There were confrontations, and it sometimes became personal. But that's okay, too,' says Gündoğan. 'The important thing is to agree on a joint way forward afterwards, so that there's no lingering resentment. With Kloppo, there were never any open questions left at the end. We always managed to get everything out of the way.'

There was a popular misconception that the Borussia manager was the players' best friend at the time, Watzke explains. 'Jürgen was more than a coach for everyone. But not a brother. Not the caring, slightly older colleague either. He commanded great authority, and it wasn't always as matey as it looked. He could change his tune. He's unpredictable. He can explode from one moment to the next, smashing everything to pieces. But he always managed to keep everything under wraps somehow.'

Dortmund, like all the best families, kept their squabbles in-house. Disagreements never went beyond the changing room, there was no falling out. The giddy, teenage love-affair between Klopp and his players of the previous years had evolved into a more regular relationship, with customary ups and downs, but the mutual adoration itself was still very much there. Klopp treated his men like a strict father would, making life uncomfortable to bring out their best, not to shift blame on to them or vent his frustrations. He never briefed against his players to the media, never played games. 'It was always about football. And everyone knew exactly where they stood with him,' says Subotić.

The coach's deep, personal connection with the supporters remained strong, too. When BVB ultra Jan-Henrik Gruszecki approached Klopp with a plea to auction off one his baseball caps in support of a crowd-funded film about Borussia's founding father Franz Jacobi, he refused, flat-out. 'But then he immediately said: "We can do much better than that. I'll give you a whole day,"' Gruszecki says. 'We "sold" him to Dortmund's biggest employers for a signing session and made €20,000, which covered a tenth of the budget.'

Watzke: 'One of the reasons we got so much out of our players was an extraordinary bond between the players and the club, and between the manager and the players. I know this might sound like a cliché but we were an extremely tight-knit group. All these players coming back to us is evidence of that. They didn't experience that combination of joy and familiarity, that backing and fairness anywhere else.' Şahin and Kagawa both returned to play for Klopp at BVB after unsuccessful spells abroad, and even Götze re-signed with Borussia in 2016, having almost made the move to join up with Klopp in Liverpool. 'He threw the odd tantrum but he was also very sensitive and understanding of his players. Everybody appreciated that.'

Buvac, responsible for the tactical details, continued to enjoy broad support, too. Klopp's right-hand man was forced to coach the team for two Champions League group games when his superior was punished with a touchline ban by UEFA. An irate Klopp had screamed 'How many more mistakes do you want to make? One more and it's fifteen today!' right into the face of the fourth official, almost dislocating his jaw in anger. Banished from the touchline, he watched the rest of the game on television in the office of the stadium green-keeper. 'My face would have warranted a five-game ban,' he ruefully admitted later, 'I don't recognise myself sometimes on the touchline.' 'We were all happy for Chucky,' says Subotić, 'he's not an extrovert, and the opposite of egotistical. It was cool that he was addressing us, for a change. We had all learned to love him.' Klopp's partial absence notwithstanding, Dortmund qualified in the top spot from another tough Champions League group (Arsenal, Napoli, Marseille).

During the winter break, they nearly pulled off an even more stunning victory. Making good use of his friendship with Real Madrid president Florentino Pérez, Watzke almost thwarted Lewandowski's Bayern move, encouraging Los Merengues to sign him up instead. Lewandowski wavered but in the end decided to honour his pre-contract agreement with Bayern. His move to the Allianz Arena for the beginning of the 2014–15 season was confirmed on 4 January 2014.

Hummels' return from injury for the second half of the season – the defender had hurt his knee at the World Cup – immediately brought more stability at the back. Since Dortmund's game was predicated on hitting opponents on the counter-attack, the ability to keep a clean sheet was absolutely vital. When other teams took the lead and could afford to sit back, BVB found it hard to find the space their explosive transitions still needed. A steady improvement in domestic results and progress to the Champions League quarter-finals vindicated Klopp's conviction that only details had been missing before Christmas. The team had enough individual and collective quality to finish second behind Bayern, make it to the DFB Pokal final and push Real Madrid very hard in the Champions League. The Spaniards just edged the tie 3-2 on aggregate, having won the first leg in Madrid 3-0. 'You're out, aren't you?' ZDF presenter Jochen Breyer had asked Klopp after the final whistle at the Bernabéu. 'How could anyone pay me for doing my job if I stood here, saying that we're out already?' Klopp replied, shaking his head in disbelief.

'My friend Florentino Pérez still gets sweaty palms thinking about that first half in Dortmund [in the second leg],' Watzke smiles. 'It was an outstanding quarter-final. On the whole, we hadn't become worse, Bayern had simply become better. Maybe 3 or 5 per cent was missing but it was okay. And we should have won the cup final, of course. That Hummels goal . . .'

A depleted Bayern had lined up with five at the back in Berlin to frustrate Dortmund. Klopp's men had destroyed Guardiola's men 3-0 at the Allianz Arena a month earlier, they were the in-form team; they had the momentum. An attritional game was heading for stalemate when on sixty-five minutes Mats Hummels saw his header cleared from well behind the line by Danté. The referee waved play on, and Bayern scored two goals in extra-time to escape with the trophy in tow.

'It was tragic,' says Watzke. 'A catastrophic refereeing mistake. There's no other word for it. The ball was thirty-five centimetres behind the line. I don't know another coach who's been this unlucky with refereeing decisions in big finals.'

Players, officials and the guests at the post-match banquet were so down that Klopp held one of his 'state of the nation' speeches, decreeing that everybody had to party, in recognition of a team that had given their all over the course of ten months and dealt with all problems – including 'the worst injury crisis in the history of football' – in 'exemplary fashion'. 'We would be crazy if we overthrew everything,' he added, in reference to the media's misgivings about his regime, Dortmund's consistency should not be taken for granted. 'Others don't even celebrate when they win something. But Borussia must be different. If anyone tells me "what a shame" tonight, I'll punch the glass out of their hands without so much as a word. Please enjoy the evening and don't worry: we will definitely be back. This is a team with a strong backbone. It doesn't matter who they take from us, we'll bring in new guys and everything will be all right.'

Everything wasn't all right, however. Far from it. Two months into the 2014–15 season, Dortmund just wouldn't stop losing games in the league. Five defeats on the trot between late September and early November pulled them down to seventeenth spot – eighteen months after contesting European club football's biggest prize, Klopp's men were heading for Bundesliga 2. No Dortmund team had ever had a worse start to a campaign, not even the side that got relegated in 1971–72. 'It's a brutal, shitty situation, crazy,' an exasperated Klopp said after the latest defeat, 2-1 in Munich. Dortmund had seven points on the board, seventeen fewer than Bayern. Every half-decent domestic result, every win in the Champions League, was taken as a clue that the nightmare was about to end. But it never did. At the halfway mark, Borussia's points tally was fifteen, and they were still seventeenth, in the drop zone. Only goal difference separated them from the worst team in the league, SC Freiburg. Bayern were on forty-five points. 'We're left looking like complete morons here,' Klopp said, 'and we deserve it.'

As a fresh-faced, occasionally clean-shaven Mainz coach in the second division, Klopp had told his players and the German public that success on the pitch had to be 'explainable, in other words: the result of objectively beneficial, repeatable endeavour'. The reasons for the disastrous lack of success in his seventh year at BVB proved much harder to ascertain. Because football is a low-scoring game, the distinction between symptoms and ills, between mere bad luck and underlying deficits often isn't an easy one to make. Did they miss so many chances due to a strength-sapping playing style that seemed 'stuck in eternal adolescence', as *Süddeutsche Zeitung* wondered? The contrast with Guardiola's Bayern, who had perfected their own version of pressing to the point that they ran less than anybody else in Germany, was especially painful. Even Watzke noted Dortmund's 'less economic, more laborious' way of playing.

A little more than two years later, officials, players and the people closest to Klopp have identified a bucket-load of explanations for the crash, some of which are conflicting. All of them, however, continue to have trouble comprehending the sheer ferocity of the slump. 'It's still an enigma to me,' says Watzke.

Robert Lewandowski's departure might not have been the single most important factor but it was something akin to the trigger for the recession. More than anyone else in the team, he could combine hard work with efficiency in front of goal. 'It was obvious that we couldn't hold on to him any more,' says Dickel. 'Jürgen knew about the club's financial possibilities, we weren't able or willing to pay somebody €15m in wages a season. I was hoping that Robert would go somewhere else but everyone knew that he would go. We only could have kept him by selling the town hall.' Dortmund had done well to find successors for previous high-profile departures before but the Polish forward proved literally irreplaceable. New Italian striker Ciro Immobile, a €18m buy from Torino, had problems adjusting to life in the Ruhr area and to Klopp's system. 'He couldn't quite make it work in its full complexity yet,' Krawietz says. 'Certain automatisms' – synced-up, instinctive moves – 'got lost.'

Why didn't they field Aubameyang in the centre-forward role instead? The pacy Gabon international was a different kind of striker, much less physical than Lewandowski, granted, but he could certainly score goals, as the two subsequent seasons under Klopp's successor Thomas Tuchel proved. Aubameyang would find the net seventy-nine times in all competitions for BVB playing through the middle.

'It was our first grave misjudgement,' Watzke says. 'In the summer of 2014, all of us – especially Jürgen, who was in charge of the line-up – were convinced that Aubameyang was not a number 9. Otherwise, we wouldn't have needed to bother with Immobile at all. Things would probably have worked out differently, it would have been easier. And so on, and so on. As it was, 2014–15 was a shit season.'

'Aubameyang is doing very well [as a striker] now,' Krawietz agrees. 'You could already see back then that he could get you goals, that he was perhaps better suited to playing as a centre-forward than on the wing, as he had problems tracking back. But on the wing is where we needed him at the time.' The loss of Lewandowski was indicative of a wider dilemma the club faced, he adds. 'On the pitch, we had grown much faster than we had developed in terms of our finances. We had young players and players that were bought for little money, who performed so well, at home and in Europe, that they were all of a sudden in a completely different league in terms of their value. The club couldn't keep them, they had to sell them. But at the same time, it was obvious that replacements of equal quality were not available, due to the finances. That led to a situation where we could only ever aim to keep our level, we couldn't actually improve. Bayern, meanwhile, were investing smartly and kept developing. Expectations at Dortmund had grown so much that we weren't able to live up to it any more.'

Watzke concurs with that macro-analysis. 'The team that we had in 2012 and 2013 would have probably gone on to make the next step if Bayern hadn't started shooting at us this much,' he says. 'That's for sure. We keep rolling the stone up the hill each year, like Sisyphus. But you can't complain, you have to live with that if you're Borussia Dortmund. I'd love to be as comfortable financially as Bayern. Unfortunately we weren't able to grow as much economically in the short space of time as would have been necessary to keep the team together.'

Watzke and Krawietz also describe Germany's World Cup win in Brazil as damaging for Borussia that season. The late arrival of the quintet of internationals – Mats Hummels, Roman Weidenfeller, Matthias Ginter, Kevin Großkreutz and Erik Durm – caused disruption, the coaching staff felt. Krawietz: 'They had a three-week holiday, which was too short, and wanted to be playing again, without having the physical foundation. That ultimately led to us not having the usual confidence in our system. On top of that, systemic errors crept into our defensive game. We were extremely vulnerable to counter-attacks. We played games where we enjoyed plenty of possession, created good chances but lost 1-0 or 2-0 because of a couple of counter-attacks. During a season, you have to rely on the basics from pre-season working in some kind of way. We realised: bloody hell, we really need to change a few things here. We needed to practise our movement on the wing and crossing, maybe for two, three weeks. No time. Or the strikers' movement through the middle, to make sure that for once somebody was going to the damn near post. All we could do is mention that in the video sessions. But when it came to a trained impulse, to *Gegenpressing*, we weren't able to get that across to make it stick.'

Psychologically, Dortmund's national team contingent seemed exhausted. 'Hummels aside, the other four hadn't played in Brazil but they were right in the middle of this huge hype,' Krawietz remembers. Watzke: 'To put it mildly, the World Cup didn't play a productive role. Our players had hardly featured in Brazil, but they all felt like world champions.'

Hummels' plight was more mundane, he says. 'I came back injured and never really recovered my form that season. As captain, my job was to lead by example but I was too busy trying to get to grips with my own problems. I couldn't be a leader and talk to others from a position of strength because I was playing crap football myself.'

The outspoken centre-back's customary calmness on the ball and his positive influence on his teammates were badly missed, which was yet another reason for Borussia's fragility. A wave of injuries, coupled with a fixture list that made neither extensive rotation nor detailed tactical repairs possible exacerbated the crisis. Dortmund's problems didn't add up – they multiplied.

'We kept losing games in the exact same way, over and over again,' says Krawietz. 'That starts to hurt your confidence as a team after a while. In the Champions League we did okay, we qualified for the knockout rounds, but that only made us wonder if we were lacking the right attitude in the league. You're in a spiral, going round in circles, going down. And we didn't manage to get out of it.'

'We all went crazy,' Dickel says. 'It was impossible to understand. We had 74 per cent possession, fifteen shots on goal, they had two shots on goal and we lost 1-0. Week after week. It was horrible.' Hummels: 'We came away thinking "we weren't that bad" after every game. You still glance at third spot in the table and you work out your points difference. You think: "We can't go down." And then you're bottom of the table with half the season gone and you realise you're in the shit, up to your neck.'

Klopp was visibly affected by the disastrous run. His job was not in danger – Watzke had given him a cast-iron guarantee – but he felt personally responsible. 'The whole thing drained him. He was in the driving seat, he took it to heart that we were not going in the right direction for some strange reason. I remember looking at him thinking: "Oh, he looks really tired and stressed," ' Subotić recalls.

'As a guy who's so emotionally involved, you knew it was hitting him very hard,' says Hummels. A coach, like any other leading figure, must project self-confidence in order to instil confidence in others. But how can you keep faith with your ideas if results continue to go the wrong way?

'Your head is full of questions,' says Krawietz. 'Is it your fault? Is it the team's? What shall we do? It was an extremely shitty situation. More than anyone could really bear. You don't wish that kind of spell on your worst enemy. It was unbelievably exhausting, unbelievably depressing. And at the same time, you're not really allowed to show your emotions. The coaching staff have to be the first ones out there the next morning, saying: "Come on, guys, we go again. Here's what we've done wrong. Two, three details, and we're back on track."'

Watzke suggests that sections of the team were maybe not as willing to adhere to Klopp's ideology as before. 'That total, complete euphoria and passion we had had in the first year wasn't there any more. That devotion. The players had become older. And richer, and more successful. Perhaps they wanted to show that things could work at a lower pace. Which is not how Jürgen operates.'

Krawietz sees it a little differently. 'It wouldn't be fair on the players and their characters to say they weren't willing or able to play *Gegenpressing* any more. I can see why some might say that. But it was much more complex than that. Don't get me wrong: we certainly didn't get everything right, not every decision that we made and that Jürgen was responsible for worked out. But it wasn't as simple as that.'

Nevertheless, the negative results bred dissent. Some of the more senior players were not shy about making their thoughts known, exchanges were rather fraught at times. And yet, the residual bond and trust between Klopp and his players was strong enough to keep things from breaking completely apart, just about. 'Whenever he went too far in an argument, he was magnanimous enough to realise that and to apologise, either to the player concerned or in front of the whole team,' says Hummels. 'With him, it always came from the heart. That won him our respect, in a huge way. He didn't just say things, he truly felt them. He also could put himself in the shoes of a player. He'd say to me: "Mats, I know how you feel, I was a player myself. How can I punish you for that?" when we disagreed on something.'

By contrast, the increasingly embattled coach did not accept outsiders casting doubts on his tactics. He scolded a local reporter for suggesting that other teams might have 'found out' his side and developed strategies for negating Borussia's high-pressing style. 'I'm not looking for a fight, so I will even answer the stupid questions,' he shot back acidly, before going on to claim that Dortmund's plight was all down to their own failings. 'If you say we've been "found out", what does that say about the work of opposition coaches for the last few years?' he added. 'Were they unable to see what our game is?' He maintained that 'pace cannot be deciphered', that winning games was merely a question of Dortmund playing to their own abilities again. Talking up the progress of the opposition in a league that had blunted his original concept by making it the new orthodoxy would have been counter-productive, he felt. Success was always a question of reconnecting with your own, inherent strengths. The right answer was already there. It just needed to be properly implemented. 'The problem isn't our problem but the solution is,' he insisted. Keeping calm when confronted by a chorus of criticism was tough, especially since he considered most of the negativity unwarranted.

'Jürgen felt he was getting a raw deal [from the media]. That was his problem,' says Schneck. 'He felt they didn't treat him right and so he made up his mind: "They have no idea, they need to fill their papers somehow." I remember a game we lost, I think away to Wolfsburg. He went hell for leather in the press conference. I said to him: "Mate, that was really shitty. That kind of tone was inappropriate." He goes: "Leave it out, you were one of those shit journos, too." He was irascible, not diplomatic at all. Of course, he later said: "Sorry, I didn't mean it that way." And I knew him too well to be offended. But his relationship with the media got more and more fractured.'

Klopp had changed, TV reporters and writers noticed. The lightness and self-deprecating humour that used to season his bluntness were gone, replaced by latent passive aggression, the natural mindset of under-pressure football coaches the world over. Vis-à-vis friends and colleagues, however, people whose loyalty Klopp was assured of, he remained his own dependable self. It would have been easy, for example, in view of Dortmund's tumble down the table, to cancel a talk on motivation that his old buddy Sven Müller had organised in Frankfurt in December 2014 but Klopp had given his word to Müller and turned up.

'To see someone feeling this bad, sitting here and laughing, that's motivating, isn't it?' he told the audience in the hotel ballroom. Throwing in the towel in the Bundesliga was not on his mind, he added. 'I'm either all in or not at all. Right now, I'm Borussia Dortmund. It's like a marriage, there are good and bad times. Why should the sun be shining out of my ass all the time?' Klopp claimed he was a better coach 'than in 2012, when we were champions. The problem is: that's not reflected in the table.'

'I hear people say that Klopp's no longer himself, that success has gone to his head and so on, but it's all nonsense,' Quast says. 'Those who really know him are aware that not a word of that is true.' Quast remembers meeting Klopp at the launch of a new car model at the Opel factory in Rüsselsheim, at the height of Dortmund's relegation worries that season. 'I had just had some very bad news about my mother's brain tumour, it was benign but beyond treatment.

Her doctor had also looked after Wolfgang Frank. Klopp says to me: "What's wrong? You don't look good." So I told him the whole story.' Quast stops, apologising for the tears in his eyes. 'Hundreds of Opel employees were there, looking down at him from five storeys. A thousand cameras. Loads of people who all want a piece of Klopp. We were standing a little to the side but I saw that everybody was staring at us, the photographers went "click, click, click". Klopp didn't care about all of that. He just hugged me really tight, not saying a word. It wasn't necessary.'

Looking back, Dortmund were saved by the bell(s) of Christmas, ringing in a six-week respite. 'I don't think we ever thought "this is the end of us" but it was so good to get to the winter break,' Subotić says. Klopp insisted that the Christmas party should go ahead as planned. There was a time to work and a time to have fun, he told Lünschermann, and without the latter, one couldn't do the former. 'He was very good at compartmentalising things,' the BVB team manager says. Krawietz remembers feeling acutely relieved after losing against Bremen, the last game in 2014: 'We knew we couldn't get any lower. We would spend six weeks in the relegation zone but we had at last a chance to regenerate and practise a few things without the pressure of competitive football. By that time, we had a pretty good idea what was missing in our game: some systematic processes that we hadn't been able to practise. It was clear that with a bit of rest for the legs and the heads, we'd be able to get it right, that this team could function again, straightaway. That's exactly what happened.'

Not exactly. Or at least, not straightaway. Dortmund drew 0-0 at Leverkusen in the first game in January but then

lost 1-0 at home to ten-man Augsburg. Borussia were so bad
in their eleventh defeat of the season that the most loyal of
supporters, those on the Yellow Wall, shouted at the players
in disgust. They were in eighteenth place now. Hummels
and Weidenfeller tried their best to placate the angry fans,
talking with them for a good few minutes through the fence.
'It would be unacceptable if we didn't understand their
frustration about us being bottom after nineteen games,'
said Hummels. The famous BVB togetherness was
beginning to crack under the pressure of relegation angst.

'That was our most difficult moment, the first time I
really started fearing for the worst,' Watzke says. 'We felt as
if we were in a horror movie.' There were rumours
that Ottmar Hitzfeld and Lucien Favre had been sounded
out to come in as 'fire fighters' but the Dortmund CEO says
'it was never an option to part ways with Jürgen, even then.
Nobody thought about that for one second.'

As Krawietz had thought, the team bounced back. The
next five games were won; they shot up the table like a
belated new year's rocket. 'Play, fun, thrill: that's Borussia
Dortmund,' Klopp said after the 3-0 win in the Ruhr derby.
The slogan was borrowed from a Kinder Surprise ad and
referenced Aubameyang's and Reus' surprise goal celebration:
the Black and Yellows' dynamic duo had dressed up as
Batman and Robin on the pitch. Suddenly, qualification for
the Champions League looked feasible once more.

The official strapline for the second half of the season
was *Aufholjagd* (race to catch up). 'Klopp always used these
terms. They weren't just empty words, they were an anchor
for us,' Subotić recalls. 'People took their cue from it and we
made it real. He was brilliant at that.' Lünschermann, who

had listened to hundreds of Klopp's team talks by then, maintains that the coach continued to find words that 'got under the players' skin'. He was able 'to bring them into line, mesmerising them. After seven years, he hadn't lost his ability to squeeze out the best of people.'

'To pick yourself up and come back so strongly is not normal,' says Sven Bender. 'It was only possible because we all pulled together. The coach had to walk through that valley of shadow, and the team had to. The club made a noble decision and kept faith with the coach, that's not a given in today's football business. Usually, the coach gets axed at this point.'

His prickly demeanour outside the dressing room notwithstanding, Klopp was still good at lightening the mood with a choice bon mot. 'We had this osteopath, Heiko. A lovely guy but a little clumsy,' Gündoğan smiles. 'Usually, he was never on the pitch with the team but that one day, he was there before Kloppo came out. He'd been at the hairdressers that morning or the day before, and Kloppo looked at him and went: "Will your hairdresser finish cutting your hair tomorrow?" All the players were on the floor laughing. Perfect delivery. Even though the mood wasn't that great any more.'

The lowest low blow was yet to come. Dortmund had come away with a 2-1 defeat from the first leg against Juventus in Italy in the Champions League. 'An almost perfect result,' said Klopp. A huge fan choreography before kick-off in the Signal Iduna Park summoned the spirit of the past – Dortmund had won the European Cup against the 'Old Lady' in 1997 – and togetherness. But when Carlos Tevez scored after three minutes for the visitors, Dortmund were rendered completely helpless, dying a slow, 87-minute-long death out on the pitch. They created next to nothing and conceded two more at the back. 'Their football was almost invisible,' *Süddeutsche Zeitung* noted after the demoralising 3-0 defeat. The manner of the capitulation left no doubt. Klopp's BVB team weren't just out of Europe. They were over. '[The club] will have to bid farewell to old habits, to nostalgic glorification – and to taboos,' the Munich-based broadsheet added. 'The coach will have to give shape to a new vision of football.' *The* coach or *a* coach?

Watzke, Zorc and Klopp met in Watzke's office not long after Easter. 'We all had this feeling of trepidation,' Watzke says. 'In principle, we all knew that it would be better if we finished it. But Michael and me couldn't say it. Eventually, Jürgen said: "Listen, we're all thinking the same here, aren't we? I'll tell you now: I'll go." We had agreed that things had run their course. It wasn't a case of his effect on the team having worn off or anything like that, but seven years was a very long time. We had felt it for a while. No one had dared to admit it. And it still felt really shit to make the decision [to part ways].'

'Could we have gone on at Dortmund?' Krawietz asks rhetorically. 'Yes. In theory. But it was best that the journey ended at that precise point. In order for it to go on, some wide-ranging decisions concerning the team would have had to be made. There are always two possibilities to develop further, to freshen up things: either the coach goes or you change the team, its important pillars at least.' The BVB triumvirate weighed up that second option but it was considered financially unviable. Two league defeats, against

Bayern and Borussia Mönchengladbach, made qualification for next season's Champions League all but impossible. The club didn't have the money to sign instant game-changers or rebuild the squad. Krawietz: 'It would have needed a revolution, a changed team with a changed playing style. But wasn't it easier to change the face up front? That was absolutely the right decision for everybody, for the club and for us as well.'

The team were shocked. 'There was a message on my phone, a push mail from a magazine, breaking news. The most important story of the year,' Subotić says. 'Klopp was leaving? You couldn't even imagine anyone else doing that job, not in the way he was doing it. At first, nobody wanted to think about it. He had established the club at the very top, not by borrowing money and buying the best players in the world. But with his strategy, his philosophy. To think that he was to go at the end of the season. Nuts. All of Dortmund was in shock. Even people who didn't support the team.' The announcement hit people in the club 'with a massive bang', Lünschermann said. 'A tough pill to swallow.'

At the ad-hoc press conference on 15 April to announce his departure in the summer, Watzke was fighting back tears. 'These talks have been very hard for us, because of our special relationship, founded on trust and friendship,' he said, before hugging Klopp. 'You can rest assured of the gratitude of all of Borussia.' Klopp explained that he was no longer certain that he was 'the right coach for such an extraordinary club' and that it had been his duty to communicate those doubts to his superiors. 'One big head needed to roll – my one,' he quipped. It was all a touch melodramatic, but it struck the right chord for the Ruhr area, where people pride themselves on saying the things other Germans dare not think. A more business-like departure wouldn't have done justice to the emotional upheaval caused by the flag-bearer's resignation.

In January 2017, Watzke is still proud of 'the most classy parting of the ways in football, ever. It wasn't an act, we all did find it very hard.' A football divorce, just like a real one, is rarely amicable. This one, he insists, was. 'Throughout those seven years, we always had some differences in opinion. But it would have been a weird friendship if that hadn't been the case. Our strength was never letting any of that leak outside. We never had a personal problem. It was never acrimonious. We never left the room in a huff, with one of us slamming the door or screaming "arsehole!" and so on. That never happened. We kept on playing cards regularly, even in that last season. I don't think we'll ever have a coach like that again.' Nevertheless, the bad run left neither party unscathed. 'The three of them were so close before that, they were all hurt,' says Dickel.

Klopp and Dortmund had amassed so many happy memories together that the pain soon gave way to a sense of contentment, Schneck says. 'It was like the end of a long-term relationship, with both sides knowing there is no other way, but also remembering all the good times they have had with each other. People could still look each other in the eye after that. And since then, the relationship [between him and the club] has become warmer again.'

In the dressing room, dismay turned into a determination to give their spiritual leader a fitting send-off. 'We didn't want to believe it at first,' says Subotić. 'But we respected him so much that we thought: "If that's what he says, it must be right." Not every manager would have created the same kind of energy. Giving our all for the last few games over the next month or so was the logical thing to do for us. We were all grateful to him, from the bottom of our hearts, for all those years we'd been able to enjoy together. He improved every single player, or almost every single player. He improved the club. We wanted to pay him back for that.'

Dortmund collected thirteen points from the last six league games to squeeze into a Europa League place: seventh spot in the table. Somewhere between disappointment and just about respectable, but not the disaster it had threatened to be.

Klopp did not trust himself to give a live farewell to address the crowd at the last home game, against Werder Bremen, for fear of breaking down. In a video message, he professed his deep gratitude at having been allowed to be in charge of the club for seven years, and for 'a sack full of happy memories'. He welled up watching himself talk in the stadium. The Yellow Wall's moving tribute gave voice to the sense of indebtedness the supporters felt towards their departing tracksuit hero. 'Thank you, Jürgen', the big banner said. 'It takes years to understand how valuable single moments can be', a smaller one underneath read.

'I think Jürgen was as afraid of that last moment as the fans were,' Dickel says. 'Seventy-five thousand people in the stadium were crying, united in mourning, and in denial as well. "Jürgen Klopp was leaving the club." People didn't want to say it because saying it made it true.'

A deep run in the DFB Pokal offered one last chance of a fairy-tale ending. Borussia managed to inflict the one defeat Pep Guardiola's Bayern suffered in three years in the cup, forcing their way into the final in Berlin on penalties. 'That game in Munich did him and us a world of good,' says Gündoğan and he picks up his phone. On a shaky dressing-room video, Klopp is grinding his hips to a rap song, beer bottle in hand. One 'super-cool game', would follow, he promised.

What was supposed to be one final, passionate night away in the German capital only confirmed that this particular love affair had run its course, however, the best efforts of an army of cheerleaders notwithstanding. Dortmund failed to capitalise on an early 1-0 lead against VfL Wolfsburg and left the pitch beaten 3-1, looking like a shadow of their former, percussively powerful selves. 'Losing against Wolfsburg . . .' Gündoğan shakes his head in mild disgust. 'Really. An embarrassment. He deserved better. It just wasn't to be.'

'The pain has set in. It hurts, extremely,' Klopp said after the game. 'Every time I embrace one of my players and think that's probably the last time, the tears are coming, immediately. I have to deal with it, one thing after the other. And I'd like to do it when the cameras are off.' At the subdued after-match party, he put on a brave face. 'Winning today would have been too kitschy, too American,' Klopp claimed on the stage. Standing ovations and cheers greeted a self-aware line about his BVB legacy: 'It's not important what people think of you when you arrive, it's important what they think of you when you leave.'

As all was said and done, Klopp made sure to drop in with Borussia's ultras for one last time. A few days after his return from Berlin, he spent four hours over drinks with members of the Unity, thanking them for their support over the years and chewing the fat. 'It was a wonderful evening,' says Jan-Henrik Gruszecki. 'I vividly remember one of the more, shall we say, sturdy fans asking him: "Why do you always play Subotić? He's thin like a herring." Klopp looked at him, raised an eyebrow and said: "He's not thin, he's in good shape." He brought the house down.'

Christian Heidel believes Klopp was more wounded by the conclusion of the Dortmund chapter than he ever let on. Not because it was over – 'they all agreed the time was right, you can't keep doing such a job with as much energy as he expends for too long' – but because the club failed to truly recognise the extent of his achievements. 'He went to Dortmund and made them champions, twice, cup winners, he got them to the Champions League final. And for all of that, they hand him a bunch of flowers in front of the south stand. I'm sure he thought of the way Mainz said goodbye to him in that moment, and my guess is that he was disappointed that Dortmund didn't really make him feel that it was him who had saved that club, him who took it from near bankruptcy to a rich club, with his ideas, and his personality. They couldn't have done it without him, not even close. He turned the whole club upside down. All of that seemed a little forgotten at the end. I'm not sure he's still emotionally very connected to Borussia Dortmund. To the people, yes, to the staff, to the kit man, to the supporters, for sure. But not to the club itself any more. When we played the [Ruhr] derby [with Schalke this season], he was crossing his fingers for me. That wasn't about Schalke or Borussia Dortmund, but about rooting for me. I know that, honestly.'

Eighteen months after Klopp left the Black and Yellows, however, it's obvious that they do miss and fully appreciate him. 'He was more than a coach, he was a coach for the whole club,' Watzke says, a little wistfully. 'Jürgen was the most resplendent ambassador any club could wish for.'

Dickel agrees. Leaving aside the way BVB played football under him, he was a huge factor in improving the club's image. 'We became much more well-known around the globe. Everywhere we go, they say: "I remember, you had a crazy manager." Everywhere. But never with any negative connotations. Kloppo and BVB will forever be linked, irrespective of where he's working.'

Süddeutsche writer Röckenhaus, whose professional working relationship with Klopp had become somewhat strained towards the end of his tenure, is convinced Borussia would take him back in a heartbeat. 'You ask anyone at Dortmund, even the groundsman, who'd been angered by Klopp, perhaps. They'd take him tomorrow. That's all down to him being the person he is. He's simply charming, in his own way. He can get on your nerves, for sure, but you can easily see yourself sitting in a bus next to him, driving for hours to get to some shitty game. Or having a drink with him after a defeat. To say nothing of the partying with him. They would all love to get him back.'

16. LFC AND BEYOND

Thanks to their late flourish in May 2017, Liverpool are once again playing in the Champions League in 2017–18, for only the second time since 2010. The fantastical riches of the Premier League's TV deal – £2.76bn per season – no longer make participation in UEFA's top competition a game-changer for a club of Liverpool's size. But, FSG's Mike Gordon explains, bringing midweek floodlit nights back to Anfield is still hugely important, financially and symbolically. 'It does make a difference in terms of revenue. And in addition, it puts your club into a different category in terms of standing. Before Jürgen's arrival, there had been questions whether the club had lost some of its lustre. Our return puts that to rest. We have a manager now who's the best in the world in my mind, and we have a squad of world-class players. Naturally, they want to play in the Champions League. It's a signal to the world that we're back. It helps us entice the best people.'

But none of the new or existing players quite connects with the fanbase in the same way Klopp has done since

October 2015, Jamie Carragher feels. 'To be honest, he's the star of the team,' the former defender says. 'If it was possible, a lot of the supporters would have his name on the back of the shirt. He's the face; he's the name of the team. When you think of Liverpool you think of Jürgen Klopp. His personality is infectious. There's no act, no games with him, he's exactly the guy you see on TV. He has a laugh, he has a joke, he's full of energy. I've been to a couple of team parties. One of them was after they had lost to Crystal Palace at the end of the season, when it looked bad for fourth place. But he was high-fiveing all the players and they were all hugging each other. That relationship he has with his players is a major part of his success as a football manager. I never had a relationship like that with any manager. He's just a big, energetic man, and you want to play for him.'

The 39-year-old was able to do just that, as part of a group of recent LFC retirees drafted in to feature in Liverpool's post-season friendly away to Sydney FC in late May. 'We were winning 2-0 just before half-time, and we should have had a penalty. It had been a very long flight and I'm thinking, this is a friendly, let's just play and get home. At the break, Jürgen was absolutely killing the referee for not giving the pen though. I thought I was very, very competitive, but he was something else. That's what you need.'

There are supporters who suspect that Klopp's winning mentality is not all that's needed if Liverpool are to catch up with Manchester United, Arsenal and the petrodollar-funded Chelsea and Manchester City. Only a significant cash injection by new investors with deeper pockets than the relatively prudent Fenway Sports Group, they believe, can re-establish Liverpool as the dominant force in the English top flight. In March 2016 and again in August of the same year, news of Chinese conglomerate SinoFortone offering hundreds of millions of pounds for a stake in the club was greeted with feverish anticipation on Merseyside. But FSG have not sold. Klopp's circumspect view on a possible change of ownership might have partially informed their stance. When the link with China hit the headlines Klopp told the Americans explicitly that it was they who had his trust.

'We chose Jürgen as manager, but we're very conscious of the fact that this was a mutual decision, that he chose us, likewise,' Gordon says. 'I don't want to use the word "legitimacy", but his decision has validated everything that those of us that have been working on the football side of the club have been seeking to achieve. He has changed the atmosphere around the club, the environment, the ethos for the place and the project is in a far more positive place. That has given hope to our supporters. I don't want to be too dramatic here but it really is true. They see what we all want to achieve as a football club. I thought we were building towards that before his arrival, but there is no doubt whatsoever that it is achievable now that he is here. That hope permeates our supporters, it permeates the atmosphere during games, it permeates almost every aspect of the football side of the club. Can you tell that I like him?' Gordon adds that there was 'a relentless tendency to try and get his time and involvement and engagement in things beyond the core of his responsibilities as the manager of our club', and that Liverpool had to actively 'resist the temptation' to seek his input, for fear of spreading him too thinly.

Back in Germany, friends and former colleagues are not in the least bit surprised that the Klopp effect has started to take hold across the channel. 'I told Jürgen when he left us that Liverpool were the only club that suited him, in terms of the history and the emotions,' says Borussia Dortmund team manager Fritz Lünschermann. 'Like Dortmund, they're a blue collar club that used to be successful and has been less successful in recent years. Jürgen will take them back to the top, I'm sure. They're as crazy about football there as we are. He will awaken their passion.' Ansgar Brinkmann, too, predicts rising temperatures on Merseyside: 'Jürgen is capable of setting fire to a city.'

Maybe to a whole country, too? Klopp has told Martin Quast that he'd be 'incredibly happy' if he only coached three clubs in his career – Mainz, Dortmund and Liverpool. That would leave taking on the German national team as his next and possibly last move – in football, anyway. Quast: 'He's a born entertainer and can get people to rally around him. After Donald Trump, I'm more convinced than ever: if he wanted to run for German president, he would get elected. He would bring people together, lead the way, make people happy. He's not a statesman, not yet, anyway. But young people would take him, 100 per cent. Schalke fans excepted, perhaps.' (In Germany, the president is elected by members of parliament and representatives of the federal states. The role is largely ceremonial.)

Many in the proudly working-class city of Liverpool will be pleased to find that the Swabian's convictions echo their own. 'I wouldn't call myself very political but I'm on the left, of course. More left than the middle,' Klopp told *taz* in 2009. 'I believe in the welfare state, I don't mind paying for health insurance. I'm not privately insured, I would never vote for a party because they promised to lower the top tax rate. My political understanding is this: if I'm doing well, I want others to do well, too. If there's something I'll never do in my life it's voting for the right.'

Klopp's religious belief has instructed him to see one's time as a chance – and a duty – to help others. 'I'd say our mission is to make our own tiny piece of land a little more beautiful,' he said to *Westdeutsche Zeitung* in 2007. In a *Stern* interview a year later, he suggested life was 'about leaving better places behind. About not taking yourself too seriously. About giving your all. About loving and being loved.'

The Kop has been too starved of shiny things of late to settle for pure romance, however. Deep and lasting love will only take hold on Merseyside if Jürgen Klopp can satisfy more material aspirations. 'It will be very difficult to win the league, it's much more competitive now than when I played. But that's what he's here for, that's what he's paid for,' says Jamie Carragher. 'I would never call him a failure if he didn't – Rafael Benítez and Gérard Houllier certainly weren't failures. They won trophies. But if he were to win the league, he'd surpass them. He'd be an absolute god. An absolute god. They would put up statutes of him.'

He's not yet a hero, but Liverpudlians have already accepted him as one of their own, Carragher adds. 'They see him walking his dog in Formby and having a meal in the local pub, he reminds them of themselves. Liverpool is very down to earth. You remember who you are, you remember where you come from. He doesn't blow his own trumpet, he gets on with the job, he's passionate about football. I know he's from the Black Forest. But to me, he's a typical Scouser.'

ACKNOWLEDGEMENTS

This version of the Jürgen Klopp story owes everything to the memories, observations and anecdotes generously shared by family members, close friends and football collaborators past and present. I'm immensely grateful for the time and thoughts of Isolde Reich, Benjamin and Sebastian Frank, Peter Krawietz, Christian Heidel, Harald Strutz, Jan Doehling, Mike Gordon, Hans-Joachim 'Aki' Watzke, Martin Quast, Josef Schneck, Fritz Lünschermann, Sven Müller, Ilkay Gündogan, Neven Subotic, Sven 'Manni' Bender, Mats Hummels, Sebastian Kehl, Dietrich Weise, Matthias Sammer, Matthias Dersch, Freddie Röckenhaus, Sandro Schwarz, Jürgen Kramny, Ansgar Brinkmann, Guido Schäfer, Ramon Berndroth, Hermann Bauer, Hermann Hummels, Ulrich Rath, Hartmut 'Hardy' Rath, Dragoslav 'Stepi' Stepanović, Adam Lallana, Thomas Berthold, Michael Theis, Marcel Reif, Jonathan Northcroft, Dominic King, Simon Hughes, Axel Schubert, Norbert Neuhaus, Jamie Carragher, Steve McManaman, Horst

Dietz, Frank Kontny, Bernd Hoffmann and Reinhard Mongiatti.

Thank you Hannes Winzer, Thorsten 'Toto' Wirth, Ronald 'Ronny' Reng, Matthias Schneider, Dr. Michael Becker, Sascha Fligge, Daniel Stolpe, Frieder Gamm, Ilhan Gündogan, Jörg Krause, Martin Hägele, Jörg Vorländer and Matt McCann for your extremely kind help and advice.

Without the tireless effort and stupendous resourcefulness of Oliver Trust, large chunks of this book simply would not have been there. Thank you so much.

Thank you Tim Broughton and Frances Jessop at Yellow Jersey Press for your belief, support and patience. And for your patience. And also for your patience.

Philip Röber: Cheers, mate.

David Luxton, Rebecca Winfield and Nick Walters at David Luxton Associates for looking after me and this book.

Talking of family . . . Elinor, Mia, Ayalah and Naomi: I love you very much. Thank you for putting up with me.

LIST OF ILLUSTRATIONS

1. Norbert and Jürgen Klopp in Bad Kreuznach; Klopp playing for TSV Glatten; Klopp, Harmut Rath and friends on a post-Abitur trip (all Hartmut and Ulrich Rath)

2. Four generations of Klopps (Isolde Reich); TuS Ergenzingen team photo (Wolfgang Baur)

3. Eintracht Frankfurt team photo (Sven Müller); Klopp and Uwe Seeler (Wolfgang Baur); Wolfgang Frank (Imago)

4. Celebrating Mainz 05's promotion to the Bundesliga (Getty); beer poured over Klopp after Mainz draw with Bayern Munich (Getty); Klopp and Christian Heidel (Imago); Klopp saying farewell at the Bruchwegstadion (Imago)

INDEX

© CI Photography

Raphael Honigstein is the author of *Das Reboot* and the top expert on German soccer. He is a columnist for the *Guardian* and ESPN, writes for Suddeutsche Zeitung and Sport 1 in Germany, and appears as a pundit for BT Sport and ESPN, as well as Sky Sports in Germany. He is also a regular fixture on the *Guardian*'s award-winning podcast *Football Weekly*.

The Nation Institute

NATION
BOOKS

Founded in 2000, **Nation Books** has become a leading voice in American independent publishing. The imprint's mission is to tell stories that inform and empower just as they inspire or entertain readers. We publish award-winning and bestselling journalists, thought leaders, whistle-blowers, and truthtellers, and we are also committed to seeking out a new generation of emerging writers, particularly voices from under-represented communities and writers from diverse backgrounds. As a publisher with a focused list, we work closely with all our authors to ensure that their books have broad and lasting impact. With each of our books we aim to constructively affect and amplify cultural and political discourse and to engender positive social change.

Nation Books is a project of The Nation Institute, a nonprofit media center established to extend the reach of democratic ideals and strengthen the independent press. The Nation Institute is home to a dynamic range of programs: the award-winning Investigative Fund, which supports groundbreaking investigative journalism; the widely read and syndicated website TomDispatch; journalism fellowships that support and cultivate over twenty-five emerging and high-profile reporters each year; and the Victor S. Navasky Internship Program.

For more information on Nation Books and The Nation Institute, please visit:

www.nationbooks.org
www.nationinstitute.org
www.facebook.com/nationbooks.ny
Twitter: @nationbooks